ROUTLEDGE LIBRARY EDITIONS:
URBAN AND REGIONAL ECONOMICS

Volume 9

REGIONAL ECONOMIC PLANNING

REGIONAL ECONOMIC PLANNING

Generation of Regional Input–output Analysis

R. C. JENSEN, T. D. MANDEVILLE AND
N. D. KARUNARATNE

Routledge
Taylor & Francis Group
LONDON AND NEW YORK

First published in 1979 by Croom Helm

This edition first published in 2018
by Routledge
2 Park Square, Milton Park, Abingdon, Oxon OX14 4RN

and by Routledge
711 Third Avenue, New York, NY 10017

Routledge is an imprint of the Taylor & Francis Group, an informa business

British Library Cataloguing in Publication Data
A catalogue record for this book is available from the British Library

ISBN: 978-1-138-09590-8 (Set)
ISBN: 978-1-315-10306-8 (Set) (ebk)
ISBN: 978-1-138-10199-9 (Volume 9) (hbk)
ISBN: 978-1-315-10322-8 (Volume 9) (ebk)

Publisher's Note
The publisher has gone to great lengths to ensure the quality of this reprint but points out that some imperfections in the original copies may be apparent.

Disclaimer
The publisher has made every effort to trace copyright holders and would welcome correspondence from those they have been unable to trace.

Regional Economic Planning

GENERATION OF REGIONAL INPUT–OUTPUT ANALYSIS

R. C. Jensen, T. D. Mandeville and N. D. Karunaratne

CROOM HELM LONDON

Croom Helm Ltd, 2–10 St John's Road, London SW11

British Library Cataloguing in Publication Data

Jensen, R C
Regional economic planning. – (Croom Helm series in geography and environment).
1. Regional planning 2. Interindustry economics
3. Regional economics 4. Economic policy
I. Title II. Mandeville, T D
III. Karunaratne, N D
338.9 HT391

ISBN 0-85664-910-4

Typeset by Pintail Studios Ltd
Ringwood, Hants.

Printed in Great Britain by offset lithography by
Billing & Sons Ltd, Guildford, London and Worcester

CONTENTS

TABLES

PREFACE

There is a widely recognised need for decision-makers at all levels to have at their disposal sufficient detailed information on regional economic structure to undertake consistent and comprehensive regional planning. Input–output models could provide this information, but the high costs of construction and the time involved have generally precluded their use as operational planning tools.

In June 1976, the Queensland Co-ordinator General's Department commissioned the authors to develop a methodology for the preparation of input–output tables for the state and regions of Queensland. This document reports on that research and on the subsequent application of the methodology.

This book is an attempt to elevate regional input–output analysis from the status of a 'research' technique to that of an operational planning technique. It presents a methodology termed the Generation of Regional Input–Output Tables (GRIT) system, designed for general use in the production of regional input–output tables from both national input–output tables and other data sources. GRIT is a 'variable-interference' non-survey based system, producing hybrid (i.e. a combination survey and non-survey) input–output tables. It is based on a combination of non-survey methods, but allows modifications of mechanically produced tables at the discretion of the analyst, to produce more realistic input–output tables.

The book reviews the literature on non-survey methods, highlights the nature of the dilemmas facing the regional input–output analyst, details the GRIT system, and reports results of the empirical application of GRIT to eleven Australian regions. GRIT is a logical extension of recent trends in the input–output literature towards the production of less costly input–output tables. It provides a facility for potential users – urban and regional planners, governments and researchers – to develop holistically accurate regional input–output tables at relatively low cost.

ACKNOWLEDGEMENTS

The completion of this project was possible only with a considerable amount of assistance from many sources, in terms of the provision of data, expert advice relating to the adjustment of prototype tables, and material support.

The project was co-ordinated by a Steering Committee with the following members: Mr K. Willett, Co-Ordinator General's Department (Chairman); Mrs J. Lee, Co-Ordinator General's Department; Mr R. Barker, Co-Ordinator General's Department; Mr A. Morrison, Co-Ordinator General's Department; Mr G. Baker, Department of Commercial and Industrial Development; Mrs D. Thomas, Department of Commercial and Industrial Development; Mr W. Moorhouse, Department of Primary Industries; Mr J. Dickinson, Department of Primary Industries; Mr L. J. Madden, Australian Bureau of Statistics; and Mr W. J. Higham, Department of Health.

The Steering Committee was a constant source of assistance and sound advice. Particular thanks are due to Mr K. Willett for his organisational assistance, to Mr G. Baker for his encouragement, to Mr J. Dickinson for his expert assistance and advice, and to Mr L. J. Madden for his willing assistance with difficult data problems. The authors also acknowledge the benefit of advice from colleagues participating in the Input–Output Workshops of the Regional Science Association meetings in Australia.

The computer program was written, and the computing task capably undertaken, by Mr M. Benjamin.

The first three stages of the project were funded by the Queensland Co-Ordinator General's Department; the fourth stage was funded jointly by that same department and the Department of Commercial and Industrial Development. The Department of Economics at the University of Queensland provided material assistance.

R. C. Jensen
T. D. Mandeville
N. D. Karunaratne

To our wives
Marion, Enid and Visvapali

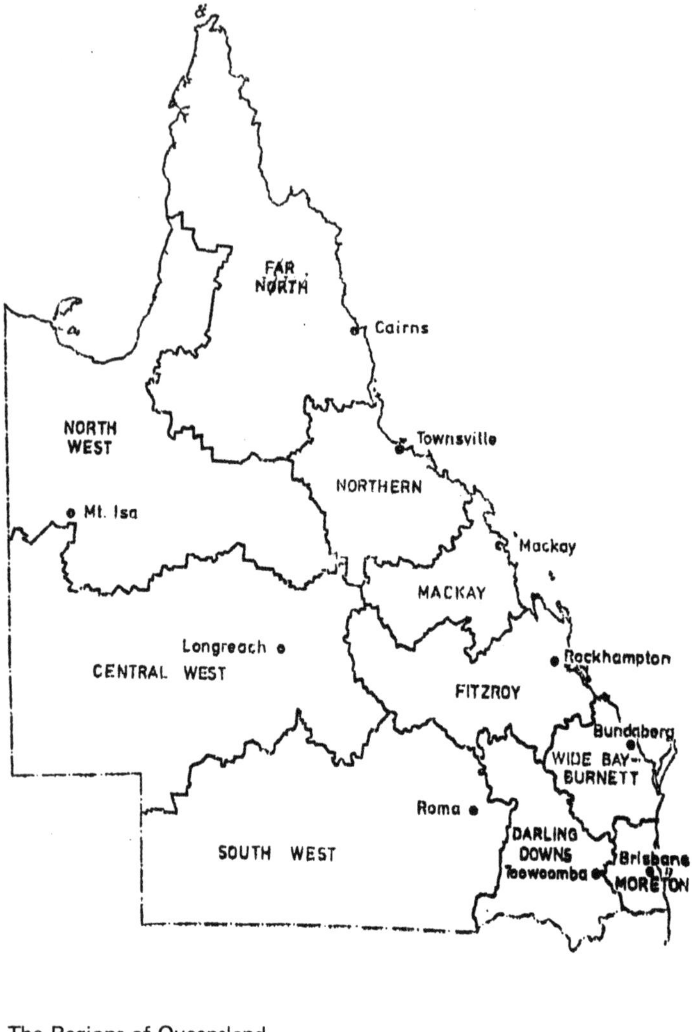

The Regions of Queensland

1 INTRODUCTION

1.1 Background and Objective of the Study

The increased concern with regional economic planning in recent years has been almost universal. Governments have shown more interest both in planning for individual regions, and in co-ordinated planning for systems of regions. This interest in economic planning has created demands for information which have presented a major challenge to the regional economist. This study is a response to a widely recognised need for governments to have at their disposal sufficient detailed information on regional economic structure to enable them to undertake consistent and comprehensive regional planning.

A comprehensive approach to regional economic planning will require that planning authorities have sufficient empirical support to enable them to: (a) consider each region individually (a 'micro' approach) in terms of its particular economic size and structure, and the likely effects on the economy of that region of economic policy decisions, significant economic events or of random factors such as climatic or industrial disturbances, and (b) consider either a state or nation as a group of regions (a 'macro' approach), so that the spatial distribution of economic activity and regional relationships might be considered in some detail.

In more specific terms, planning for regional development for the 'macro' approach requires a series of relatively detailed and compatible regional accounts; the 'micro' approach requires structural detail on individual regional economies and the capability to assess the regional impact of a given economic change on the component industries of each region. In many countries, such information is conspicuously lacking, and this has made a consistent approach to regional economic analysis a difficult task. For example, regional impact studies have tended to be somewhat haphazard, employing a variety of approaches:

(a) to 'assume' multipliers to be of a certain magnitude or within a given range of magnitudes. The assumed multipliers are normally gained from informed opinion and represent 'best-guesstimates' in the absence of data from comparable regions, or resources to complete an empirical study in detail;

(b) to 'borrow' multipliers from a previously completed study from a region of similar industrial structure;

(c) to 'calculate' multipliers by a variety of questionable

techniques, often in the face of an almost complete lack of suitable regional data. In this case the multipliers derived must be of dubious value, but are often accepted as 'reasonable estimates' and assume an aura of authenticity which is not warranted.

In some circumstances the 'borrowing' or the 'best-guessing' of multipliers may be appropriate, for example in tentative or preliminary studies, or studies of relatively insignificant events which do not warrant a professional level of attention. Where the size or the importance of the impacting agent has warranted serious attention, regional Keynesian multipliers, economic base multipliers or input–output multipliers have been developed. Recent development in the calculation of regional Keynesian multipliers (Brownrigg, 1971, 1974; Greig, 1971) will ensure a wider and more productive use of this method of impact calculation. However, in common with the economic base approach, the Keynesian approach is suited best to measurement of total changes in the level of economic activity occasioned by an event, rather than an examination either of absolute levels of activity, or of the effects of the change on the individual sectors of the economy.

Another important disadvantage of the existing situation in the regional planning context is the inability of planning authorities to compare the multipliers derived by analysts in the various empirical studies. Inconsistencies appear not only in the approach of the analysts, i.e. 'best-guesstimates' versus an empirical approach, but also within the definitional context of multipliers with the same apparent meaning, and within the calculation procedures for similarly defined multipliers. It has been shown, for example, that variation in the method of reconciliation (Jensen and McGaurr, 1978) and in the methods of accounting (Jensen, forthcoming) can result in substantial variations in multipliers from the same input–output tables.

The objective of this study was the development of techniques to provide an empirical base for general application in regional economic planning, and to apply those techniques to the regions and state of Queensland, Australia. It was intended to devise a system which facilitated the examination both of the economic structure of individual regions in reasonable detail, and of the regional structure of the state economy. It was considered that such a requirement could be met only by the development of a series of input–output tables relating to the state and its constituent regions defined for the study. It was further recognised that the development of such a system of input–output tables would be feasible only if suitable techniques could be developed, or existing techniques modified, to derive the series of regional input–output tables largely from national input–output tables.

Input–output analysis is potentially an excellent descriptive device and a powerful analytical technique. In practice, the time and expense required to complete survey-based tables has restricted the application of the technique to 'research' rather than operational applications. Certainly input–output techniques appear to have played a relatively insignificant part in most regional planning decisions made by governments, due largely to the inability of analysts to produce input–output tables in the time span within which most decisions must be made.

Recent literature, reviewed in Chapter 3, describes attempts to produce input–output tables by non-survey, or largely mechanical means. These methods have the advantage of relative speed and low cost, but have attracted severe criticism for their apparent inaccuracies. The current 'state-of-the-art' appears to offer a choice between the more expensive and professionally respected survey-based table and the cheaper, less respected non-survey tables. The only further alternative is the so-called 'hybrid' table, which attempts to supplement mechanically produced elements of the table with insertions of survey-based data to improve the acceptability of the resulting table.

This study is the result of efforts by the authors to elevate input–output analysis from the category of a 'research' technique to one of operational application for regional planning and analysis. A system has been developed, termed the Generation of Regional Input–Output Tables (or GRIT) system which produces variable-interference non-survey based tables, essentially hybrid in nature. GRIT relies on a series of mechanical steps to produce regional coefficients, but provides the opportunity at three stages for the insertion of 'superior data', i.e. data considered by the analyst to be more reliable than those produced by the mechanical processes. The system is 'variable-interference' to the extent that the analyst is able to determine the extent to which he interferes with the mechanically produced tables by insertion of these superior data at various stages in the development of the tables. In this way, the judgement of the analyst is incorporated into the tables. It is argued later in Chapter 4 that such a system incorporates the advantages of both survey-based and non-survey tables, and avoids the cost extravagances of the former. The GRIT system allows the calculation of tables to the degree of accuracy which we would simply claim as 'free from significant error'. It is later argued that since the smaller coefficients in an input–output table have an insignificant effect on the analytical uses of the tables, the method of calculation of these coefficients is seen as operationally irrelevant. The more significant coefficients in the tables warrant more attention, and may be corrected by the insertion of superior data. It is, therefore, argued that the analytical reliability of GRIT tables could be similar to that of survey-based tables.

The GRIT system was designed to incorporate the following features:

(a) that input–output tables and their attendant multipliers could be calculated for any region for which certain minimum levels of data are available,[1] for example local government areas, planning regions, or any *ad hoc* region devised for a specific purpose;

(b) that the regional tables be consistent with the table developed for the economy as a whole;

(c) that, although the basic GRIT methodology for producing both state and regional tables is a combination of procedures for converting national tables to regional tables, sufficient flexibility exists to allow the insertion of other data at the discretion of the analyst. This facility will be applied where users have 'superior data',[2] i.e. estimates of higher quality than those generated from national tables;

(d) that the system be capable of updating with minimum effort, as new data sources become available;

(e) that the input–output tables and multipliers derived for each region be directly comparable, both conceptually and by sector definition, and internally consistent within the system;

(f) that the application of the system in an empirical context involve a minimum of expense and time, consistent with a reasonable degree of accuracy, while allowing the subjective judgement of the analyst to be incorporated without difficulty;

(g) that the application of the system be sufficiently uncomplicated to encourage adoption by analysts without a high level of expertise in 'conventional' approaches in the preparation of input–output tables;

(h) that the system be designed as a series of modular components, each of which might be modified by the analyst.

1.2 Overview of the Study

Chapter 2 provides a brief introduction to input–output tables and multipliers, and refers to the main analytical uses of the technique. It is provided for readers with less familiarity with input–output, and to express formally the methods used for multiplier calculation in this study. Since this study is essentially a 'hybrid' approach, incorporating both the selective use of survey or superior data and non-survey methods of preparing input–output tables, Chapter 3 provides a brief introduction to the 'survey versus non-survey' debate, and discusses in some detail the literature relating to non-survey based tables. It is intended to provide a background to the non-survey techniques, some of which have been selected for use in this study.

Chapter 4 is the basic statement of approach adopted by the authors. It provides a broad perspective for the GRIT system; some thought is given in this chapter to the problems facing the regional input–output analyst, particularly with respect to the choice of techniques for table construction. The aims and features of the GRIT system are outlined, and some thoughts on the concept of accuracy in input–output tables are provided.

The remaining chapters focus more directly on the application of the GRIT system. Chapter 5 discusses the accounting conventions and constraints placed on the project. Chapter 6 describes in some detail the GRIT methodology, and Chapter 7 presents the empirical results of the study. The presentation of this book has been designed so that Chapter 7 is not overwhelmed with detail; the extensive use of appendices to record detailed empirical results leaves Chapter 7 in a more readable form. Finally, Chapter 8 undertakes a brief review of the GRIT system.

Notes

1. i.e. in this application, to the state regions of Queensland.
2. These 'superior data' are available from various statistical sources, and would be actively sought for industries known to be of special significance in each region.

2 INPUT–OUTPUT TABLES AND MULTIPLIERS

2.1 The Input–Output Transactions Table

An input–output table represents the economy to be studied in terms of aggregated industrial or commodity groups or sectors. They trace out the transactions in dollar terms between the sectors for a given year. Industries sell goods and services to other industries and to final users or 'final demand' and buy their inputs from other industries and primary sources. The transactions table summarises the inter-sectoral flows in a given period and is conventionally presented in matrix form. A hypothetical and much-simplified transactions table for a 3-sector economy is shown in Table 2.1. Each row indicates the flows from one sector to other sectors and to final demand. From Table 2.1, sector 1 sells $25,000 of its output to firms in the same sector, $20,000 to firms in sector 2, $15,000 of its output to sector 3, and $40,000 to final users. The columns show the purchasing pattern of each sector. Thus sector 3 purchases $15,000 of goods or services from sector 1, $10,000 of goods from sector 2, $43,000 from firms in sector 3, and $32,000 in the form of primary inputs.

It is convenient to define four quadrants (Quadrants I to IV) and consider each in turn. Quadrant I is termed the 'processing' or 'intermediate' quadrant and it shows the flows of transactions between the sectors defined for the purpose of the study.

Quadrant II indicates sales by each sector to final demand. Final demand traditionally includes columns relating to personal consumption, investment, some government expenditure and exports. Quadrant III lists the primary inputs into each industry and represents mainly value added in production. This quadrant normally includes rows for depreciation, indirect taxes, wages and salaries, gross operating surplus imports and 'other value added' items. Quadrant IV shows primary inputs which are absorbed by final demand.

In practice the number of sectors shown in a particular table is determined mainly by the availability of data and the objectives of the study. All endogenous sectors of the economy are included within the intermediate quadrant (Quadrant I) of the table and all exogenous sectors in other quadrants. Endogenous sectors are those which are assumed to be influenced by the internal structure of the economy. Exports, capital expenditure and government spending are usually

Table 2.1: Hypothetical Transactions Table (thousands)

Selling Sectors \ Purchasing Sectors	1	2	3	Final Demand	Total Output
	(Quadrant I)			(Quadrant II)	
1	25	20	15	40	100
2	14	6	10	20	50
3	20	12	43	25	100
	(Quadrant III)			(Quadrant IV)	
Primary Inputs	41	12	32	12	97
Total Outlay	100	50	100	97	347

treated as exogenous since these are influenced primarily by factors external to the regional economy. Personal consumption expenditure is treated as exogenous in one type of input–output table, the standard or 'open' model, but as endogenous in the 'closed' or induced-consumption model.

The transactions table provides a concise, descriptive snapshot of a particular economy at a point in time. It is also a disaggregated and consistent accounting system for an economy. The final demand components (minus imports) are considered to indicate the equivalent of what GNP or GRP (Gross Regional Product) measures on the expenditure side, and primary inputs (minus imports) are the same as the receipts side. Since GNP or GRP accounting seeks to avoid the double counting involved in all the transactions leading up to final demand, it contains only part of the information represented in an input–output table. In the regional policy and planning context, the transactions table gives both a general understanding of the economy of a particular region, and important information on particular aspects of the region's economy.

Before discussing the output, income and employment multipliers in some detail, it is necessary to distinguish between the treatment of the household sector in 'open' and 'closed' input–output models. In open input–output models, household personal consumption is located as a column vector in the final demand portion of the table, and the row vector comprising wages, salaries and other household income is included in the primary inputs quadrant. Alternatively, the input–output table may be closed with respect to households by incorporation of the household row and column into the endogenous matrix. The implications of 'open' and 'closed' models are discussed in the following section.

2.2 Input–Output Multipliers

Once the transactions table has been compiled, simple mathematical procedures can be applied to derive output, income and employment multipliers for each sector in the economy. These procedures are illustrated briefly with accompanying explanatory comment.

The transactions table may be represented by a series of equations thus:

$$
\begin{aligned}
X_1 &= X_{11} + X_{12} + \ldots + X_{1n} + Y_1 \\
X_2 &= X_{21} + X_{22} + \ldots + X_{2n} + Y_2 \\
&\;\vdots \\
X_n &= X_{n1} + X_{n2} + \ldots + X_{nm} + Y_n
\end{aligned}
$$

where

X_i = total output of intermediate sector i (row or column totals)
X_{ij} = output of sector i purchased by sector j (elements of Quadrant I)
Y_i = total final demand for the output of sector i.

It is possible, by dividing the elements of the columns of the transactions table by the respective column totals, to derive coefficients which represent more clearly the purchasing pattern of each sector. These coefficients are variously termed 'direct' or 'input–output' coefficients or, less appropriately, 'technical coefficients'. They are normally notated as a_{ij}, and represent the direct or first round requirement or inputs from each sector i following an increase in unit output of any sector j, i.e. $a_{ij} = X_{ij}/X_j$, a_{ij} is the input–output coefficient. This may be represented in matrix terms as:

$$\underset{n \times 1}{X} = \underset{n \times n}{A}\underset{n \times 1}{X} + \underset{n \times 1}{Y}$$

where $A = [a_{ij}]$, the matrix of input–output coefficients

By transposition we obtain

$$X(I - A) = Y.$$

By solving the above system we derive the general solution:

$$X = (I - A)^{-1} Y.$$

$(I - A)^{-1}$ is termed the Leontief inverse.

Sector Output Multipliers

Let

$$Z = (I - A)^{-1} = [z_{ij}].$$

The matrix Z is termed the matrix of interdependence coefficients. Each element z_{ij} indicates the total direct and indirect requirements from sector i arising from an increase in sales of one dollar to final demand by sector j. The Z matrix provides, therefore, extremely important structural information relating to the economy under study, by indicating the strength of intersectoral economic linkages. The coefficients z_{ij} indicate the extent to which changes in the level of activity of one sector will affect the level of output of all other sectors. The indirect effects could appropriately be termed 'local industrial support' effects.

Each element z_{ij} shows the direct and indirect effects on the output of each sector from an increase in sales of one dollar to final demand by sector j. It follows that the $\Sigma_i z_{ij}$, or the column sums of the inverse of the open model, will show the total effect on all sectors in the table (i.e. the total output effect on the local economy) of an increase in sales of one dollar by sector j to final demand. For this reason $\Sigma_i z_{ij}$ is termed the *simple output multiplier*.

When the model is closed with respect to households, i.e. the household rows are included in the processing sector, the inverse $Z^* = [z^*_{ij}] = (I - A^*)^{-1}$ may be obtained where each element z^*_{ij} provides, in the non-household rows of the inverse, the direct, indirect and induced effect on the output of each sector of an increase in sales to final demand by sector j. The column sums of the non-household z^*_{ij} provide a measure of the *total output multiplier* for each sector.

Hence it is possible to distinguish three effects in the output multiplier:

(a) the *direct* effect. This is shown by the direct coefficients a_{ij}, and represents the immediate or first-round effects on each sector of an increase in output of sector j;

(b) the *indirect* effect. This is shown, together with the direct effect in the z_{ij}, or elements of the inverse of the open model, and represents the second and subsequent-round industrial support requirements from each sector following an increase in sales to final demand of any sector. The indirect effect for any sector can be calculated simply as $z_{ij} - a_{ij}$;

(c) the *induced* effect. This is shown, together with the direct and indirect effects in the non-household rows of the z^*_{ij}, or elements of the inverse of the closed model, and represents the effect on the output of each sector occasioned by increased household consumption as a result of increased sales to final demand of any sector. The induced effect for any sector can be calculated simply as $z^*_{ij} - z_{ij}$.

The facility to disaggregate multipliers into direct, indirect and induced effects is an important advantage of the input–output approach, in that the different components of an impact may be identified and compared. This facility is applicable also to both income and employment multipliers.

Sector Income Multipliers

Income multipliers measure increases in income occasioned by a specified change in the economy. In this study, 'income' is interpreted as household income, and specifically as wages, salaries and supplements. This definition of income excludes some items normally classified as household income, namely dividends and interest received; the narrower definition of income was adopted because of the difficulty of isolating other components of household income at the regional level and of achieving consistency between regions in this respect.

The direct effect of increases in output on household income is given by the household row coefficient a_{Hi} for each sector, where a_{Hi} is the appropriate entry in the household row of the A matrix. The direct and indirect effect of an increase in sales of any sector to final demand is derived by multiplying the direct and indirect output changes (the elements of the Z matrix) by the corresponding household row coefficient, i.e. obtaining $z_{ij}a_{Hi}$ for each element. The direct and indirect income multiplier for sector i is obtained simply as $\Sigma_i z_{ij}a_{Hi}$. The indirect income effect on each sector is calculated as $z_{ij}a_{Hi} - a_{Hi}$.

The direct, indirect and induced income multiplier (total regional income multiplier) is obtained from the household row of the Z^* matrix. The induced effect can be calculated as $z^*_{ij} - z_{ij}a_{Hi}$.

Sector Employment Multipliers

Both output and income multipliers are calculated from elements within the input–output tables. These tables, however, do not contain elements relating to employment *per se*. It is necessary therefore to derive, independently of the tables, an employment coefficient. The simplest method of obtaining this coefficient is the expression of the number of employees per unit of output. Once this coefficient has been obtained, the calculation of employment multipliers parallels to some extent the calculation of income multipliers. The direct effect on employment in each sector of a change in output of sector i will be given by a_{Ei}, the 'employment equivalent' of the household row. The direct and indirect employment effects will be shown as $z^{i}_{ij}a_{Ei}$ for each sector and as $\Sigma_i z_{ij}a_{Ei}$ for all sectors. The direct, indirect and induced effects are calculated as $z^{*}_{ij}a_{Ei}$, and as $\Sigma_{i=1}^{n-1} z^{*}_{ij}a_{Ei}$, i.e. over non-household sectors for the total employment multiplier.

Type I and Type II Multipliers

It has been conventional in input–output analysis for some time to calculate Type I and Type II income and employment multipliers.

$$\text{Type I multiplier} = \frac{\text{Direct and indirect effects}}{\text{Direct effects}}$$

$$\text{Type II multiplier} = \frac{\text{Direct, indirect and induced effects}}{\text{Direct effects}}$$

It is important to establish the distinction between the types of multipliers which have been mentioned. For example, the income multipliers described in the sections above measure the direct and indirect, or direct, indirect and induced effects of a change in *sales* of one dollar of the output of a sector to final demand. Type I and II income multipliers measure the income generated following a dollar change in *household payments*, as a result of a change in final demand for the relevant sector. In other words, the regional income multipliers measure the income impact of a change in *sales* to final demand, while the Type I and II income multipliers measure the income impact of a change in *income*. Similarly the regional employment multipliers measure the employment impact of a change in *sales* to final demand, and the Type I and II employment multipliers measure the employment impact of a change in *employment.*

When interpreting input–output multipliers, it is important to bear in mind that their use is subject to the following important assumptions:

(a) fixed coefficients of production – the production function is assumed to be linear, implying constant returns to scale;
(b) homogeneity – each sector has a fixed set of products that are not produced by any other sector;
(c) additivity – the total effect of carrying on several types of production is assumed to be the sum of the separate effects. Thus external economies and diseconomies, along with the synergistic effect, are assumed away.

The assumptions, although restrictive, simplify the model and thereby make the empirical derivation of multipliers feasible.

2.3 Some Analytical Uses of Input–Output Tables

The input–output transactions table is simply an accounting statement of the transactions between sectors in the economy under study for a given time period. As such, it contains a great deal of information which can be used for a descriptive study of the economy in question, or for comparative purposes when tables for several regions are available. The tendency in input–output work has been for analysts to concentrate on analytical aspects; it should be remembered, however, that the transactions tables can contribute substantially to an understanding of the nature of the regional economy and that comparative studies of transactions tables can provide a valuable basis for studies of regional economic development. The authors, after a long period of examination in detail of several regional economies, feel that input–output analysis could be developed more fruitfully and more consistently if more research attention was devoted to the nature and 'shape' of transactions tables, before proceeding to analytical work.

Despite these reservations, the real analytical power of input–output is evident only when we proceed to the derivation of the inverses (both open and closed) and multipliers. The analytical applications of input–output have been manifold – too numerous to detail in a brief survey of this nature. An attempt is made, however, to summarise the major categories of analytical use for which the technique has been used:

1. Projections of Economic Activity

Once the inverse has been derived, the relationship between the level of final demands and sector outputs can be represented simply through the equation $X = (I - A)^{-1} Y$. In an indicative planning context, for example, it is possible to project or to estimate future levels of final demand, Y, for each sector and to calculate the levels of output, X, from each sector required to achieve the required goals. Alternatively, it is equally simple to estimate from given levels of output, X, for each sector, the levels of final demand, Y, which may be satisfied. Modifications of the relationship to account for imports are common. Many variations of this basic input–output relationship have been employed in empirical work.

2. *Impact Analysis*

It is possible to use input–output tables and multipliers to measure the result in terms of output, income and employment, of any change in the local economy due to an 'impacting agent'. This analysis may require manipulation, extension or adjustment of the input–output model. It is convenient to distinguish impacts according to the analytical operation which has been developed to accommodate the impact, namely:

(a) the use of the inverse in the original form. The impacts of changes in final demand in the short or long term, on sectoral output may be measured in a manner, similar to the projection techniques discussed in (1) above;

(b) modification of the existing entries in the input–output coefficients matrix. The impact of some development may provide cause for alteration of the A matrix. For instance, the entry of new firms can cause changes in sales and purchases patterns, or changes in input–output coefficients, if their entry (or the exit of existing firms) affects the level of technology in the local industry. In particular, the entry of a firm or industry to produce import substitutes could be important. Richardson (1972) suggests that most changes in the A matrix will be connected with changes in the geographical distribution of sales and purchases, rather than with changes in the input requirements pattern;

(c) expansion of the transactions table. The impact of a new firm, industry or sector can be handled by augmenting the original transactions table with a new row and column representing the added industry. The augmented table is converted to an augmented inverse for impact measurement.

3. *Market and Structural Analysis*

The input–output tables provide a substantial amount of information relating to the market of the various sectors. Apart from the use of the transactions table as a market information system (Schaffer, 1976), it is possible (Parker, 1967) to determine the extent to which the final demand sales by each sector are responsible, directly or indirectly, for absorbing the output of all sectors individually.

Other useful structural investigations may be undertaken. For example, the analyst may be interested in determining the extent to which imports contribute to the satisfaction of local final demand. In particular, the import content (direct and indirect) of regional exports could be an important factor in the planning of industrial location. It is a simple matter also to calculate the extent to which the local economy contributes, in terms of value added, to each category of final demand; in particular the planning authorities may be interested in the local direct and indirect labour content of regional exports.

4. Economic Intelligence

The term economic intelligence, applied by Schaffer (1976), refers to the ability of the planning authorities to examine strategic questions relating to regional economic development, by a detailed study of the nature of the regional industries. By the use of self-sufficiency analysis, it is possible to identify apparent 'missing links' or 'bottlenecks' (Schaffer, 1976, p. 80) in an economy, and thus facilitate strategic planning.

5. Other Uses

Among many applications, input–output models have been employed in the calculation of environmental effects, interregional multipliers, and the separation of price and output effects on income. The number of situations to which the technique has been applied continues to increase.

2.4 Résumé

This chapter has attempted to provide a brief introduction to input–output tables and analysis. The concepts involved are inherently simple and subject to some important assumptions. Once the transactions table is derived, the manipulation of the table to allow the substantial analytical power of the technique to be exercised is a lesser task in terms of resources. For a more comprehensive understanding of input–output analysis and its potential, the reader is referred to books by Richardson (1972) and Schaffer (1976).

3 NON-SURVEY REGIONAL INPUT–OUTPUT TABLES

The preparation of an input–output transactions table means, in effect, attempting to account in a disaggregated form for virtually all of the transactions which occur in an economy in a given time period. Even though these are identified as groups of transactions between sectors, this is a major undertaking. The step from the simple input–output table as an expository device as described in Chapter 2, to the completion of the table in a consistent form is, to say the least, a very large one indeed. The sheer volume of information required for the data-ravenous table, and the detailed treatment of these data, demands a massive input from the input–output analyst.

The preparation of national tables is facilitated by the existence of detailed national accounts and commodity data. Even in these circumstances, several man years of patient and painstaking work is required to produce transactions tables. Access to such detailed data and to a team of workers familiar with the various official statistical collections provide the 'ideal' circumstances for the production of authoritative and 'accurate' input–output tables.

Analysts faced with the task of preparing sub-state regional tables are usually seriously disadvantaged both with respect to data availability and access to research resources. Data collections by national statistical collection agencies, and by other official or unofficial data-collection institutions, are designed primarily for purposes other than the preparation of regional input–output tables and often provide only some of the basic control totals for this task. Prior to this study, the preparation of regional tables has been regarded in Australia as appropriate only for the occasional regional analyst with sufficient tenacity of purpose and patience to complete the task alone or with limited research assistance. This study is the first recognition by a government agency in Australia of the need to produce a series of consistent and detailed regional tables for use in a policy context.

The literature on regional input–output tables would suggest that past Australian experience is by no means unique. Most regional input–output analysts in the United States and the United Kingdom appear to have faced similar problems with respect to the availability of suitable data and research resources. Consequently, the preparation of regional tables has been unable to follow a fairly well trodden and well defined path in a manner which is available to those engaged in the preparation of national tables. Various approaches to the preparation of regional tables have been adopted in the search for methods which provide satisfactory results. These are discussed in more detail in the remainder of this chapter.

3.1 Deriving Regional Input–Output Tables: Survey and Non-Survey Approaches

The various approaches to the derivation of regional tables can best be broadly categorized as 'survey' or 'non-survey'. The clear distinction between the two approaches lies in the fact that the former attempts to determine the elements of the transactions table from collections of primary data by various 'survey' methods, and the latter attempts to derive these elements from other (usually national) tables by various modification techniques. The literature, however, leaves no doubt that the term 'survey' is loosely interpreted by analysts. It is reasonable to conclude from a reading of many 'survey-based' studies that the term has been interpreted to include visits to firms selected either at random or by necessity, or simply sufficient firms to provide the analyst with information which may be regarded as 'satisfactory' in some way. Certainly it appears to be unusual for analysts to follow the conventions required by sampling theory, and to express the results in statistical terms. It is also unusual for analysts to draw attention to the possible sources of non-sampling errors such as bias in their estimates due to non-response.

Despite the apparent variations within the survey approach, the general procedure has been followed by most analysts to date, and will probably remain in general use in input–output research for some time. The presumption that survey-based approaches provide more 'accurate' tables will be discussed in more detail in Chapter 4.

In contrast to the survey approach, non-survey methods attempt to estimate transactions without recourse to primary data, by procedures which are largely mechanical in nature. Each approach has its proponents, and each approach is subject to valid criticism. For example, Miernyk (1969) expressed early doubts about non-survey approaches and repeated these doubts more recently (Miernyk, 1976), while Smith and Morrison (1974) have contributed substantially to an understanding of the non-survey approach.

Historically, the relative emphasis given to survey and non-survey techniques by regional analysts has tended to vary. In the early 1950s, when attention was first turned to applying the Leontief input–output system to sub-national areas, non-survey techniques were applied. Throughout the sixties, analysts concentrated on constructing survey-based regional input–output tables. However, in the late sixties and early seventies, attention has again focused on the non-survey techniques as the demand has grown for a wider application of the input–output approach in regional and urban planning. Given the dearth of regional statistics, the survey approach has proven to be too costly in terms of time and resources for widespread application to regional planning problems. Boster and Martin (1972) indicate the cost comparisons between a survey and non-survey model constructed for the state of Arizona. They found budget differences of a magnitude of 20:1. The large difference in cost essentially means that in most problem-oriented situations there is no alternative between a survey or non-survey input–output model; it is 'non-survey or nothing'. Clearly such estimates of regional structure will be better than none at all, and if the analyst is interested in the overall structural view of a regional economy, rather than in individual input–output coefficients, a non-survey model will be quite adequate. Preliminary work by West and Jensen (1977) suggest that errors in input–output coefficients have much less impact on sector multipliers than has traditionally been thought to be the case.

Boster and Martin (1972, p. 35) argue that *a priori* assumptions that the survey approach is more justifiable are unwarranted: 'Poorly drawn samples, sampling errors, inadequate or poorly-trained field workers, and poorly conceived schedules are among possible sources of error to balance against the possibility of secondary data (especially national model coefficients) being inapplicable to a region.'

If any consensus in the matter of survey and non-survey approaches were to emerge from input–output analysts, it would probably be that the survey approach is the most attractive both theoretically and intuitively. However, on practical grounds and cost considerations there are strong arguments for devoting increased attention to non-survey techniques.

Other workers have suggested a hybrid approach as a compromise between the two approaches, in order to gain the advantages of both and to avoid the main disadvantages. Richardson (1972) and Cutbush (1973) refer to the possibility of using non-survey techniques to estimate the elements of the initial transactions table, but to replace the entries in this matrix relating to a few key or problem industries with survey-based estimates.[1] The approach adopted in this study goes beyond this suggestion by the systematic insertion of 'superior data' into a table developed by non-survey methods. Later chapters describe the techniques in some detail. The remainder of this chapter is concerned with the non-survey techniques developed by input–output workers, as a basis for an appreciation of the choice of methods for this study.

3.2 Non-Survey Methods: An Overview of the Literature

This section provides a brief outline of the several alternative non-survey techniques which have been used for the construction of regional input–output tables. This outline is intended primarily as background for later chapters, rather than as a comprehensive evaluation of non-survey techniques.

Use of Unadjusted National Coefficients

The earliest and simplest non-survey method involved representing the regional economy by use of essentially unmodified national technical coefficients. The Isard and Kuenne (1953) study to evaluate the impact of steel upon the Greater New York–Philadelphia area and Miller's (1957) similar analysis of the aluminum industry impact on the Pacific north-west are two US examples. In Australia, Mules (1967) used national coefficients to construct an input–output matrix for South Australia.

Since regional coefficients are known to vary considerably from national coefficients, the use of unadjusted national coefficients is regarded as being highly questionable. Isard (1953) was led to issue a 'stern warning' that the input requirements generated by this method were 'crude estimates' only of the regional transactions table. This argument has been further developed by others, including Richardson (1972). The largest source of variation between regional and national coefficients arises from the greater 'openness' of regional economies; the import component of any industry will normally be much greater at the regional level than at the national level. Further, the industrial mix within any sector may vary considerably between the region and the nation, and regional technical production functions may differ from those observed nationally. With regard to the latter, Hewings (1971a) notes there has been almost no work on measuring regional production functions and comparing them to national production functions.

An enumeration of the following non-survey methods is provided here:

(a) location quotient approach;
(b) commodity balance approach;

(c) constrained matrix techniques;
(d) regional weights and aggregation techniques;
(e) representative regional coefficients;
(f) semi-survey methods;
(g) miscellaneous techniques.

Location Quotient, Commodity Balance and Constrained Matrix Techniques

The location quotient, commodity balance and constrained matrix procedures have been applied, compared and contrasted in the literature; it is convenient to discuss these techniques together. All three methods attempt to adjust the national coefficients to the regional level. The assumption has been that the regional trade coefficients differ from the national technical coefficients only by the magnitude of the regional import coefficient. Let $r_{ij} = a_{ij} - m_{ij}$, where a_{ij} is the national technical coefficient, r_{ij} is the regional trade coefficient, and m_{ij} $(0 \leqslant m_{ij} \leqslant a_{ij})$ is a regional import coefficient. It should be noted that these three techniques cannot account for a region-unique product mix or sector production function.

The location quotient (LQ) method consists of a variety of refinements which utilise the LQ to estimate regional imports. The LQ is a measure which compares the relative importance (in terms of output or employment) of an industry in a region to its relative importance in the nation, or $LQ_j = (X_j^r/X^r)/(X_j^n/X^n)$ where X represents output and superscripts r and n, the region and nation respectively. Operationally, the regional coefficients for row j are estimated by multiplying the national coefficient by LQ_j, and apportioning the difference to imports, i.e. $r_{ij} = a_{ij} LQ_j$ where $LQ \leqslant 1$. This means that the region produces less than its share of national output in industry j and imports are therefore required.

In attempts to overcome some of the deficiencies of the simple LQ, other types of location quotients have been developed for application in a similar manner. The main variations to the simple LQ are:

(a) Purchases Only Location Quotient.

This has been suggested by Tiebout (CONSAD, 1967) who recommended that the summation of total output in the calculation of the quotient for industry i should be carried out only over those industries which make purchases from industry i. However, the impact of this modification upon the results is comparatively slight (Schaffer and Chu, 1969a, p. 95).

(b) Cross-Industry Location Quotient (CILQ).
Attributed to Leven by Schaffer and Chu (1969a), the CILQ attempts to take into account the relative local importance of the purchasing industry as well as the selling industry. Thus the CILQ compares the proportion of national output of selling industry i in the region to the proportion for purchasing industry j, or

$$\mathrm{CILQ}_{ij} = \frac{X_i^r / X_i^n}{X_j^r / X_j^n}$$

(c) Logarithmic Cross-Industry Location Quotient (LCILQ).
Smith and Morrison (1974, p. 73) give Round the credit for this technique, which takes the form $\mathrm{LCILQ}_{ij} = \mathrm{LQ}_i / \log_2 (1 + \mathrm{LQ}_j)$. According to Round, the logarithmic cross-industry LQ refines the CILQ by taking into consideration the relative size of the region compared to the nation.

The supply–demand pool (SDP) technique proposed by Schaffer and Chu (1969a) is based upon regional commodity balances, which were first derived by Isard (1953). This method relies upon subtracting total regional requirements (row vectors of output distributions to regional industries and final demand estimated from national coefficients) from total regional output in each industry to obtain a net surplus or deficit. If a surplus is obtained for industry i, then local supply is sufficient to cover local demand, and the national coefficients may be used in row i of the regional coefficients matrix. If, however, a deficit is obtained, the implication is that local demand is greater than local supply, and importation of goods/services from other regions will be necessary. In this situation, the national coefficients of row i are reduced: $r_{ij} = a_{ij}(X_i^r / R_i^r)$ where R_i^r is total regional requirements. This technique was used in the Utah study (Moore and Petersen, 1955).

The SDP technique can be modified in several ways, two of which will be discussed here. First, Kokat (1966) adjusted the SDP technique to account for a predetermined final demand, that is, no imports are computed for the final demand sector. Smith and Morrison (1974) suggest that Kokat's method may be considered as a formalisation of earlier work, such as that by Miller (1957), which aimed at estimating the proportion of local input requirements expected to originate in the region. Second, Schaffer and Chu (1969a) developed an iterative procedure as a refinement to the SDP technique, referred to as Regional Input–Output Table (RIOT) Simulator, which assumes national technology applies and 'attempts to distribute local production according to both the national sales pattern and local needs' (p. 92). Required inputs for producing regional output of the sectors were calculated by using national coefficients. Regional final demands were assumed as a proportion of national final demand. Regional sales were distributed initially according to the national sales pattern. Requirements and sales allocations were compared, and for each row a 'pool' of surplus for re-allocation, and a pool of 'needs' were computed. For rows with pools greater than needs, the excess was considered as exports; for rows with needs greater than pools, the pool was spread in an iterative process until it diminished to zero. Imports were calculated as negative residuals.

The main weakness of the commodity balance approach (as well as the LQ approach) is that balances are stated in net terms. Thus the possibilities of accounting for cross-haulage (the import and export of similar goods by an individual sector) are denied, implying the assumption that within-region trade is maximised (Jones, Sporleder and Mustafa, 1973). This in turn implies that the SDP technique will tend to overstate sector multipliers. Moore and Peterson (1955) argue that the assumption that local goods will satisfy input requirements wherever possible is only reasonable for regions insulated by a 'space buffer', i.e. relatively isolated regions. Another limitation of the SDP and LQ techniques is that the rows of the region's export sectors cannot be adjusted for imports. The problem here is that national coefficients may overstate these industries' sales to local processing industries.

The constrained matrix procedures refer to iterative adjustment techniques used to estimate an input–output matrix, given row and column totals and an input–output table which may be taken as providing information with respect to the internal structure of the required matrix. Of the alternative constrained matrix procedures,[2] the RAS technique (Stone and Leicester, 1966) has received the most attention in the literature. Lecomber (1971), in his critique of constrained matrix techniques, attributes the popularity of RAS to its relative simplicity, and the fact that it preserves signs. RAS has been used by Czamanski and Malizia (1969), and Smith and Morrison (1974) to estimate regional input–output coefficients from national input–output coefficients, respectively for Washington state and the city of Peterborough in the UK. Detailed discussion of RAS and other constrained matrix techniques is not provided in this book.

Weighting Techniques

Regional weighting and aggregation techniques have been utilised by Shen (1960) and Czamanski and Malizia (1969) in an effort to account for differences in industry mix in the region *vis-à-vis* the nation. These techniques involve using regional weights (employment, value added, or output) to group the highly disaggregated national input–output table into a more aggregated regional table. This approach relies on the principle that the sectors in a highly disaggregated national table may be grouped together by a weighting method, and that the resulting more aggregated sector is an improved representation of the regional sector.

Richardson (1972, p. 118) reports a further study by Walderhaug (1972) using the Washington economy (Bourque *et al.*, 1967) and weighting the columns of national input coefficients by estimates of gross regional output in each industry. The 'errors' in the form of differences between estimates and 'true' coefficients were measured.[3] The size of these errors fell in most cases within acceptable limits; the exceptions were thought to be due to poor quality of the 'true' coefficients.

The general consensus would appear to suggest that techniques aimed at the conversion of national coefficients to regional coefficients by aggregation and weighting remain in the tentative and development stage. While it is possible for tables derived by these methods to be employed in a general descriptive manner, the wisdom of using them as the sole conversion technique for precise analytical purposes would appear to be questionable.

Representative Coefficients

Mandeville (1975) advocates the use of 'representative' regional input–output coefficients, that is, when constructing a non-survey regional table, the analyst 'borrows' selected coefficients from survey-based tables already constructed for a similar region. The rationale would be that survey-based tables already in existence are likely to provide reasonable estimates of regional 'foreign' trade, product mix and production functions in selected cases. In the context of GRIT, representative coefficients could be applied only as an adjunct to other techniques, allowing economies to be achieved from existing regional input–output studies. Following Czamanski and Malizia's findings that national coefficients are least appropriate for primary industries and industries in which the region specialises, representative coefficients could be substituted for national coefficients in these sensitive and important sectors.

It is difficult to gauge the extent to which the 'borrowing' of coefficients has been practised by regional input–output analysts, even in so-called survey-based tables. This borrowing could take the form either of the insertion of the borrowed coefficients or their transactions equivalent *in toto*, or by the judicious use of other studies as a check on the 'reasonableness' of tables in preparation. In either case, if the borrowed coefficients provide, in the judgement of the analyst, an opportunity to improve the quality of a table, the procedure must have merit. It may transpire that a lack of research resources forces an analyst to 'borrow' from other tables if his own research is to reach fruition. Another argument suggests that the structure of some sectors may vary little from one region to another, and that in these circumstances, borrowing should be encouraged.

Semi-Survey Techniques

It has already been mentioned that the RAS technique as applied in the conversion of national to regional coefficients can incorporate survey data. Su (1970) proposed a technique emphasising the direct estimation of imports. A survey of regional firms requested respondents to identify the proportion of required inputs which were imported into the region. These proportions were then applied to the national a_{ij}'s in order to compute the regional imports row. Alternatively, the direct estimation of exports was suggested by Schaffer (1970). This approach amounts to a simplified version of the Hansen–Tiebot (1963) 'rows only' approach. Regional firms were surveyed for annual sales and the proportion of sales to purchasers outside the region. This information can then be applied to calculate regional coefficients in a similar manner to the commodity balance approach.

Miscellaneous Adjustment Techniques

This listing can be concluded with a brief mention of a small number of 'miscellaneous' national coefficient adjustment techniques mentioned in the literature. Smith and Morrison (1974) record an improvement in their results after the insertion of zeros into the principal diagonal of the national technical coefficients matrix before the various reduction procedures were applied. The argument for this procedure is that a national sector is far more heterogeneous in character than the equivalent local sector. In the region it is unlikely that all subsectors of the nationally defined sector will be represented locally, implying that the intra-industry linkage will tend to be overstated unless specific allowance is made for this factor. Another technique employed by Smith and Morrison (1974) and Moore and Petersen (1955), in conjunction with other reduction techniques, was to allocate the coefficients of national sectors not present in the region to imports. The rows of the national matrix which relate to sectors not present in the region are removed because local requirements from these sectors must clearly be met wholly by imports.

The final technique that will be mentioned here can be simply termed 'subjective adjustments'. It is virtually impossible to assess the degree to which subjective adjustments have entered into the preparation of published regional input–output tables. Our judgement would be that the subjective opinions of the analyst and his expert and experienced advisers has influenced the structure of virtually all regional tables, apart from those experimentally constructed by purely mechanical means. That this should happen is no cause for concern; one would claim with some justification that it is not only the right of the analyst to incorporate the subjective opinions of those familiar with the region under study but that he has an obligation to do so in the interests of the ultimate users of his tables. To do less, it would seem, may often be simply striving for 'respectability' at the expense of honest and informed attempts to produce more accurate and representative tables.

3.3 Evaluations of the Location Quotient, Commodity Balances and Constrained Matrix Techniques

The preceding section refers to a number of techniques which are wholly or partly 'non-survey'. The evaluation of any technique must rest on the ability of the technique to produce regional input–output tables which satisfactorily represent the regional economy. So far, most of these techniques have not been subjected to rigorous evaluation; the evaluation literature is restricted largely to the location quotient, commodity balance and constrained matrix techniques. Since this literature influenced the design of GRIT, it is briefly summarised here.

Three major studies have been undertaken to evaluate selected reduction techniques by comparing the alternatively produced synthetic matrices with survey-based input–output tables for the same region. The 1963 survey-based table for Washington state (Bourque, 1967) was used by Czamanski and Malizia (1969) to test the RAS method, and by Schaffer and Chu (1969) to evaluate the major variations of the location quotient and commodity balance approaches. More recently, Smith and Morrison (1974) evaluated the RAS, location quotient and commodity balance approaches using a survey-based table for the city of Peterborough as a bench-mark for the purposes of comparison using five statistical criteria. Discussion of these efforts to evaluate the national coefficient reduction techniques follows.[4]

Czamanski and Malizia

Starting with the 1958 US national input–output table, and regional estimates of gross sector outputs and vectors of the intermediate outputs and inputs, Czamanski and Malizia have applied the RAS method to generate a 1963 regional table for Washington state. Some adjustment was also made for relative price changes between 1958 and 1963. Using statistical tests based upon information content and upon mean percentage errors, the authors experimented with difficult levels of aggregation; they also attempted to evaluate the impact of making adjustments for price differentials and for domestic imports. They examined in detail the quality of results obtained in respect of individual sectors and found that the largest errors were manifest in the primary sectors and also in sectors in which the region specialised.[5] Czamanski and Malizia suggest that it seems important to exclude tertiary sectors through aggregation and to use field surveys in order to obtain input–output coefficients for primary industry and industry in which the region is specialised. Price adjustments and adjustments for domestic imports had little effect on the quality of results.

Schaffer and Chu

In their comparison of simulated input-output tables with the Washington survey-based matrix, Schaffer and Chu (1969a) computed chi-square statistics for each column of the tables. The authors found that the best results, in terms of simulating acceptable coefficients, were obtained with the simple location quotient, followed (in rough order) by the cross-industry location quotient, RIOT simulation and SDP. No attempt was made to evaluate the tables as a whole by using chi-square statistics, but they did compare estimates of income multipliers. In every case the non-survey-based multipliers overestimated those derived from the survey table. Here again, the best estimates were those resulting from the application of the simple LQ technique.

In a later paper (Schaffer and Chu, 1969b), the study was widened so as to include an examination of three states – Washington, Utah and New Mexico, and the chi-square test was supplemented by the use of regression and of information content procedures. Results presented in this paper confirm that the best estimates arise from the simple LQ procedure. On balance, the second-best estimates resulted from the pool technique, followed by the iterative RIOT procedure and the cross-industry location quotient technique.

Hewings (1971a,b) also applied variations of the LQ and SDP

technique to the British national input–output tables in order to derive regional tables for the West Midlands (Hewings, 1969) and also for south-east Kent (Hewings, 1971b). However, since survey-based tables do not exist for these areas, no objective evaluation of the techniques has arisen from Hewings' work.

Smith and Morrison

Smith and Morrison (1974) tested what was in their view the most promising of the non-survey methods: simple LQ, purchases-only LQ, cross-industry LQ, logarithmic cross-industry LQ, supply demand pool, and RAS. The simulated matrices and multipliers were compared with the survey-based equivalent. The following observations were made.

(a) Matrix Comparisons. Statistical test procedures were applied to each of the simulated matrices and the non-survey techniques were ranked as to their relative 'closeness' of the resulting tables to the survey-based matrix. The RAS technique gave far superior results to the other reduction methods; a conclusion that the authors qualify in the light of the methodology employed, i.e. their version of RAS incorporated some survey material (the intermediate input and output vectors). Among the remaining methods, there was less variation in the results; the tables were grouped more closely together. The ranking among the location quotient and commodity balance techniques placed the simple LQ approach first, followed by purchases-only LQ, supply demand pool, and finally the logarithmic cross-industry LQ and the cross-industry LQ.

(b) Multiplier Comparisons. Type I and Type II income multipliers were calculated and compared with those from the survey table. It is significant that of the various LQ and commodity balance approaches tested, the simple LQ approach was the most successful in both the Smith and Morrison and Schaffer and Chu studies.

The RAS Technique

The use of the RAS technique as a single-step approach to the derivation of input–output coefficients has been examined by a number of analysts. On one hand, the Morrison and Smith (1974) results suggest that the basic RAS approach, supplemented by survey or other exogenous data, can provide greatly improved, perhaps superior results. On the other hand, the evidence assembled by Miernyk (1976) establishes that the RAS should, in this context, be treated with caution. Citing the work of Malizia and Bond (1974) in comparing the Washington state tables with one derived by the use of RAS, Miernyk concludes (1976, p. 48) that 'in spite of its elegance and mechanical nature, which obviates the need for judgement, the RAS is not a satisfactory way of deriving a regional input–output table from a national counterpart.' Miernyk reinforces suspicion of the RAS by reference to the work of Barker (1975) and work carried out at the Regional Science Institute, relating to the use of RAS in projecting national coefficients. Although the latter comparison has little relevance in the derivation of regional tables, the case for treating the single-step RAS approach with considerable reserve has been established.

Notes

1. See Richardson (1972), p. 129.
2. See Cambridge Department of Applied Economics (1963), Friedlander (1961), Matuszewski *et al.* (1964), Stone and Leicester (1966) and Theil (1967).
3. The 'true' coefficients were taken from the 1963 Washington study (Bourke *et al.*, 1967).
4. This discussion relies heavily on the excellent review by Smith and Morrison (1974).
5. The authors defined sectors in which the region specialised as those having a location quotient in excess of 2.0.

4 THE GRIT SYSTEM IN PERSPECTIVE

This chapter is basically a statement of intent. It summarises the dilemma facing regional input–output practitioners at this point in the development of the technique, and provides in the form of general statements the background and 'philosophy' of approach which resulted in the production of GRIT.

4.1 The Dilemmas of Regional Input–Output

'The truth is that our capacity to develop highly sophisticated regional models has far outrun our ability to implement them, given the primitive nature of available data and data-gathering techniques' (Miernyk, 1976). These words epitomise one of the basic dilemmas shared by regional input–output workers and other applied economists. Tools of economic analysis, potentially powerful and valuable in a policy and planning context, frequently remain virtually the playthings of academics or at best find application in a limited context, with their potential contribution bypassed by events. Governments and planning authorities with legitimate demands for applied economic analysis have had to be satisfied with inferior but more readily obtainable advice, drawn from more primitive techniques of analysis.

It is disappointing that input–output, with its vast potential for regional economic analysis, remains primarily a research tool and is not yet readily implementable at an operational planning level. There are, of course, good reasons for this. As Miernyk suggests, the primitive data situation places severe limits on the applicability of the technique. While analysts with experience in producing survey-based tables would readily concur with the serious nature of the data problem, it is nevertheless a fact of life which must be accommodated. Miernyk (1976, p. 54) would have analysts wait for 'better basic data collected on a uniform basis'. This solution can be achieved only in the (very) long run and implies that data-gathering resources are at present misallocated, a question worthy of considerable debate. Other input–output workers have attempted to accommodate the data problem by varying the basic input–output approach and using some 'mechanical' means to produce regional tables. Most of these workers appear to be motivated by a desire to see the input–output technique adjust to data problems and develop towards operational usefulness. Any technique can be operationally useful only if it is capable of application before the decision it should affect has been made, rather than being restricted to *ex post* or hypothetical situations. The second dilemma is reflected then in the apparent conflict between the statement that 'there is still no substitute for a good survey-based study' (Schaffer and Chu, 1969) and the earlier statement in Chapter 3 of this study that it is 'non-survey or nothing'.

The second dilemma lies at the very heart of this study – whether it is better to wait (almost inevitably in vain) for the data-gathering authorities to produce data to remove all doubts about the quality of the input–output tables, or whether it is better to produce tables of an apparently lower degree of accuracy than the ideal to which we might aspire. If we follow the former approach, we have the satisfaction of professional purity but remain necessarily unable to respond to the call by governments and planning authorities for guidance in the affairs of the nation at the stage when this guidance is needed. If we follow the latter approach, we must accept the risk of providing this guidance based on models whose accuracy we are unable to guarantee in detail. We have adopted the latter approach; this study is the result. Inevitably the approach adopted is subject to criticism, inevitably it will be improved, but it represents the efforts of the authors to take regional input–output to an operational level.

4.2 Aims and Features of the System

The GRIT system is a response, taken in the context of the two dilemmas facing regional input–output, to the challenge to provide an operational method, free from 'significant error', for regional economic analysis. The test of operationality implies that the system must be capable of producing an input–output table and its multipliers in a fairly short time span, that is, sufficiently short to enable the analytical implications of the tables to be incorporated into the decision-making processes of government. It implies also that the derivation of the table(s) not be costly in money terms, since to provide a system expensive to operate would simply discourage its use. In both time and money terms, the distinct advantage lies with non-survey techniques of input–output, the so-called 'mechanical' techniques, and therefore selected non-survey techniques form the basis of the GRIT system.

The test of accuracy is more difficult to apply since no input–output analyst has produced a table without error, or one in which the analyst is able to indicate clearly the margin or direction of errors. The concept of accuracy is discussed more fully in section 4.3. At this stage, it is sufficient to say that the GRIT system was designed to ensure that the table(s) were free from significant error, by the introduction of 'superior data' where this could be obtained, and by the retention of facilities for the analyst to exercise his judgement in the formation of the final tables.

In the final analysis the GRIT system is a variable-interference non-survey technique, producing tables which could be termed hybrid tables. It is variable-interference to the extent that the operator might exercise discretion regarding the amount of superior data from survey or other exogenous sources, to be inserted into the tables. This feature directly incorporates a trade-off at the discretion of the operator between survey and non-survey sources of coefficients, and consequently a trade-off between a time-and-cost component and the satisfaction of knowing that data has been gathered by the more 'respectable' survey methods. The application shown in the following chapters reflects a level of interference close to the minimum-interference operation of the GRIT system; superior data was inserted into the table where this was directly available from the Australian Bureau of Statistics or other major sources, where dominant regional industries occurred, or the prototype tables disclosed errors to workers with a degree of familiarity with the regional economies.

GRIT was designed for general use in analysis of a wide range of economies. It has been applied in this study to the regions of Queensland, and inevitably reflects therefore the Queensland and Australian data context. However, the changes that would need to be made to implement GRIT in other countries are considered to be relatively minor. GRIT was designed for application either to single *ad hoc* regions, or to a system of regions such as a state or nation. In more specific terms the features of the system are:

(a) Input–output tables with their attendant multipliers can be calculated for any region for which certain minimum levels of data are available. The minimum data required for regions in the Australian context relate to the sources of output for the manufacturing, rural and mining industries for the relevant year, and employment data by region for all sectors.[1] The region would normally be defined as a statistical unit such as a local government area, a grouping of local government areas, statistical divisions, or as any *ad hoc* region designed for a specific purpose.

(b) If GRIT is applied to a system of regions, the regional tables will be consistent with the table of the economy of the whole, i.e.

the state or nation. The application illustrated in later chapters shows the tables for the economies of the regions of Queensland consistent with the table for the economy of the state.

(c) The basic methodology, outlined in Chapter 6, is a combination of selected non-survey and survey-procedures. At various stages in the programme, facilities exist which allow insertion of superior data at the discretion of the analyst.

(d) The system relies in the first instance on the availability of a national table, and of data reflecting regional levels of output and employment. As these sources are replaced by more recent figures, these may replace the original data for updating with a minimum of effort.

(e) The input–output tables and multipliers derived for the state economy and for each of the component regions are directly comparable. In terms of sector definition, and in terms of accounting procedures and conceptual definition, each table is consistent with others and with the table of the whole. This feature was imposed to avoid the difficulties faced when attempting to compare existing input–output studies using different definitions and conventions.

(f) The application of the system in an empirical context will involve limited expense in terms of money and time, consistent with an apparently reasonable degree of accuracy. In its 'native' environment, with a minimum-interference approach, a regional table could be provided in a matter of weeks and a system of tables in a few months. With increasing levels of operator interference in the mechanical aspects of the programme, the required time increases.

(g) The application of the system is sufficiently uncomplicated to encourage use by analysts without a high level of expertise in the preparation of conventional survey-based tables. It is probably true to say that the experience of preparing a survey-based table forces the analyst to develop a high level of expertise in many aspects of input–output, and that conversely a high level of expertise would be very difficult to acquire without this experience. GRIT was designed so that its application would not be restricted to the few individuals with such experience.

(h) GRIT, as outlined in detail in Chapter 6, proceeds in a number of clearly defined phases, each with modular components. It is likely that other analysts may prefer a different combination of procedural components to that comprising the basic GRIT system. In this event, an individual module could be replaced by one preferred by the analyst, by rewriting the appropriate part of the computer program shown in Appendix IV.[2]

4.3 Accuracy and Approaches to Table Construction

The second dilemma of regional input–output, i.e. the 'survey *v*. non-survey' dilemma, discussed in section 4.1, deserves further discussion. Two facts, eminently clear from the literature, are central to the dilemma. First, if the preparation of regional input–output tables were restricted to the more 'respectable' survey methods, then input–output would in most countries contribute a minor role to planning and decision-making. The long delays and high cost of such studies would ensure this. Second, it has been demonstrated that purely mechanical methods of producing input–output tables have not yet resulted in 'satisfactory' tables. Even though the procedures to assess the success of mechanically produced tables, namely comparison with survey-based tables, may be suspect,[3] the weight of evidence supports this case. This has led to the suggestion (Richardson, 1972; Cutbush, 1973) that the hybrid table is the logical next step in regional input–output.

There is a strong argument, however, that the survey *v*. non-survey debate, based mainly on the current comparison of single-shot mechanically produced non-survey tables and the 'purer' survey tables, has failed to address the most crucial question, namely the prime requirement of a regional input–output table. If the prime requirement of the table is to present accurate details of intersectoral transactions, i.e. that each cell in the table be presented within close tolerances of accuracy, then presumably there can be no substitute for fully detailed and scientifically designed survey-based tables, and we can relegate input–output to the high-budget institutions essentially divorced from operational economic analysis. A further relevant argument would be that such an approach to regional input–output would be extravagant in terms of resource use. Work in progress at the University of Queensland suggests that a substantial portion of an input–output table, perhaps 50 per cent (or more) of the smallest coefficients, have quite insignificant effects on the multipliers, and could be safely ignored. The converse of this suggestion is that research resources should be concentrated on the larger coefficients, with the smaller coefficients left as unworthy of attention, once it has been established that they are, in fact, small. An extension of this argument is that the simple comparison of coefficients between survey and non-survey tables (Miernyk, 1976, p. 49) is not a suitable comparison in terms of the ultimate uses of the tables; if the errors appear mainly in the smaller coefficients, the differences may be operationally meaningless.

If, on the other hand, the purpose of the input–output table is seen primarily as the substantially accurate representation of an economy *in toto*, in relation to its general 'shape' and structure, and that analytical applications of the table can provide order-of-magnitude measurement only, a different emphasis on table construction is warranted. Detailed attention to larger coefficients is necessary, with less attention deserved as the coefficients decrease in size. Certainly, purely mechanical techniques in this respect are unsatisfactory, but hybrid techniques which involve the replacement of mechanically produced larger coefficients by survey or other 'superior data' could well be adequate in assuring the general operational accuracy of the tables. This approach assumes that the general accuracy of the table as a whole will be greater than that of each part.

If the latter approach is adopted, and the research team believes it to be the most reasonable interpretation of regional input–output, the case for non-survey techniques, coupled with the subjective judgement of the analyst, is stronger, and to some extent the distinction between survey and hybrid tables becomes less important. Both the survey and the hybrid approach (at least as interpreted in this study) will ensure that the more important coefficients are reasonably accurate by substantially the same means, and since the smaller coefficients are insignificant in the formation of multipliers, the method of calculating these coefficients is largely irrelevant for operational purposes.

The crucial question becomes then the extent of interference in the mechanical process or the extent to which superior data is sought for insertion into the mechanically produced table. It is tempting to conclude that this interference should be maximised subject to the resources available for the study and this would be an appropriate conclusion. An alternative approach, and one adopted in this study, was to ensure that the characteristics of major or dominant industries were faithfully represented, and to search the prototype tables for any anomalies apparent to those familiar with the economic structure of the individual regions.

The concept of accuracy embodied in GRIT is one which implies 'freedom from significant error', rather than accuracy in detail. It implies also a holistic concept of accuracy, that the table present a representative overall picture of the regional economies concerned. Such a concept creates difficulties in the measurement of accuracy, since the concern is with the internal structure of the matrix and with identifiable principal components. One measure which is relevant lies in the comparison of multipliers derived from GRIT with those derived from survey-based tables. Such comparisons were made and allowed the authors to conclude that either freedom from significant 'error' had been achieved, or that both sets of tables were subject to the same relative errors.

Notes

1. This requirement reflects the data normally available in Queensland without long delay.
2. For example, GRIT employs a simple location quotient approach to calculate competitive imports. The use of other techniques for this calculation could readily be incorporated into the computer program.
3. The procedures assume that survey-based tables are a suitable reference point for accuracy measurement; such an assumption may be difficult to justify in view of the shortcomings of many survey-based tables (Boster and Martin, 1972, p. 35).

5 ACCOUNTING PROCEDURES

Previous chapters have been concerned with a review of regional input–output and of the background to the GRIT system. The following chapters concentrate specifically on the GRIT methodology and application. It is necessary at this stage, however, to define the accounting constraints which faced the research team and the accounting procedures and conventions adopted for the implementation of GRIT.

The literature relating to the building of non-survey regional input–output tables provides scant discussion on the accounting conventions used in the 'parent' national tables employed in producing regional tables. The problems of dealing with national imports, purchasers' *v.* producers' prices, secondary products and so on, do not appear to have been considered by most workers in this area. Hewings (1971a) used the national import coefficient to represent the regional category 'international trade'; unfortunately no justification or discussion was presented on this procedure. Goldman (1969), commenting on the work of Czamanski and Malizia (1969), argues that the effect of statistical and methodological idiosyncrasies employed in the national tables needs to be considered. It is difficult to compare non-survey-based regional tables with survey-based tables constructed under different conventions, without first determining the implications of these conventions.

5.1 The Australian National Input–Output Tables

The most recent Australian national tables available for this study were those for 1968–9.[1] The Australian tables are normally available in a number of forms, in terms of the degree of aggregation and the treatment of imports. The research team was given the choice of employing either 30-sector or 109-sector tables for the GRIT base; the latter was chosen to achieve a higher degree of flexibility in the definition of sectors for the regional tables, and to enable adjustments to be carried out in finer detail. The national tables were available in either purchasers' prices with indirect allocation of competing imports, basic values with indirect allocation of competing imports or basic values with direct allocation. In all tables transactions were net of intrasectoral transactions, although it would have been possible to estimate intrasectoral transactions.

The sectors of the national tables are defined in terms of the Australian Standard Industrial Classification (ASIC). The classification used in the 1968–9 tables is attached as Appendix II to this report. The sector content in the national tables was determined from three sources. Establishment statistics were used as the source of data in the mining, manufacturing and gas and electricity industries. The sector content for agriculture, forestry, fishing and hunting relate to commodities. In wholesale and retail trade, the sectors represent the activity of merchandising; the merchandising activities of establishments classified to other sectors is included in the wholesale and retail sectors. Similarly, sectors in the construction, service, government and other tertiary areas are conceptually on an activity basis.

5.2 Valuation of Transactions

In the preparation of the Australian national tables, the distinction was drawn between three methods of valuation of transactions.[2]

(a) *Purchasers' prices*, where transactions are valued at the prices actually paid by the purchaser, including delivery and distribution charges. Transport and distribution costs are shown as direct inputs to the producing sector. Output, including these costs, is distributed along the row of the producing sector.

(b) *Producers' prices*, where transactions are valued at the prices received by the producer. Marketing and distribution costs in this case are shown as direct inputs from the marketing and distribution sectors to the purchasing sector.

(c) *Basic Values.* Basic values are producers' prices net of commodity taxes. Where either producers' or purchasers' prices are used, commodity taxes are, of course, included in the valuation of the transactions, and are shown as paid by the producer of the commodities on which the taxes are levied. Transactions presented in basic values are net of commodity taxes; these are shown in a separate row and paid by the purchaser of the commodities on which the taxes are levied.

It should be noted that the definition of producers' prices used commonly in input–output work appears to correspond with the 'basic values' concept outlined above,[3] in that net commodity taxes have been deducted in the transactions table. To avoid confusion on this point, these terms are used in this report in the context defined in the Australian national input–output table.

The Australian national tables are presented in both purchasers' prices and basic values. When considering the choice between these methods of valuation for regional tables, the ultimate use to which the tables will be applied suggests initially a preference for the former. Purchasers' prices are probably more readily understood by users less familiar with input–output tables. Also they perform the very important function in a number of tables representing various regions of the state, of illustrating more realistically the local costs of the various categories of inputs, if accompanied by indirect allocation of imports.[4] In a state such as Queensland which is geographically dispersed and where distance is an important factor in determining the nature of regional economic activity, purchasers' prices would demonstrate the substantial differences in the local costs of the various categories of inputs. They would in effect provide within each column the locational effects on production costs for each sector.

The research team considered the conversion of national tables given at purchasers' prices to regional tables in the same prices. Such a method would require the incorporation into the national table (for each region) of adjustments for marketing and distribution costs for the output of each sector, i.e. correction of national tables at purchasers' prices by a matrix of marketing and distribution costs for each region. This was regarded as not possible in practice, and undesirable in principle, where regional tables were calculated partly by mechanical means. The alternative was to accept the purchasers' prices from national tables as representing purchasers' prices at the regional level; for the geographic reasons stated above this was not regarded as acceptable.

On the other hand, since locational factors do not influence basic values, they are likely to be more uniform between regions than purchasers' values, and could be accepted as a reasonable starting point for the calculation of regional tables. Although less easily understood by many users of the tables, it was considered that basic values could be more accurately portrayed at the regional level than purchasers' prices. The study team therefore chose to develop GRIT in basic values.

The decision to choose a particular method for valuing transactions appears to be more significant in terms of the ultimate use of the table than has been recognised in the literature. Jensen (1977) has carried out experiments with a regional table and the 30-sector version of the Australian national tables and has demonstrated that multipliers derived from different forms of the same table (purchasers' prices and basic values) can differ significantly in both absolute size and ranking. The paper suggests caution in the comparison of multipliers which have not been derived from tables in precisely the same form.

5.3 Treatment of Imports

Conventionally, input–output analysts distinguish between competitive and non-competitive (or complementary) imports. The former are usually described as those which are close substitutes for locally produced commodities and are normally recorded as an addition to the local value of output. The latter are those for which no suitable substitute is produced locally. Two important questions are associated with the treatment of imports, namely the method of allocation of imports within the table and the method of distinguishing between competitive and non-competitive imports. These are briefly considered in turn.

In general terms, imports may be allocated directly or indirectly within the table. When allocated directly, they are recorded in the column of the purchasing sector; when allocated indirectly they are recorded in the column of the sector which would have produced them within the region, and distributed within the row of that sector. An established convention in input–output is that non-competitive imports should be directly allocated. The method is accepted since non-competitive imports, which are a function of sector output, are appropriately included at c.i.f. cost in the relevant sector cost structure. No such widely accepted practice exists, however, with respect to the allocation of competitive imports; published tables show both direct and indirect allocation in common use.

The argument for indirect allocation of competitive imports has been that it produces more stable direct coefficients. However, Matuszewski *et al.* (1964) refute the stability argument by pointing out that the assumption that the coefficients of such a column are constant implies that the ratio of imports to domestic output for the industry is constant. They address the question that indirect allocation of competitive imports produces an input–output model which is a better predictor than a model employing direct allocation of all imports. Comparing the performance of input–output models in Canada based on 1949 data in predicting the performance of that economy in 1956, the authors concluded that the method of allocation of imports made no significant difference to predictive results.

Work by McGaurr (1977) has established that it is important to consider together the valuation of transactions and the method of allocation of imports. If the advantages of purchasers' prices (the identification of regional costs of production) are to be presented in the table, it is required that the total purchases by each sector be shown in the columns. This implies the use of indirect allocation of competitive imports. GRIT was, for reasons previously outlined, committed to the use of basic values, and the choice of direct or indirect allocation of non-competitive imports needed to be made on this basis.

Other factors support the use of direct allocation of both competitive and non-competitive imports in this study. *First*, direct allocation ensures that the level of imports varies only with the change in sector output. The indirect allocation method could result in variation of the level of imports for a purchasing sector, with variation in the level of output of the supplying sector. *Second*, the use of the indirect method is traditionally regarded as being more suited to a table attempting to present technical relationships and coefficients; this study is concerned more with trade flows and trade coefficients.[5] *Third*, when direct allocation is used, the intermediate quadrant refers specifically and exclusively to actual regional inter-industry transactions, and contains no elements of import content; these are separately provided in the primary inputs quadrant. Indirect allocation produces intermediate coefficients containing some elements of imports; the resulting multipliers therefore contain these elements. Supplementary structural analysis of the input–output table would be required to isolate the significance of imports. *Fourth*, direct allocation had been used by Huxley (1973), which provided some important checks on the calculation of regional trade in this study. This major work provides information on interregional trade flows in Queensland. *Fifth*, direct allocation allows adjustments to be made more easily since a change in the import/local ratio in the output of a sector involves a single proportionate adjustment. *Sixth*, direct allocation is a simpler concept for users of the tables.

The second major question relates to the distinction between competitive and non-competitive imports. The difficulty of distinguishing competitive from non-competitive imports, as an exercise in determining which commodities are 'satisfactory' substitutes for others, even in a reasonable data situation, has been well documented. The difficulty is compounded in a regional context when data relating to regional trade is scarce, and when mechanical means for calculating first estimates of imports are necessary. To accommodate this problem, GRIT incorporates the definition of competitive and non-competitive imports adopted in the Central Queensland study (Jensen, 1976). It was assumed that if firms in a particular statistical classification have been recorded as existing in the region by the Australian Bureau of Statistics, that these firms produce, or are capable of producing, those commodities normally considered as the output of the firms in that classification. Imports of these commodities were therefore regarded as competitive.

Clearly, commodities listed as the output of firms in a classification not recorded in the region were to be considered as non-competitive imports. Such a distinction inevitably inflates the proportion of imports recorded as competitive, since the mere existence of some firms in the region in a statistical classification does not ensure that all of the commodities associated with that classification of firms could, or will, be produced within the region.

In the light of these problems, GRIT encompasses this distinction between competitive and non-competitive imports in the procedures for calculating imports, but aggregates both categories of imports for presentation in the tables. Since non-competitive imports were directly allocated, the desire to avoid the rather arbitrary distinction between the two categories of imports provided a further persuasive reason for direct allocation of competitive imports.

5.4 Treatment of Intrasectoral Transactions[6]

The concepts of gross output (including intrasectoral transactions) and net output (excluding intrasectoral transactions) were illustrated in input–output use long ago (Evans and Hoffenberg, 1952). Analysts have employed both approaches; the former appears to be more common in regional tables.

It is possible (Parker, 1967) to identify three types of intrasectoral transactions, namely: (i) commodities which are produced and used in own works, and which are not normally recorded in official value of output estimates; (ii) transactions which occur between establishments which are grouped in the same sub-class; and (iii) transactions which occur between establishments classified to different sub-classes which have been aggregated to the same sector for the purpose of the study. Inevitably input–output studies ignore category (i) items for obvious data reasons, but the question of inclusion of category (ii) and (iii) items requires further discussion.

Generally, tables are considered to be in gross terms if categories (ii) and (iii) of intrasectoral transactions are recorded in the table. A general principle expressed by Evans and Hoffenberg (1962, p. 114) is that gross tables are desirable since 'gross output remains constant and additive'. Tables are considered to be in net terms if these categories are excluded.

Any classification of sectors is necessarily arbitrary; the 109-sector Australian tables would not provide a sufficient degree of disaggregation to avoid some category (iii) transactions occurring in different amounts in different sectors if the tables were recorded in gross terms. The arbitrary nature of the sector classification system must impose a similarly arbitrary nature on the intrasectoral entries in a gross table. While this is a disadvantage, the removal of these entries to form net tables imposes a similarly arbitrary adjustment on sector output in net tables. It is inevitable that both gross and net output levels are to some extent a function of the classification system used.

The problem is compounded when reduction of national to regional tables is contemplated. Items which constitute intrasectoral transactions at the national level in a more diverse economy might not, in fact, be intrasectoral transactions in the simpler regional economies, and may be items of interregional trade. It would appear that inferring regional intrasectoral transactions from national intrasectoral transactions coefficients would considerably overstate the actual regional cell entries in this respect.[7]

The choice facing the GRIT team was between: (a) the use of gross national tables, in the knowledge that gross tables have some advantages when aggregating from larger to smaller tables, but were likely to produce exaggerated estimates of regional intrasectoral transactions; and (b) the use of net national tables, knowing that the aggregation procedure in GRIT would produce estimates of intrasectoral transactions, i.e. that the net national table would produce a regional table which was gross in some respects. The latter was chosen for a number of reasons. *First*, the advantage of the use of gross tables in aggregation was seen as limited to the case where the aggregated table referred to the original (disaggregated) economy, and did not extend to aggregation to produce regional tables from national tables. *Second*, the above-mentioned exaggeration of regional intrasectoral transactions was regarded as unacceptable. *Third*, the net output concept in the national tables would be preserved in the regional tables, despite the fact that aggregation to produce smaller regional tables would result in entries on the diagonal of the regional tables, i.e. the tables remained 'net' as defined in the national tables. Removal of the cell entries on the main diagonal, which occurred as a result of aggregation at the regional level would have destroyed the consistent valuation throughout the regional tables.

The resulting tables, presented in Chapter 7 and Appendices, show an apparent inconsistency. When sectors have been taken from the national tables in net form and not subjected to aggregation, the relevant diagonal element is zero. This occurs in a few important sectors, but should be interpreted in the light of this discussion.

5.5 Summary

The reasoning outlined in this chapter led to the production of GRIT tables in the following form:

(a) transactions valued in basic values;
(b) both competitive and non-competitive imports allocated directly;
(c) use of the 'net' treatment of intrasectoral transactions at the 109-sector level.

Notes

1. At the time of writing (late 1977), the first national tables for the 1968–9 year were recently made available. The Australian Bureau of Statistics kindly made available, prior to publication, to the authors a form of the national tables necessary for this project to proceed.
2. Commonwealth Bureau of Census and Statistics (1973), pp. 25–7, based on United Nations standards (United Nations, 1968).
3. Examination of the input–output literature shows that few analysts precisely define the concept of producers' prices which they employ. Exceptions are Evans and Hoffenberg (1952, p. 103) and O'Connor and Henry (1975).
4. Methods of allocating imports are discussed in section 5.3.
5. We distinguish between technical coefficients arising from the technical characteristics of production functions, and trade coefficients calculated from transactions data.
6. This section draws heavily on Jensen (1977).
7. The reader is referred to the decision by Smith and Morrison (1974) to remove intrasectoral transactions from the national table before deriving regional tables.

6 METHODOLOGY

This chapter outlines the GRIT methodological sequence. The sequence is expressed in fifteen steps which are arranged in five phases. These are summarised in Table 6.1, detailed operationally in Appendix I, expressed in the form of a computer program in Appendix IV, and discussed in appropriate detail in this chapter.

The methodology focuses on the conversion of national *coefficients* to regional *coefficients*, rather than on the conversion of the national transactions table to a series of regional transactions tables. In principle, of course, there is no difference; the authors have chosen to describe and specify the methodology in terms of coefficients. The coefficients are described in terms of the following general framework:

		Intermediate Sectors	Final Demand	
Intermediate Sectors	n	A	F	n
Primary Inputs	h	B	G	h
		n	k	

where A is a matrix of input–output coefficients of dimension $n \times n$,
B is a matrix of primary inputs of dimension $h \times n$,
F is a matrix of final demand of dimension $n \times k$, and
G is a matrix of primary inputs absorbed by final demand, of dimension $h \times k$.

The matrices and coefficients are notated in the text and in the flowchart (Appendix I) by superscripts in parentheses to indicate the stage of adjustment. The initial coefficients of the national table are denoted $A^{(0)} = [a_{ij}^{(0)}]$, those resulting from the first step of the adjustment procedure $A^{(1)} = [a_{ij}^{(1)}]$, and so on.

6.1 Outline of the GRIT Methodological Sequence

Phase I of the sequence provides for adjustments to the national table which supplies the basic input into GRIT; these comprise adjustments

Table 6.1: The GRIT Methodological Sequence

Step No.	
	PHASE I ADJUSTMENTS TO NATIONAL TABLE
1	Start with national input–output table. (109-sector table with direct allocation of all imports, basic values, net of intrasectoral transactions.)
2	Adjustment of national table for price levels and updating.
3	Adjustment for international trade.
	PHASE II ADJUSTMENT FOR REGIONAL IMPORTS
	(Steps 4–14 apply to *each* region for which input–output tables are required)
4	Calculation of non-competitive imports.
5	Calculation of competitive imports.
	PHASE III DEFINITION OF REGIONAL SECTORS
6	Insertion of disaggregated superior data.
7	Aggregation of sectors.
8	Insertion of aggregated superior data.
	PHASE IV DERIVATION OF PROTOTYPE TRANSACTIONS TABLES
9	Derivation of initial transactions tables.
10	Manual or iterative adjustments to initial tables to derive prototype tables.
11	Aggregation if uniform tables are required.
12	Derivation of inverses and multipliers for prototype tables.
	PHASE V DERIVATION OF FINAL TRANSACTIONS TABLES
13	Final superior data insertions and other adjustments.
14	Derivation of final transactions tables.
15	Derivation of inverses and multipliers for final tables.

for price changes, updating and for international trade. In Phase II the difficult task of estimating regional imports for each region for which tables are desired is attempted. This is achieved by assuming that the coefficients referring in the national table to sectors which do not exist in the region(s) indicate the level of regional non-competitive imports. Further, some of the coefficients of the sectors which exist in the region are adjusted downwards to eliminate that portion of purchases ascribed to these sectors in the national table, which become imports at the regional level. Phase III provides for the insertion of 'disaggregated superior data', i.e. estimates which the operator considers superior to those produced by the mechanical operations of Phases I and II, and which are available at the disaggregated (109-sector) level. Adjustments are also made for region-unique industrial mix and production functions by weighted aggregation to smaller tables which are more commensurate with the simpler economic structure of the regions. Phases II and III, then, attempt adjustments for the main differences between a national and its corresponding regional sector, namely the level of imports, the component industry mix and the production functions.

Phase IV provides a further opportunity for the insertion of superior data, when these data are available only in a more aggregated form. From the coefficients developed from earlier phases, an *initial transactions table* is developed for each region by applying regional ouput estimates to the coefficients to produce first estimates of transactions. Either manual or constrained-matrix iterative adjustments are applied to produce a consistent *prototype transactions table*. Finally, Phase V allows for the inspection of each table, the insertion of superior data and other adjustments to improve the accuracy of the table or to remove anomalies. This phase produces *final transactions tables* and their associated multipliers.

The following convention has been applied throughout the text:

(a) National trade coefficients are derived, and are subjected to a series of adjustments to produce regional trade coefficients. Hence Phases I, II and III are discussed only in terms of coefficients.

(b) The regional coefficients derived in Phases I to III are converted into regional transactions in Phase IV by the application of regional gross output levels. Phases IV and V are therefore discussed in terms of transactions.

The remainder of this chapter describes each phase of the GRIT sequence in more detail.

6.2 Phase I: Adjustments to the National Table

The GRIT sequence begins with the national input–output tables; the objective of Phase I is to ensure that these tables are developed to the most appropriate form for the calculation procedures designed to produce regional tables in subsequent phases.

For reasons outlined in Chapter 5, the authors chose the 109-sector version of the Australian tables, with direct allocation of all imports, in basic values and net of intrasectoral transactions. Other analysts following the GRIT system might choose, or be forced through circumstances, to adopt other forms of national tables. In this case some variation in one or more of the steps may be required.

Step 2: Adjustment for Price Levels and Updating

Step 2 was inserted as an 'optional' step by the research team. Procedures to adjust for relative prices and other updating methods are available, and could be incorporated at the discretion of the analyst. In this application to develop regional tables for the state of Queensland, Step 2 was omitted and the 1968–9 national tables were accepted as appropriate. More recent national tables could be substituted when they become available. The implementation of updating and price adjustment procedures at the 109-sector level were, in any case, beyond the resources available to the GRIT team. An alternative would have been to apply these procedures to the simpler and more aggregated regional tables. The significance of Step 2 in the formation of regional multipliers has not been empirically examined. It is important to consider the marginal gains from updating and price adjustment procedures, given the time involved in applying these procedures and the fact that the opportunities provided for insertion of superior data should ensure that imports and local industries are suitably represented in the regional tables, and that noticeable anomalies are removed.

Step 3: Adjustment for International Trade

The extent to which a nation and any of its constituent regions trade with the 'rest of the world' differs significantly, both in terms of the relative importance of trade, and the trading pattern of the various sectors. Normally, trade measures for the nation and the region are expected to be empirically inconsistent and incapable of conversion from one to the other, except in quite unusual circumstances. There is no *a priori* reason for the patterns of imports or exports to be consistent from a national to a regional basis. For example, in the Queensland context, our knowledge of the trading patterns of Queensland regions suggests that there are important and substantial differences between national and regional import patterns. This has been demonstrated by Huxley (1973), and reflects an identifiable pattern. Regions outside the metropolitan areas typically export primary products through local ports before or after processing; primary products form a substantial proportion of the local economic base of these regions. Typically, non-metropolitan regions also import the large majority of durable and non-durable household commodities and investment goods, most of which are manufactured in the metropolitan area, other states or overseas. Conversely, the metropolitan area exports large quantities of consumer and investment goods to the rural regions, and re-exports goods imported from rural regions. The metropolitan region imports both processed and non-processed primary commodities from the rural regions, and a high proportion of investment goods used in the state. From the point of view of international trading patterns, most imports will be destined for the metropolitan region, industrial exports will derive largely from the same region, and primary exports from rural regions.

Since the concept of international trade in the national table is empirically incompatible with regional trade in the tables to be produced, it was considered necessary to make adjustments to the national table. This involved adjustment for those measures of international trade which are inconsistent with the concept of regional trade. However, since imports at the national level contribute substantially to the output of sectors at the national level, and the national sectors form the reference base for deriving regional sectors, it was also seen as necessary to retain the national imports within the table. An attempt was therefore made to produce a table which represented a closed national economy, i.e. one in which the imports originally shown in the national tables were assumed to be domestically produced.

Prior to a determination of procedures for adjustment of the national tables to remove the effects of international trade, some consideration was given to the following issues. As indicated in section 5.3, imports are normally distinguished as competitive and non-competitive. It is clear that those imports which are non-competitive at the national level must remain non-competitive in any table derived for a region. However, it is possible for imports which are competitive at the national level to be either competitive or non-competitive at the regional level. Since we desire to estimate both regional competitive and non-competitive imports as a means of estimating total regional imports, the question should be raised of the extent to which the distinction between competitive and non-competitive imports at the national level is a guide to the same distinction at the regional level. Clearly there is no *a priori* empirical connection between the two, except as stated above, items which are non-competitive at the national level will be also non-competitive at the regional level, and in this respect might provide some *minimum* level of regional non-competitive imports with respect to the specific commodities or groups of commodities. Given the aggregation processes and the differing industry mixes in various regions, attempts to translate national competitive and non-competitive imports to their regional counterparts were considered and rejected. Further, since Phase II is specifically aimed at calculation of regional competitive and non-competitive imports, the distinction at the national level was discontinued and all imports were therefore treated in a similar manner.

Accepting that imports should not be removed from the national table, and also the consideration that national imports should not remain in the national tables as estimates of regional imports, the remaining possibility was the allocation of imports over the non-import entries in the relevant column of the national table. This raised the question of the appropriate allocation method. Examination of the national tables indicated that the bulk of imports were of inputs to, or of finished products of, secondary industries. This invited the suggestion that accuracy would be served more by restricting the reallocation of the import coefficient in each column to those coefficients representing purchases from secondary industries within that column. The suggestion was considered of general validity and was adopted as a standard reallocation procedure. However, it was recognised that the general procedure could produce serious distortions in some sectors where it was known that national imports to the sector were not mainly of secondary commodities. A procedure was therefore implemented to allow interference in the general reallocation procedure to allow the operator to reallocate imports over any combination of the three groups i.e. primary, secondary and tertiary sectors.

Step 3 involves in notation terms, the conversion of $A^{(0)}$ to $A^{(1)}$ and $B^{(0)}$ to $B^{(1)}$, as shown in the flow chart (Appendix I).

6.3 Phase II: Adjustment for Regional Imports

Phase I provides the reference base for that part of the GRIT system which is mechanical in nature, and from which the calculation of any number of tables referring to regions within the nation can be initiated. Phase II and subsequent phases will be required with respect to each regional table to be developed.

Phase II attempts the conversion of national trade coefficients to the first approximations of regional trade coefficients. We begin with the 109-sector matrix of national coefficients adjusted for international trade, $A^{(1)}$ and $B^{(1)}$ and seek to produce a matrix of regional coefficients, by applying two adjustment procedures. The first adjustment procedure (Step 4), producing matrices $A^{(2)}$ and $B^{(2)}$, attempts to identify regional non-competitive imports. The second adjustment procedure (Step 5), producing matrices $A^{(3)}$ and $B^{(3)}$, attempts to identify, from $A^{(2)}$ and $B^{(2)}$, regional competitive imports.

Conventionally, it is not acceptable to use a national coefficient as a regional coefficient without making adjustments for interregional trade. The conversion of national coefficients to regional coefficients has been discussed in the literature; this discussion has been outlined in Chapter 3. The problem is usually stated simply in terms of decomposing the national technical coefficient a_{ij} into a regional input coefficient r_{ij} and a regional import coefficient m_{ij}. The process of decomposition is usually based on the assumption that national and regional technical coefficients are identical, and that the decomposition will provide estimates of regional input–output coefficients r_{ij} and imports m_{ij} which are closer to survey-based coefficients than to national coefficients. We argue that since national tables are derived, in Australia at least, from transactions or flows rather than physical quantities, it is inappropriate to suggest that these national coefficients are technical coefficients in any real sense. The process of regionalisation of national coefficients should then be seen as adjusting national flow or trade coefficients to coefficients which can reasonably be expected to represent regional flows in a substantial way.

Step 4: Calculation of Non-Competitive Imports

We begin by assuming that the national flow coefficients are a first indication of regional coefficients, and apply for each region for which a table is required, a procedure similar to that proposed by Smith and Morrison (1974). Where data from the statistical authorities indicate that no activity in a statistical classification exists in the region, the $a_{ij}^{(1)}$ associated with that classification was removed from the $A^{(1)}$ matrix and entered as a regional import. This step is in effect the complete allocation of the $a_{ij}^{(1)}$ coefficient to imports, and from the regional point of view, calculates non-competitive imports. The vacated cells are entered as zero in the table.

On the surface the question of determining whether or not a sector displays economic activity in a region is not a difficult matter. This could be achieved satisfactorily by simply noting the presence or absence in the region of either firms or employment in the sectors as defined for the national table. Since employment data by sectors were required for later adjustment procedures, the employment criterion was chosen. It should be mentioned also that Australian statistical authorities do not record the number of firms or the number of employees in all sectors; however, employment is available in detail for census years and reasonable estimates of employment statistics in intercensal years can be developed.

Estimates of non-competitive imports could be improved if the process of defining non-competitive imports could be applied with a finer classification than that provided in the 109 sectors of the national tables. For example, it would be possible to apply the criterion at the four-digit ASIC level. With finer classification it would have been possible to allocate proportions of the $a_{ij}^{(1)}$ remaining in the table to non-competitive imports. Problems of confidentiality of data at the local level suggested that the finer classification was not operational. The confidentiality problem at the 109-sector level was noticeable and was expected to be severe with finer classification. One result of the decision to incorporate the coarser classification shown in the national tables would be that estimates of non-competitive imports will be lower relative to competitive imports, compared to those which would have resulted from a finer classification.

Step 5: Calculation of Competitive Imports

Following the calculation of non-competitive imports, matrices $A^{(2)}$ contain national coefficients for industries known to exist in each region. An adjustment procedure must now be applied in Step 5 to convert these national coefficients to regional trade coefficients for each industry by determining that part of the national coefficient which should be allocated to competitive imports.

The various methods which have been adopted for this conversion have been discussed at length in the literature. The procedures adopted and an evaluation of the procedures are outlined in Chapter 3. The selection of a technique for decomposing the national coefficient has received more attention in the literature than other aspects of developing regional non-survey tables; in fact, apart from the work of Smith and Morrison (1974) and Schaffer (1976), it has been regarded by most previous analysts as the sole method of developing non-survey tables. Certainly the selection of a procedure is important to the ultimate accuracy of the regional tables. While later steps provide further modifications to the regional coefficients determined by Step 5, these later modifications are expected to be relatively minor in effect in most industries, unless superior data insertions occur.

It has been suggested by Smith and Morrison (1974) and Czamanski and Malizia (1969) that the simple location quotient (LQ) would produce regional tables closer to survey-based tables than the alternative location quotient and commodity balance procedures. These analysts measured the 'closeness' of the survey-based and derived non-survey tables in terms of the distance between coefficients of the two tables.

The authors were not able to apply this method of comparison due to time constraints; we would have valued the opportunity to execute Step 5 with several alternative procedures, in order to test the sensitivity of the results according to the procedure adopted. In these circumstances, the location quotient was chosen as the appropriate procedure for the GRIT system. Analysts using GRIT could well express a preference for other methods of calculating competitive imports, and these could be substituted at this stage.

Some criticisms have been levelled at the location quotient technique for the measurement of interregional trade, and are therefore relevant to the context of this study. An important criticism of the location quotient rests on the implicit assumption of uniformity in demand and consumption patterns between regions. This assumption is inevitable in the absence of studies of consumption on a spatial basis. This problem is overcome to some extent by allowing the analyst the freedom to insert more appropriate consumption data for any region, should this be available.

Another criticism of the location quotient procedure for calculating imports is that it fails to account for cross haulage. The authors were satisfied that in the context of the rather simple trading patterns of the Queensland economy, a minimum of cross haulage occurred.

The location quotient in the GRIT sequence is applied as follows:

(a) calculation of location quotients on employment data alone for the 109 sectors of the national tables;

(b) isolation of those sectors where $LQ_i < 1$, and the application of the location quotient across the rows of the appropriate sectors to decompose the national trade coefficient into the regional trade coefficient, and the regional import coefficients, the latter to be collected as competitive imports for each column.

The completion of Phase II provides new matrices $A^{(3)}$ and $B^{(3)}$, with non-competitive and competitive imports aggregated to a single imports row.

6.4 Phase III: Definition of Regional Sectors

Phase III begins with a series of coefficient tables, each with 109 sectors, relating to regions of the state. These tables have been derived by the application of techniques for the conversion of national to regional coefficients.

Phase III is seen as applying procedures to convert the 109-sector tables into more representative regional tables, by (a) the insertion of more appropriate data where these are available in disaggregated, i.e. 109-sector, format and (b) aggregation. Aggregation is carried out on a weighted basis, both to reduce the number of sectors to a number more consistent with useful and operational regional tables, and to incorporate at least in part the differences in industry mix apparent in the range of regions under study.

Step 6: Insertion of Disaggregated Superior Data

As indicated earlier, the term 'superior data' is used in this study to refer to data which are considered by the analyst to be more accurate with respect to the regional tables than the estimates mechanically derived from the table of national coefficients. Data may be considered 'more accurate' if obtained from a source such as official statistical collection agencies, or from research sources such as surveys, or simply if the skilled resources available to the analyst consider one estimate to be 'better' than another.

This step provides a facility for superior data to be inserted before the sector aggregation process is undertaken. It therefore allows superior data in a disaggregated form to replace elements of matrices $A^{(3)}$ and $B^{(3)}$ as considered appropriate. In the application of GRIT to the regions of Queensland, superior data of various types were incorporated. These are classified and detailed in Appendix VI.

Although Step 6 is considered by the research team to be crucial to the development of realistic regional tables, it is also considered important that the operational insertion of superior data should be limited to those occasions where the insertion can be expected to contribute substantially to an improved table. The concept of GRIT, that is the development of regional tables in a less time-consuming and less expensive manner, will be weakened if the insertion of superior data is extended to a large number of marginal improvements. To this end, we confine the insertion of superior data to relatively major regional sectors. In this study, insertion of superior data is kept to a minimum consistent with realism in the regional tables and freedom from significant error. Other analysts may choose to increase the level of operator interference, depending on their objectives and resources.

Step 7: Aggregation of Sectors

There was clearly a need to reduce the 109-sector tables relating to rural regions (resulting from Phase II) to a size which is commensurate with the simpler economic structure of these regions. On the other hand it is important to enable the complexity of the metropolitan region and provincial city regions to be adequately represented. There was, of course, the important additional need to retain conformity of sector definition between regional tables to allow direct comparison of the tables and to facilitate comparative studies. On the other hand, the process of aggregation should be designed to highlight, and not to subdue, the significant differences in regional economic structure which is a feature of most national economies.

The question of aggregation was seen to require consideration of three aspects:

(a) the selection of an appropriate number of sectors for the derived regional tables;

(b) the choice of the appropriate combinations of national table sectors for the selected regional sectors;

(c) the choice of an appropriate mathematical aggregation procedure.

To some extent these aspects, particularly (a) and (b), are interrelated.

The wide range of regions, in terms of economic complexity, was mentioned briefly at the beginning of this section. The more isolated regions of the state exhibit a simple economic structure, with a tendency to monocultural primary industries (either beef or sheep) providing the export base, very restricted local manufacturing (restricted to establishments such as bakeries, automotive services, light engineering) and importation of most consumer goods. On the other hand, the metropolitan region, with a population of over one million, exhibits the characteristics and complexities of a modern city-region. Between these two extremes can be identified a range of regions of varying degrees of complexity of economic structure, but which do not approach the complexity of the metropolitan region.

The desire to represent the different levels of economic complexity of the individual regions and the desire to retain conformity of sector definition are clearly in conflict. The former implies producing input–output tables at different levels of aggregation; the latter implies a series of tables at a uniform level of aggregation. This conflict was resolved by producing *two* sets of regional tables, one set with three different levels of aggregation to accommodate to some degree the variety in regional economic complex, and one set at a uniform level of aggregation to allow direct comparisons between regions and between the regions and the state, for all sectors. The first set is termed in this text the *non-uniform* tables; the second is termed the *uniform* tables.

In the calculation of non-uniform tables, three types of regions were identified:

(a) the Metropolitan (Moreton) region, representing the only metropolitan region in the state, and considered to exhibit an economy sufficiently diverse to warrant special attention in its own right;

(b) rural regions, representing those regional economies of a simpler structure, i.e. consisting of few primary industries and whose manufacturing sector consists of a small number of basic activities;

(c) provincial regions, where the existence of at least a medium-sized urban area suggests the presence of a wider range of manufacturing activity, and where the primary sectors tend to be more diverse in nature.

The regions of Queensland were categorised as shown in Table 6.2. Based on this categorisation, the sectors of the regional tables will be defined as shown in Appendix III. The first step in the aggregation procedure combines the national sectors listed in the right-hand column of Appendix III to sectors defined for the Metropolitan region. At this stage the aggregation procedure ceases for the Metropolitan region, defining 36 sectors for this table. For non-metropolitan regions, the aggregation proceeds until the 19 sectors for the Provincial regions have been formed. At this stage the aggregation ceases for the Provincial regions, and continues to form eleven sectors for the Rural regions. This method was designed to cater for the detail required for different types of regional economies and also to produce comparability of definition of the sectors between regions of different types. The latter is achieved by the fact that sectors in the smaller tables are aggregates of identifiable sectors in larger tables, as indicated by the alpha-numeric sector identification system in Appendix III.

Table 6.2: Categorisation of Queensland Regions

Metropolitan	*Provincial*	*Rural*
Moreton	Wide Bay—Burnett	
	Darling Downs	Central West
	Fitzroy	South West
	Mackay	
	Northern	
	Far North	
	North West	

The GRIT computer program allows for the aggregation process to be continued to produce uniform tables if these are required by the analyst. This occurs in Step 11 following manual adjustments to ensure that the regional tables are consistent. The uniform tables are, therefore, aggregations of adjusted tables.

The aggregation system described above, including that foreshadowed in Step 11, produces the following variety of tables: (Table 6.3). The mechanics of sector aggregation proceed by aggregation of coefficients weighted by employment data.

Alternative aggregation procedures were considered in the light of the extensive discussion in the literature on the problems of aggregation in linear models. It is not proposed to repeat or outline this discussion here, but simply to draw attention to the fact that GRIT shares the problems and hazards normally faced by input–output analysts in considering appropriate levels and procedures for aggregation, and that as far as possible these have been considered. There are, however, some points regarding aggregation which are particularly relevant to this study. First, it is believed (with Shen, 1960) that some form of weighting of national coefficients by regional data will be more likely to produce coefficients closer to 'true' regional coefficients. While Shen used the weighting technique as a 'one-shot' method to produce regional from national tables, GRIT uses the weighting technique as a marginal improvement to already estimated 'regional' coefficients. Secondly, we recognise that other weights, in particular value added or output, would be more acceptable weights to incorporate in the aggregation process. Neither value added nor output data were available at the 109-sector level for all regions and this fact precluded the use of these as weights. Some difficulty was experienced in obtaining employment in 109-sector detail for all regions but, as mentioned earlier, these were inferred from census data with some confidence.

A third constraint on the aggregation procedures exists in a study of this type. For reasons stated previously, it is necessary that the sectors appearing in the various regional tables be defined consistently in terms

Table 6.3: Summary of Types of GRIT Input–Output Tables Produced

Input–Output Tables of:	*Non-Uniform Tables*	*Uniform Tables*
State of Queensland	36-sector	11-sector
Metropolitan Region	36-sector	11-sector
Provincial Regions	19-sector	11-sector
Rural Regions	11-sector	11-sector

of component industries. It was therefore necessary that any aggregation procedure should produce this consistency. Aggregation bases other than ASIC could not be guaranteed to produce the required conformity in sector definition between tables. This was considered to be the case particularly with respect to aggregation procedures such as the use of 'cluster analysis' (Blin and Cohen, 1976).

Following Step 7 new matrices $A^{(5)}$ and $B^{(5)}$ with respect to each region are produced. These matrices will now vary in dimension according to the categorisation of the region concerned.

Step 8: Insertion of Aggregated Superior Data

The use of superior data was mentioned briefly in the discussion of Step 6 and is detailed with respect to the application of GRIT to the regions of Queensland in Appendix VI. Step 8 provides an opportunity for the insertion into matrices $A^{(5)}$ and $B^{(5)}$ of superior data which are available only in a more aggregated form consistent with the sector definitions adopted. Together with Step 6, this facility maximises the potential use of the various forms of superior data, some of which are available on a detailed 109-sector basis, and some of which are available at a regional level only with respect to combinations of industries.

Following Step 8, coefficient matrices $A^{(6)}$ and $B^{(6)}$ are produced for each region.

6.5 Phase IV: Derivation of Prototype Transactions Tables

The aim of Phase IV is the conversion of coefficient tables $A^{(6)}$ and $B^{(6)}$ into prototype transactions tables for each region. These prototype tables are 'next-to-final' regional transactions tables, to be subjected to the detailed scrutiny of the analyst in Phase V of the GRIT sequence. The development of the prototype tables and their multipliers is essentially the production of the 'interim results' of the GRIT system.

Step 9: Derivation of Initial Transactions Tables

As outlined, Step 8 concludes with coefficient matrices $A^{(6)}$ and $B^{(6)}$ referring to the intermediate and primary inputs quadrants of each regional table. Two steps are required for expansion of these matrices into conventional transactions tables, namely the conversion of the coefficients to transactions and the completion of the final demand quadrants, namely matrices F and G. Step 9 provides for the former, and Step 10 for the latter.

Step 9 simply involves multiplying the elements of each column by estimates of output for each sector to convert the coefficients to first estimates of transactions. The tables produced are termed *initial transactions tables*, and as suggested above, refer to intermediate and primary inputs quadrants *A* and *B* only.

The derivation of output levels for the implementation of Step 9 presented some problems. Official statistics of output were available for several sectors at the regional level. For those sectors for which these output statistics were not available, estimates were derived from other input–output studies or by the use of indirect methods of calculation.

Step 10: Manual or Iterative Adjustments to Initial Transactions Tables to Derive Prototype Tables

Step 10 produces, from the initial transactions tables (detailing the intermediate and primary inputs quadrants only), the prototype transactions table, detailing the four quadrants of each table, by calculation of estimates for the elements of final demand quadrants *F* and *G* for all regional tables. Conventionally the components of final demand in a regional input–output table include household consumption, exports, public authority net current expenditure, inventory accumulation and capital formation. The derivation of estimates by region of these components is, in effect, the estimation of their spatial distribution within the state – these are aspects of economic activity in which there is almost a complete lack of useful data in Australia.

Two questions need to be considered at this stage:

(a) the choice of a level of aggregation in final demand sectors which will be consistent with the ultimate uses to which the regional tables will be put;

(b) the choice of technique for the estimation of the final demand sectors chosen in (a).

These questions are now addressed in turn.

Previous experience in the compilation of regional input–output tables in the Australian context (Jensen, 1976) has highlighted the difficulty of obtaining estimates of final demand elements (excluding exports) at a regional level, without surveys or detailed analysis of government and semi-government expenditure patterns. This experience showed also that such time-consuming effort did not necessarily produce useful or reliable estimates in all components of final demand. The GRIT team considered in any case that such an approach was not consistent with the objectives of the project, and concluded that an alternative approach was necessary.

It is necessary for the ultimate production of multipliers for the regional tables to contain estimates of household consumption. It was considered a necessary and achievable object of the study for regional exports to be included in the tables. Beyond these two components, no further components of final demand were considered individually measurable for individual regions, and these were therefore aggregated under the heading 'Other Final Demand'.

Two approaches to the estimation of final demand in the regional tables were considered. First, it is possible to use final demand as a residual item to achieve the necessary row and column consistency within each table. Second, it is possible to incorporate independent estimates of final demand. The latter procedure would almost certainly produce inconsistent tables, i.e. column and row totals of intermediate sectors which were not equal, and it would be necessary to enforce consistency using an appropriate mathematical technique, for example the RAS technique.

The decision between these two alternatives must depend on the availability and reliability of data relating to regional final demand. If reliable data relating to final demand are not available for each region, as was the case in the GRIT application to the regions of Queensland, the use of final demand as a residual item seems the obvious solution. The tables presented in Chapter 7 were derived on this basis.

However, circumstances might exist where analysts are able to develop estimates of final demand for regions, and have an equal or higher degree of faith in these estimates, compared to those produced by earlier phases in the GRIT sequence. In this case it would be important for these estimates to be entered in the regional transactions tables and some operations undertaken to ensure consistency within these tables. These operations might be carried out manually, or by the use of some iterative constrained matrix technique such as the RAS.

The GRIT sequence allows for the operator to choose between the two alternatives – use of final demand as a residual, or incorporation of final demand estimates followed by the application of the RAS technique. Minor adjustments to the sequence would allow other techniques to achieve consistency to be included.

The RAS model has been applied in various areas of input–output analysis and needs no comment in detail in this study. It has been widely applied to generate an updated and consistent national matrix given minimal information in the form of marginal constraints and an earlier input–output matrix. A catalogue of such applications is reviewed by Lecomber (1971). Two published applications of the RAS model in regional input–output economics are the previously mentioned Czamanski and Malizia (1969) and Smith and Morrison (1974) studies which generated regional tables for Washington state and Peterborough (UK) from national coefficients. The RAS technique has also been invoked for the reconciliation of purchases and sales estimates of regional transactions by Jensen and McGaurr (1976).

The application of the RAS technique as part of the GRIT sequence would be different from the earlier applications. Unlike the Washington and Peterborough studies, we chose not to rely solely on RAS to do the 'long jump' from the national to the regional table. Instead, the previously described series of adjustments have been marshalled to produce what is in our opinion the best possible regional matrix estimate in the context of the available data.

Some sensitivity analysis relating to the various steps of the GRIT sequence was carried out. Some independent estimates of final demand were crudely estimated, and the resulting differences between row and column totals resolved by the RAS constrained to the column totals. The procedure resulted in large, apparently random and unwarranted changes in both transactions and multipliers. The procedure was therefore abandoned in the application to the regions of Queensland, but retained as an option for other users of GRIT.

It will be noted that in the detailed flow chart (Appendix II) Steps 9 and 10 are operationally merged.

Estimation of Final Demand

In the Queensland application of GRIT, final demand was estimated as a residual. Since equivalence of total final demand and total value added exists in an input–output table, total final demand is indirectly estimated by the GRIT procedures. The problem still remains to decompose aggregate final demand into its constituent components, namely household consumption, exports and other final demand. Existing regional input–output studies provided estimates of that proportion of each sector output into the three final demand categories. These proportions were used as allocators to allocate the sales from each sector. Procedures for final demand estimates are further detailed in Appendix VI.

Step 11: Aggregation if Uniform Tables are Required

The discussion of Step 7 drew attention to the possibility that the analyst might require uniform tables for each region, i.e. uniform in the sense that each table contains the same number of similarly defined sectors. Step 11 allows the aggregation process outlined in Step 7 to proceed to achieve this end. The application to the regions of Queensland produced 11-sector tables for the regions and for the state of Queensland. This aggregation has been delayed until this stage so that the advantage of the insertion of aggregated superior data (Step 8) can be incorporated into the uniform tables without duplication of effort.

Step 12: Derivation of Inverses and Multipliers for Prototype Tables

This step derives the inverses, with output, income and employment multipliers for both uniform and non-uniform input–output tables for each region and for the state. Conventional techniques for multiplier calculation were employed for this purpose.

6.6 Phase V: Derivation of Final Transactions Tables

It may be helpful to summarise briefly the total effect of Steps 1–12 in producing regional input–output tables. The basic component of GRIT is a multi-stage mechanical sequence for adjusting the national table, calculation of regional imports and weighted aggregation of sectors. Important modifications to this mechanical procedure ensure that where any data, other than those generated by the mechanical processes, are available, these data could be incorporated to improve the general level of accuracy. The prototype tables represent therefore the 'best' tables which can be produced by the variable-interference mechanical processes. Phase V, the final stage in the GRIT sequence, shifts the responsibility for adjustment from modified mechanical procedures to the analyst and his expert advisers. At this stage, the analyst is faced with a series of non-uniform tables (and probably a uniform series) which he must examine in detail.

Step 13: Final Superior Data Insertions and Other Adjustments

There is, of course, a limit to the extent to which a mechanical process, even though supplemented by additions of superior data, can be expected to produce tables which reflect accurately the peculiar features of the economies of individual regions. In many, in fact most, sectors there can be a reasonable expectation that the estimates generated in Phases I–IV are free of substantial error. These cases will include sectors which do not differ substantially in structure between regions; these will include certain categories of manufacturing; service industries and the like. The identification of such sectors by the analyst should be possible as an exercise of his professional judgement.

However, the analyst cannot be absolved of the responsibility, either in the use of the GRIT system or in the development of survey-based, or indeed any input–output tables, to exercise his professional judgement in the detection of inappropriate entries in the table, and other apparent anomalies. Whichever method of table construction is employed, the ultimate responsibility for assessment and final adjustment must be accepted by the analyst, and there should be no professional refuge in mechanically produced figures. To take such refuge is to abdicate from professional responsibility.

The experience of the GRIT team was that inspection of the final tables showed that few adjustments were required. However some of these adjustments were significant, and the tables would have been inadequate representations of these economies if this examination had been avoided. The GRIT team drew on the extensive knowledge of other input–output workers, government officers skilled in economic interpretation of the various facets of the regional and state economies, and other useful sources of opinion. From this consultation emerged a series of tables which were accepted as conforming with the original main criterion of GRIT, namely as 'free of significant error'.

Two points should be made at this stage. First, the number of 'major' adjustments to the prototype tables was relatively few, and restricted to sectors which showed either unique regional characteristics, or which had been 'submerged' by dominant national industries outside the region through their effect on the national coefficients. Second, it follows that most entries in the prototype tables were acceptable and conformed to expected magnitudes. Examination of the multipliers of the prototype tables and comparison of these multipliers with those from other studies assisted in highlighting potential 'problem areas'.

Superior data insertions and action, including those adjustments which were made during the execution of Step 13, in application to the Queensland tables, are outlined in Appendix VI.

Step 14: Derivation of Final Transactions Tables

This step completed the development of the final transactions tables, after incorporation of the adjustments outlined in Step 13. The completion process involved some of the inevitable 'juggling' which seems to be a usual part of the preparation of input–output tables to ensure consistency.

Step 15: Derivation of Inverses and Multipliers for Final Transactions Tables

The final step applied conventional techniques for the calculation of the inverses, with accompanying output, income and employment multipliers for the final transactions tables.

The tables and multipliers derived for the regions of Queensland are shown in Chapter 7 and in the various Appendices VII to XII to this text.

7 EMPIRICAL APPLICATION OF THE GRIT SYSTEM

Previous chapters have outlined relevant regional input–output economics, the objectives of the GRIT system, and have described in detail the GRIT methodology. This chapter provides some of the empirical results of the application of the GRIT system to the regions and the state of Queensland, Australia.

As outlined in section 6.4, *two* sets of transactions tables with accompanying tables of coefficients and multipliers were produced. A series of 11-sector tables, termed *uniform* tables, was produced for the regional and state economies. Second, a series of *non-uniform* tables was produced, including 36-sector tables for the Metropolitan (Moreton) region and the state of Queensland, and 19-sector tables for those regions defined as Provincial regions for the purposes of this study. The presentation of the tables of transactions, coefficients and multipliers required the preparation of approximately ninety tables. The disposition of these tables throughout this book is itemised in Table 7.1 to assist the reader with ready reference to the results of the study.

These tables contain an enormous amount of information relating to the economic structure of the state and regions of Queensland. The sheer volume of the information prevents comment in detail on each table. This chapter therefore is restricted to general comment on the 11-sector *uniform* transactions tables and associated multipliers. Non-uniform transactions tables and multipliers, and all Leontief inverse tables have been presented in appendices. However, the general comment on the uniform tables in this chapter is relevant also to the non-uniform tables which should, of course, be considered simply as providing more detail relating to those sectors which are shown in a more disaggregated form.

In both the uniform and non-uniform transactions and coefficient tables, sectors are represented by numbers in the interests of space. These numbers represent sectors as defined in Appendix III. It will be noted that the same sector number is retained throughout uniform and non-uniform tables, and the numbering is modified to denote disaggregation for non-uniform tables. For example, Sector 4 in the uniform tables refers to the manufacturing sector; in the 19-sector tables of provincial regions, Sector 4 is disaggregated to Sectors

Table 7.1: List and Location of GRIT Input—Output Results for the State of Queensland

Form of Results	*Uniform Tables* (11-Sector Tables for State and Regions)	*Non-Uniform Tables* (36-Sector Tables for State and Metropolitan Region, 19-Sector Tables for Provincial Regions)
Transactions Tables	Chapter 7 (Tables 7.2 to 7.12)	Appendix VII (Tables VII.I to VII.9)
Direct and Indirect Coefficients (Inverse of Open Model)	Appendix IX (Tables IX.I to IX.II)	Appendix XI (Tables XI.1 to XI.9)
Direct, Indirect and Induced Coefficients (Inverse of Closed Model)	Appendix X (Tables X.I to X.II)	Appendix XII (Tables XII.1 to XII.9)
Output Multipliers	Chapter 7 (Table 7.13)	Appendix VIII (Tables VIII.1 to VIII.2)
Income Multipliers	Chapter 7 (Table 7.14)	Appendix VIII (Tables VIII.3 and VIII.4)
Employment Multipliers	Chapter 7 (Table 7.15)	Appendix VIII (Tables VIII.5 and VIII.6)

4A–4F. In the 36-sector tables, these may be further disaggregated as 4A1–4A5, and so on.

For convenience in the reading of this chapter the sector titles for the eleven-sector tables are provided below:

Sector No.	*Title*
1	Animal industries
2	Other primary industries
3	Mining
4	Manufacturing
5	Electricity, gas and water
6	Building and construction
7	Trade
8	Transport and communication
9	Finance
10	Public administration and defence
11	Community services and entertainment, recreation

7.1 Eleven-Sector Tables for the Regions of Queensland

The discussion is now focused on the uniform transactions tables for the regions of Queensland. These are presented as tables 7.2–7.11 for the ten regions of the state.

The tables summarise the inter-industry transactions in dollar terms at basic values for 1973–4 for the regions of the state. The first eleven entries in each row indicate the sales to other sectors in the same region; the last three entries in each row indicate the sales of each sector to households, other final users in the region and to markets outside the region. For example, the sales of the animal industries sectors in all tables are virtually restricted to the manufacturing sector (including rural processing factories), with a small volume of sales to local households. The proportion of the output of this sector exported reflects the type of activity in this sector which is carried out in the region. This sector in the Moreton Region table (Table 7.2), producing mainly dairy and beef products, exports only a small proportion of total output; the bulk of sector output requires some local processing by the manufacturing sector. On the other hand, the output of Sector 1 in the North West region (Table 7.9) is almost entirely exported in a non-processed form from the region.

A more detailed study of the rows of the regional tables draws attention to some important economic characteristics of Queensland regions. *First*, some sectors, particularly 'service' type sectors, export only a very small proportion of total output. Sectors such as Public Administration, Community Services, Finance, Trade and Building and Construction tend to be established in each region at the level sufficient to provide the amounts of services required locally; few regions will reach the stage of becoming major exporters of services. *Second*, the heavy reliance on some form of primary activity for regional exports is demonstrated in these tables. The tables for some non-metropolitan regions show exports from the mining sector to be very high, in fact higher than the exports of rural sectors in the Fitzroy Region (Table 7.5), the Mackay Region (Table 7.6), the Far North Region (Table 7.8) and the North West Region (Table 7.9). The table for the Darling Downs Region shows the dominance of rural industries over mining industries at this stage. The dominance of the mining sectors as the source of regional exports should, however, be carefully interpreted. This dominance is a relatively recent phenomenon in some regions? the economic infrastructure of most non-metropolitan regions remains largely influenced by the requirements of the rural industries.

Table 7.2: Eleven-Sector Transactions Table: Moreton Region, 1973–4 (thousands)

	1	2	3	4	5	6	7	8	9	10	11	House-holds	Other Final Demand	Exports	Total
1	0	0	0	43555	0	1	0	0	0	0	0	491	0	4550	48597
2	1250	2243	849	39562	61	10	1	569	0	3	65	23843	0	44940	113396
3	0	20	1117	15442	6121	4821	735	815	13	29	449	0	0	42485	72047
4	5901	16104	14346	394502	6916	210753	31072	54579	3463	37849	21728	457368	82519	602413	1969513
5	695	1887	2135	33897	4321	2598	6111	3363	25005	4132	18830	52664	32861	0	188499
6	696	1391	740	19399	8774	0	9495	20153	20539	28896	9332	13671	467316	0	600402
7	2137	5872	6277	108688	3090	55466	28118	22056	32226	2454	17582	390940	0	34179	709085
8	1014	3652	3268	90028	8365	21881	24752	8856	6706	3835	3070	105956	115344	27094	423821
9	25	141	4210	32718	718	1817	78685	4958	52833	8222	7160	237157	139907	55546	624097
10	0	0	1	3	6	0	1	10	0	0	0	5585	273627	0	279233
11	136	15	52	48	77	51	1347	1034	928	2929	528	185473	146479	34529	373626
Households	2173	11570	7574	434027	48396	176947	271165	146853	233587	166391	198241	0	0	0	1696924
Other Value Added	29633	56646	19155	294725	97199	74760	223171	120788	237966	3600	76212	0	0	0	1233855
Imports	4937	13855	12323	462919	4455	51297	34432	39787	10831	20893	20429	479139	0	0	1155297
Total	48597	113396	72047	1969513	188499	600402	709085	423821	624097	279233	373626	1952287	1258050	875729	

Table 7.3: Eleven-Sector Transactions Table: Wide Bay-Burnett Region, 1973–4 (thousands)

	1	2	3	4	5	6	7	8	9	10	11	House-holds	Other Final Demand	Exports	Total
1	0	0	0	13326	0	0	0	0	0	0	0	607	0	41863	55796
2	3724	9472	74	40471	9	2	0	152	0	0	8	18454	371	19926	92663
3	0	12	68	268	257	407	26	35	0	0	18	0	0	6224	7315
4	3406	1833	372	6116	348	9107	365	293	17	517	494	57648	24845	61250	166611
5	541	1003	152	1252	273	246	351	199	852	201	1155	3815	6359	0	16389
6	836	1158	54	917	694	0	662	3084	1154	1837	860	1820	52531	0	65597
7	2649	4649	701	4342	245	4333	3615	1723	1543	124	1109	25691	1750	0	52474
8	983	2694	253	6433	758	1870	1162	274	337	76	213	11417	1801	5410	33681
9	12	52	194	1181	33	85	3214	70	1355	336	268	16842	6842	3683	34167
10	0	0	0	24	1	0	0	0	0	0	0	722	15428	0	16175
11	137	2	4	237	5	7	127	16	43	153	35	10236	19262	1705	31969
Households	2526	10402	963	34964	4248	20112	20254	12550	13346	10176	17446	0	0	0	146987
Other Value Added	33000	48725	1686	19466	8336	8182	16017	83271	13105	248	6205	0	0	0	238241
Imports	6993	12661	2794	37614	1182	21246	6691	7014	2415	2507	6665	112748	0	0	218023
Total	55796	92663	7315	166611	16389	65597	52474	33681	34167	16175	31969	260000	129189	140061	

Table 7.4: Eleven-Sector Transactions Table: Darling Downs Region, 1973–4 (thousands)

	1	2	3	4	5	6	7	8	9	10	11	House-holds	Other Final Demand	Exports	Total
1	0	0	0	35199	0	0	0	0	0	0	0	913	0	62912	99024
2	8295	12547	70	8102	3	2	0	159	0	0	9	6208	31	113343	148769
3	0	7	32	161	30	266	16	13	0	0	10	0	0	2452	2987
4	4405	3065	87	6729	16	7966	499	223	14	476	797	48129	26905	42799	142110
5	675	1095	41	824	66	135	329	145	784	135	1070	290	482	0	6071
6	1450	2071	33	1110	314	0	1069	3251	1213	2021	1183	1967	43160	0	58842
7	5247	8344	316	5867	83	4666	5987	2746	2103	186	1732	42533	2898	0	82708
8	1825	4104	110	7477	243	1888	1946	264	472	155	329	14184	2240	6718	41955
9	26	79	71	669	6	93	4919	31	1711	419	258	20890	8487	4571	42230
10	0	0	0	0	0	0	0	0	0	0	0	864	18432	0	19296
11	279	6	2	2	2	5	160	8	57	144	44	13677	25695	2280	42361
Households	5323	11895	257	31266	1539	17776	31841	15142	16717	11380	23045	0	0	0	166181
Other Value Added	59645	84025	791	14858	3200	7335	25463	11372	15840	240	8247	0	0	0	231016
Imports	11854	21531	1177	29846	569	18710	10479	8601	3319	4140	5637	131345	0	0	247208
Total	99024	148769	2987	142110	6071	58842	82708	41955	42230	19296	42361	281000	128330	185075	

Table 7.5: Eleven-Sector Transactions Table: Fitzroy Region, 1973–4 (thousands)

	1	2	3	4	5	6	7	8	9	10	11	House-holds	Other Final Demand	Exports	Total
1	0	0	0	24254	0	0	0	0	0	0	0	451	0	31097	55802
2	4436	3006	1673	3516	3	1	0	25	0	0	8	9252	4	10273	32197
3	0	6	1524	4666	2000	1143	93	100	1	2	65	0	0	175816	185416
4	2075	743	8238	18279	173	17346	646	1910	22	438	871	61787	58067	34818	205413
5	460	303	6932	3451	192	309	370	137	658	152	1230	2938	3696	1203	22031
6	852	412	3548	1230	732	0	793	2625	881	1488	1109	1526	81624	0	96820
7	2834	1697	9396	6806	288	6998	4312	972	1309	107	1421	23724	1620	0	61484
8	811	698	4992	5328	768	2355	1346	211	196	75	201	3224	509	1529	22243
9	15	20	1237	1209	43	153	4073	108	1199	290	337	11155	4532	2437	26808
10	0	0	6	375	1	0	0	0	0	0	0	569	12139	0	13090
11	134	1	133	351	10	10	148	24	36	164	43	12310	23937	2024	39325
Househblds	3094	3307	21273	46990	5571	29436	23674	8637	10315	8243	21783	0	0	0	182323
Other Value Added	33546	17295	81468	37371	11036	12072	18915	4572	10231	201	7436	0	0	0	234143
Imports	7545	4709	44996	51587	1214	26997	7114	2922	1960	1330	4821	91064	0	0	246859
Total	55802	32197	185416	205413	22031	96820	61484	22243	26808	13090	39325	218000	186128	259197	

Table 7.6: Eleven-Sector Transactions Table: Mackay Region, 1973–4 (thousands)

	1	2	3	4	5	6	7	8	9	10	11	House-holds	Other Final Demand	Exports	Total
1	0	0	0	5604	0	0	0	0	0	0	0	222	0	15307	21133
2	1423	6177	974	43739	2	1	0	13	0	0	5	3585	4	3975	59898
3	0	3	689	211	517	375	43	32	0	1	39	0	0	47998	49908
4	1782	2897	1374	1751	80	5974	163	174	8	137	318	38805	3001	54690	111127
5	194	674	2067	753	180	252	193	59	436	87	833	1721	2866	0	10315
6	327	721	1043	399	440	0	376	722	387	773	505	868	58238	0	64799
7	1128	2980	2354	2472	179	5011	2093	564	778	55	777	10020	781	0	29092
8	275	1179	1208	2529	326	1462	544	108	88	37	98	1162	184	552	9752
9	6	48	142	782	13	118	1296	34	424	123	147	6561	2664	1437	13795
10	0	0	2	28	0	0	0	0	0	0	0	295	6299	0	6624
11	39	1	25	278	3	7	72	21	14	61	22	8076	10692	1489	20800
Households	1209	7443	5263	13932	2683	19952	11198	3493	5360	4260	11012	0	0	0	85805
Other Value Added	12675	31617	23354	13064	5205	8085	8961	2517	5089	108	4259	0	0	0	114934
Inputs	2075	6158	11413	25585	687	23589	4153	2015	1211	982	2785	52685	0	0	133338
Total	21133	59898	49908	111127	10315	64799	29092	9752	13795	6624	20800	124000	84729	125448	

Table 7.7: Eleven-Sector Transactions Table: Northern Region, 1973–4 (thousands)

	1	2	3	4	5	6	7	8	9	10	11	House holds	Other Final Demand	Exports	Total
1	0	0	0	13080	0	0	0	0	0	0	0	109	0	7519	20708
2	1389	7482	171	37876	9	2	0	215	0	1	21	15501	70	17113	79850
3	0	4	107	1879	1487	874	139	410	1	10	105	0	0	5152	10168
4	967	1693	581	7500	493	22489	992	7675	28	2693	906	56561	9174	74999	186751
5	253	1236	505	2240	346	612	878	955	2434	719	3105	5954	9923	0	29160
6	325	878	169	934	980	0	1279	9866	1685	5333	1629	1680	115035	0	139793
7	1263	4405	824	7048	440	13484	7214	6085	3415	768	2308	44453	3030	0	95237
8	415	2272	407	8037	1340	4732	3169	1664	565	1103	431	19838	3132	57304	104409
9	8	69	136	1137	48	299	6282	554	2967	1060	615	28076	11406	6140	58797
10	0	0	0	23	1	0	0	2	0	0	0	2673	56970	0	59669
11	53	1	7	233	14	13	209	197	79	394	94	23347	23332	13745	61718
Households	1320	12719	1151	33577	7320	41680	36510	38940	22528	31073	32398	0	0	0	259216
Other Value Added	12312	40961	3875	21456	15951	17416	29732	24159	21816	443	12788	0	0	0	200909
Imports	2403	8130	2235	51731	731	38192	8833	13687	3279	16072	6818	41808	0	0	193919
Total	20708	79850	10168	186751	29160	139793	95237	104409	58797	59669	61718	240000	232072	181972	

Table 7.8: Eleven-Sector Transactions Table: Far North Region, 1973–4 (thousands)

	1	2	3	4	5	6	7	8	9	10	11	House-holds	Other Final Demand	Exports	Total
1	0	0	0	14147	0	0	0	0	0	0	0	89	0	6160	20406
2	1436	9620	407	59194	11	2	0	76	0	0	10	11431	38	12656	94881
3	0	12	1034	608	0	514	2	6	1	0	6	0	0	55991	58174
4	1321	3371	2117	6039	392	6904	297	1467	11	512	519	57524	15713	91884	188071
5	238	1349	1638	1836	270	200	419	237	1079	241	1419	906	1510	5862	17204
6	314	1152	288	1023	660	0	646	1578	936	1660	768	1456	38685	0	49166
7	1125	5100	6563	5391	253	4096	3596	1636	1519	134	1236	17453	1189	0	49291
8	358	2528	2265	6772	672	1430	1370	528	296	150	190	7420	1172	3515	28666
9	6	68	1608	1499	30	80	2676	196	1078	276	297	12890	5237	2820	28761
10	0	0	0	35	1	0	0	1	0	0	0	659	14042	0	14738
11	52	2	42	350	7	5	120	105	35	182	35	10499	17921	1808	31163
Households	1147	11103	8237	28256	4363	14668	18947	10079	11122	9210	17078	0	0	0	134210
Other Value Added	12255	50044	12599	23115	9182	6125	15252	7659	10825	221	6018	0	0	0	153295
Imports	2154	10532	21376	39796	1363	15142	5966	5098	1859	2152	3587	80130	0	0	189155
Total	20406	94881	58174	188071	17204	49166	49291	28666	28761	14738	31163	200457	95507	180696	

Table 7.9: Eleven-Sector Transactions Table: North West Region, 1973–4 (thousands)

	1	2	3	4	5	6	7	8	9	10	11	House-holds	Other Final Demand	Exports	Total
1	0	0	0	744	0	0	0	0	0	0	0	471	0	45885	47100
2	2404	205	0	27	0	0	0	0	0	0	5	688	0	5590	8919
3	0	0	7779	72	0	342	1	3	0	0	3	0	0	259750	267950
4	88	16	1230	65	1	1034	13	10	0	31	60	3316	2893	2761	11518
5	80	18	2388	28	4	25	25	17	61	13	118	143	237	0	3157
6	704	36	1584	94	89	0	185	1010	214	418	251	525	26552	0	31662
7	1045	273	7397	247	14	897	463	267	162	11	156	3216	221	0	14369
8	560	109	6827	266	103	658	234	100	62	18	54	1531	242	724	11488
9	10	2	1162	28	2	39	375	8	150	55	56	3889	1580	848	8204
10	0	0	0	0	0	0	0	0	0	0	0	158	3370	0	3528
11	71	0	139	1	1	3	36	40	7	49	16	5483	6299	0	12145
Households	3434	1420	65435	2637	786	9519	5532	4136	3345	2298	6297	0	0	0	104839
Other Value Added	27634	4260	77225	1638	1765	3946	4421	2791	2997	60	2564	0	0	0	129301
Imports	11070	2580	96784	5671	392	15199	3084	3106	1206	575	2565	55580	0	0	197812
Total	47100	8919	267950	11518	3157	31662	14369	11488	8204	3528	12145	75000	41394	315558	

Table 7.10: Eleven-Sector Transactions Table: Central West Region, 1973–4 (thousands)

	1	2	3	4	5	6	7	8	9	10	11	House-holds	Other Final Demand	Exports	Total
1	0	0	0	167	0	0	0	0	0	0	0	867	0	59756	60790
2	6280	517	0	32	0	0	0	2	0	0	2	0	0	93	6926
3	0	0	0	2	0	74	0	1	0	0	1	0	0	0	79
4	49	11	1	12	0	115	4	3	0	10	17	866	1296	0	2384
5	404	102	1	34	21	56	72	37	71	53	287	113	187	0	1438
6	806	59	1	23	56	0	99	319	51	326	119	203	7875	0	9937
7	2476	217	8	114	12	464	495	232	67	15	130	3540	241	0	8011
8	913	162	4	81	65	326	169	64	41	16	39	1880	296	889	4945
9	6	1	0	0	0	6	18	0	6	29	0	1414	575	307	2362
10	0	0	0	0	0	0	0	0	0	0	0	123	2612	0	2735
11	129	0	0	0	1	1	21	8	1	27	8	2541	1935	545	5217
Households	5591	1719	8	382	361	3139	3096	1749	1057	1790	2631	0	0	0	21523
Other Value Added	34680	3350	13	339	783	1241	2432	1364	829	47	1157	0	0	0	46235
Imports	9456	788	43	1198	139	4515	1605	1166	239	422	826	17453	0	0	37850
Total	60790	6926	79	2384	1438	9937	8011	4945	2362	2735	5217	29000	15017	61589	

Table 7.11: Eleven-Sector Transactions Table: South West Region, 1973–4 (thousands)

	1	2	3	4	5	6	7	8	9	10	11	House-holds	Other Final Demand	Exports	Total
1	0	0	0	4492	0	0	0	0	0	0	0	1025	0	70676	76193
2	8299	1769	108	975	1	1	0	37	0	0	3	4376	0	4863	20431
3	0	3	63	17	18	177	5	5	0	0	4	0	0	2538	2830
4	713	152	28	652	3	555	33	21	0	30	55	5528	0	8209	15979
5	379	185	70	114	30	44	66	42	136	42	286	311	519	0	2224
6	1056	216	49	138	120	0	188	754	157	518	194	406	10332	0	14128
7	3592	879	177	646	25	867	974	524	276	30	27[illegible]	5985	408	0	14660
8	1198	552	113	800	87	460	336	109	98	2[illegible]	67	3816	603	1809	10070
9	14	8	10	14	0	15	382	2	110	89	15	3775	1536	827	6797
10	0	0	0	0	0	0	0	0	0	0	0	197	4186	0	4383
11	176	0	1	0	1	2	37	9	7	29	11	4250	3239	910	8672
Households	6794	3560	297	2664	564	4405	5649	3646	2875	2847	4421	0	0	0	37722
Other Value Added	43657	10401	1064	1917	1165	1764	4499	2659	2486	74	1891	0	0	0	71577
Imports	103[illegible]5	2706	850	3550	210	5838	2491	2262	652	702	1448	28331	0	0	59355
Total	76193	20431	2830	15979	2224	14128	14660	10070	6797	4383	8672	58000	20823	89832	

Table 7.12: Eleven-Sector Transactions Table: Queensland, 1973–4 (thousands)

	1	2	3	4	5	6	7	8	9	10	11	House-holds	Other Final Demand	Exports	Total
1	0	0	0	312095	0	3	0	1	0	0	0	10111	0	183319	505529
2	41501	61382	11322	311877	120	23	1	1588	0	9	174	140640	0	88879	657516
3	1	111	14804	67588	13766	11884	1645	2196	21	61	1063	0	0	543733	656873
4	60789	72830	85791	420063	9253	334401	37132	75589	3130	42875	28133	848860	89780	839402	2948028
5	6151	9741	25764	46326	6411	4793	9633	5793	32798	6236	30219	87448	25673	0	296986
6	7461	8102	7540	24123	13642	0	15024	46367	28008	44375	15683	24136	857362	0	1091823
7	21512	29699	47977	136475	4674	99505	41522	34593	43209	3606	28104	625540	0	0	1116416
8	10485	20670	29268	138035	13708	40517	38181	14232	9542	5725	5041	180514	174734	41405	722057
9	221	660	19923	32921	829	2750	105563	5745	59842	11708	9295	324634	0	280210	854301
10	0	0	11	163	9	0	2	14	0	0	1	8381	410464	0	419045
11	1446	29	476	1644	124	103	2360	1514	1261	4404	853	290400	270889	39409	614912
Households	28669	77514	85392	621261	75983	325614	427912	256711	323647	249265	326882	0	0	0	2808850
Other Value Added	303288	345281	205746	420407	154542	136021	348767	193972	324300	5371	124989	0	0	0	2562684
Imports	24005	31497	122859	415050	3925	136209	88674	83742	28543	45410	44475	908881	0	0	1933270
Total	505529	657516	656873	2948028	296986	1091823	1116416	722057	854301	419045	614912	3449545	1828902	2016357	

Third, it is important to understand the different roles performed by the manufacturing sector in each region (row 4 in each table). The Moreton region table shows a high level of exports of manufactured goods; these are largely exports of finished goods to the other regions of Queensland. Where non-metropolitan regions show high levels of exports from this sector these represent either processed primary products which have been locally produced or processed mining products.

The first eleven entries in each column show the purchases which each sector makes from other intermediate sectors in the same region; the remaining three entries show the purchases of labour (in the households row), the imports of that sector, and the components of other value added (depreciation, indirect taxes, interest, profits etc.). In general terms, the relative size of the entries in the intermediate and primary inputs quadrants indicates the extent to which each sector obtains its inputs from other local sectors.

The column structure of the regional tables is important. Since the columns show the pattern of purchases of each sector, they are the basis for the calculation of tables of coefficients for the analytical application of the table described in the next section. An examination of the columns of the transactions tables is an important prerequisite to the analytical stage, and highlights some important points with respect to Queensland regions.

First, the column shows, within the household row, the sources by sector of the wages, salaries and supplements paid within the region, and indirectly the importance of each sector as a source of local employment. It shows, for example, the dominance of the manufacturing sector as the source of employment in most regions but in more isolated regions, for example the Northern and North West Region, the dominant employing industries tend to be the trade (wholesale–retail) and building and construction sectors and mining if this is appropriate. *Second*, the columns show the importance of imports by sector for the regions of the state. Almost inevitably, the highest level of imports for each region is shown by the manufacturing sector; for the non-metropolitan regions, these represent imports of semi-finished and finished goods as inputs into the manufacturing process; the manufacturing sectors of these regions tend to comprise the lower-order manufacturing processes, and imports tend to be of the middle and higher-order, more specialised commodities.

Each cell entry in the transactions table represents, of course, the sum of the transactions between two sectors for the time period under study. Consequently each cell entry is important, it indicates whether the economic linkages between the sectors concerned are strong or weak, i.e. whether or not a change in the level of output of one sector will affect the other. While it is important to identify weaker linkages, it is the stronger intersectoral linkages which are more important in identifying those characteristics of an economy which determine its response to changing economic circumstances. The relative size of each cell entry, the distribution of these relative sizes over the table, and the tendency for larger entries to appear in particular sectors are therefore important in understanding the nature of each regional economy and the variation between regional economies.

The tables for the regions of Queensland present some predictable contrasts in this respect. The Far North region shows a table (Table 7.8) of relatively small transactions, dominated by one cell (cell 2, 4) representing mainly sales of sugar cane to local sugar mills. By far the largest intersectoral transaction in the table, the cell shows not only the extent to which the region has specialised in sugar production, but the extent to which the region and its component industries relies on the local processing of sugar cane for support of other sectors; some of the remaining elements in column 4 are amongst the relatively large entries in the table. The Northern Region displays similar characteristics. These tables describe rather simple economies, which import most consumer goods and industrial inputs, conduct lower-order services and manufacturing locally, and export mainly processed primary products.

The table of the Fitzroy region (Table 7.5) provides an important variation to the tables of rural regions. The largest cell entry in the table (cell 1, 4) shows the importance of the sale of beef cattle to the processing sector, and the contribution of this sector to the regional economy. However, of almost equal importance[1] were the activities of the coal mining in the region.

Table 7.2 of the Moreton (metropolitan) region provides a contrast to the tables of other regions. A much larger proportion of the cell entries is relatively large in magnitude, reflecting the more numerous intersectoral linkages which are characteristic of a more diversified economy. The region contains some significant linkages between the rural and rural processing industries, of the same magnitude as many 'rural' regions, but these are relatively small compared to the activities of other sectors such as manufacturing, building and construction, trade and finance. The Moreton region table tends to be less dominated by particular sectors and to display numerous linkages which could be described as significant.

The important distinction between the regional tables lies in the number of 'significant' cell entries; few significant entries denote a regional economy dominated by one or two sectors, whereas several significant entries describe a highly developed and more complex economy with a high degree of intersectoral interaction.

7.2 A Queensland State Table

An eleven-sector transactions table for the state of Queensland is provided as Table 7.12; and a 36-sector table as Table VII.9 in Appendix VII.

Table 7.12 is in effect a summation of Tables 7.2–7.11, in terms of sector output levels and most non-trade components of primary inputs and final demand. Many items which comprise interregional trade in the regional tables were not components of trade at the state level and adjustments were made for these items. Those items which comprised overseas or interstate trade at the regional level were retained in the state table, and appear as state imports or exports in Table 7.12.

The Queensland state table is typical of input–output tables describing advanced economies; it shows the many significant linkages expected in a highly diversified economy. In the same way as regional tables illustrated the facets of the industrial regional economies, Table 7.12 demonstrates the features of the state economy in terms of sources of inputs of each sector and the sales pattern of these sectors for the state as a whole.

The choice between the use of state or regional tables for an analyst will be influenced by the problem he faces and the point of view from which the study must be carried out. If the analyst is concerned with the repercussions of an event or policy on the state as a whole, Table 7.12 provides the appropriate analytical base; if the question of interest concerns the spatial incidence of the effects of an event, one or more of the regional tables will provide the appropriate base.

7.3 Regional and State Input–Output Multipliers

Chapter 2 outlined the procedures adopted in this study for the calculation of input–output multipliers, and briefly discussed the interpretation of these multipliers. Output, income and employment multipliers were calculated; these appear respectively in Tables 7.13, 7.14 and 7.15. The inverse tables for both open and closed versions of the uniform tables are presented in Appendices IX and X respectively.

This section provides only a brief discussion of the multipliers derived by the GRIT procedure for the state and regions of Queensland.

Table 7.13: Eleven-Sector (Uniform Tables) Output Multipliers: Regions and State of Queensland

Sector	Moreton		Wide Bay—Burnett		Darling Downs		Fitzroy		Mackay		Northern	
	Direct & Indirect	Total	Direct & Indirect	Total	Direct & Indirect	Total	Direct & Indirect	Total	Direct & Indirect	Total	Direct & Indirect	Total
1. Animal ind.	1.368	1.600	1.297	1.412	1.297	1.450	1.274	1.397	1.347	1.494	1.308	1.555
2. Other primary	1.416	1.766	1.291	1.470	1.271	1.451	1.279	1.450	1.334	1.540	1.301	1.708
3. Mining	1.678	2.163	1.333	1.563	1.325	1.556	1.269	1.463	1.258	1.440	1.388	1.771
4. Manufacturing	1.593	2.206	1.584	1.891	1.609	2.010	1.448	1.770	1.701	1.955	1.571	2.086
5. Electricity, gas, water	1.317	1.880	1.211	1.525	1.162	1.539	1.251	1.567	1.214	1.545	1.246	1.786
6. Building & construction	1.760	2.573	1.350	1.740	1.364	1.861	1.404	1.818	1.291	1.689	1.439	2.146
7. Trade	1.359	2.180	1.224	1.682	1.222	1.802	1.243	1.717	1.201	1.681	1.277	2.097
8. Transport & communication	1.424	2.189	1.227	1.663	1.212	1.746	1.379	1.878	1.229	1.679	1.376	2.194
9. Finance	1.319	2.107	1.193	1.641	1.185	1.758	1.204	1.661	1.189	1.665	1.245	2.041
10. Public admin. & defence	1.502	2.711	1.270	1.966	1.247	2.073	1.282	2.001	1.251	2.005	1.287	2.318
11. Community services, entertainment	1.308	2.329	1.168	1.753	1.166	1.906	1.177	1.787	1.169	1.778	1.209	2.214

Table 7.13 (continued)

Sector	Far North		North West		Central West		South West		Queensland	
	Direct & Indirect	Total	Direct & Indirect	Total	Direct & Indirect	Total	Direct & Indirect	Total	Direct & Indirect	Total
1. Animal ind.	1.332	1.479	1.116	1.149	1.210	1.295	1.247	1.369	1.467	1.732
2. Other primary	1.330	1.544	1.081	1.140	1.188	1.343	1.225	1.410	1.483	1.852
3. Mining	1.359	1.637	1.119	1.209	1.202	1.300	1.264	1.409	1.565	2.016
4. Manufacturing	1.691	1.990	1.152	1.236	1.238	1.348	1.618	1.842	1.780	2.380
5. Electricity, gas, water	1.183	1.521	1.076	1.164	1.123	1.283	1.152	1.393	1.328	1.879
6. Building & construction	1.399	1.835	1.107	1.213	1.120	1.315	1.194	1.488	1.744	2.520
7. Trade	1.233	1.752	1.102	1.237	1.123	1.360	1.161	1.517	1.319	2.104
8. Transport & Communication	1.284	1.762	1.140	1.270	1.151	1.373	1.177	1.513	1.421	2.177
9. Finance	1.216	1.725	1.088	1.228	1.113	1.379	1.134	1.510	1.290	2.055
10. Public admin. & defence	1.297	2.085	1.186	1.414	1.205	1.589	1.208	1.780	1.467	2.631
11. Community services entertainment	1.187	1.857	1.065	1.238	1.130	1.428	1.126	1.564	1.288	2.278

Table 7.14: Eleven-Sector (Uniform Tables) Income Multipliers: Regions and State of Queensland

Sector	Moreton			Wide Bay—Burnett			Darling Downs			Fitzroy		
	Direct	Direct & Indirect	Total	Direct	Direct & Indirect	Total	Direct	Direct & Indirect	Total	Direct	Direct & Indirect	Total
1. Animal ind.	0.045	0.141	0.216	0.045	0.117	0.148	0.054	0.123	0.162	0.055	0.123	0.158
2. Other primary	0.102	0.212	0.325	0.112	0.182	0.231	0.080	0.145	0.192	0.103	0.170	0.219
3. Mining	0.105	0.294	0.451	0.132	0.234	0.296	0.086	0.186	0.246	0.115	0.192	0.248
4. Manufacturing	0.220	0.372	0.570	0.210	0.313	0.397	0.220	0.323	0.428	0.229	0.320	0.412
5. Electricity, gas & water	0.257	0.342	0.523	0.259	0.320	0.406	0.254	0.304	0.402	0.253	0.314	0.404
6. Building & construction	0.295	0.494	0.756	0.307	0.397	0.503	0.302	0.399	0.528	0.304	0.412	0.530
7. Trade	0.382	0.499	0.764	0.386	0.467	0.591	0.385	0.466	0.617	0.385	0.471	0.607
8. Transport & communication	0.347	0.464	0.711	0.373	0.443	0.564	0.361	0.429	0.568	0.388	0.496	0.638
9. Finance	0.374	0.479	0.732	0.391	0.457	0.578	0.396	0.461	0.610	0.385	0.454	0.585
10. Public admin. & defence	0.596	0.734	1.123	0.629	0.709	0.898	0.590	0.664	0.880	0.630	0.715	0.921
11. Community services & entertainment	0.531	0.620	0.948	0.546	0.597	0.756	0.544	0.595	0.788	0.554	0.607	0.781

Table 7.14 (continued)

Sector	Mackay			Northern			Far North			North West		
	Direct	Direct & Indirect	Total	Direct	Direct & Indirect	Total	Direct	Direct & Indirect	Total	Direct	Direct & Indirect	Total
1. Animal ind.	0.057	0.131	0.162	0.064	0.145	0.220	0.056	0.132	0.167	0.073	0.103	0.116
2. Other primary	0.124	0.196	0.242	0.159	0.238	0.362	0.117	0.192	0.244	0.159	0.184	0.206
3. Mining	0.106	0.173	0.214	0.113	0.224	0.341	0.142	0.250	0.318	0.244	0.282	0.316
4. Manufacturing	0.125	0.241	0.299	0.180	0.301	0.458	0.150	0.269	0.341	0.229	0.262	0.294
5. Electricity, gas & water	0.260	0.315	0.390	0.251	0.316	0.481	0.254	0.304	0.386	0.249	0.274	0.307
6. Building & construction	0.308	0.378	0.468	0.298	0.413	0.629	0.298	0.392	0.498	0.300	0.333	0.373
7. Trade	0.385	0.456	0.565	0.383	0.480	0.730	0.384	0.466	0.592	0.385	0.423	0.474
8. Transport & communication	0.358	0.427	0.529	0.373	0.477	0.727	0.352	0.430	0.546	0.360	0.406	0.454
9. Finance	0.389	0.452	0.560	0.383	0.465	0.708	0.387	0.458	0.581	0.408	0.438	0.490
10. Public admin. & defence	0.643	0.716	0.887	0.520	0.602	0.917	0.625	0.708	0.899	0.651	0.711	0.797
11. Community services & entertainment	0.529	0.578	0.716	0.525	0.587	0.894	0.548	0.602	0.765	0.519	0.540	0.604

Table 7.14 (continued)

Sector	Central West			South West			Queensland		
	Direct	Direct & Indirect	Total	Direct	Direct & Indirect	Total	Direct	Direct & Indirect	Total
1. Animal ind.	0.092	0.155	0.186	0.089	0.153	0.191	0.057	0.164	0.242
2. Other primary	0.248	0.301	0.362	0.174	0.234	0.291	0.118	0.228	0.337
3. Mining	0.107	0.179	0.215	0.105	0.181	0.226	0.130	0.279	0.412
4. Manufacturing	0.160	0.219	0.263	0.167	0.280	0.350	0.211	0.371	0.548
5. Electricity, gas & water	0.251	0.292	0.351	0.254	0.301	0.376	0.256	0.341	0.503
6. Building & construction	0.316	0.355	0.427	0.312	0.368	0.458	0.298	0.479	0.708
7. Trade	0.387	0.431	0.518	0.385	0.445	0.555	0.383	0.485	0.717
8. Transport & communication	0.354	0.405	0.487	0.362	0.421	0.525	0.356	0.467	0.690
9. Finance	0.447	0.485	0.583	0.423	0.470	0.586	0.379	0.473	0.699
10. Public admin. & defence	0.655	0.719	0.864	0.650	0.716	0.893	0.595	0.719	1.062
11. Community services & entertainment	0.505	0.544	0.654	0.510	0.549	0.684	0.532	0.612	0.904

Table 7.15: Eleven-Sector (Uniform Tables) Employment Multipliers: Regions and State of Queensland[a]

Sector	Moreton			Wide Bay—Burnett			Darling Downs			Fitzroy		
	Direct	Direct & Indirect	Total	Direct	Direct & Indirect	Total	Direct	Direct & Indirect	Total	Direct	Direct & Indirect	Total
1. Animal ind.	0.122	0.146	0.164	0.089	0.116	0.126	0.051	0.075	0.087	0.051	0.076	0.085
2. Other primary	0.091	0.117	0.145	0.089	0.118	0.134	0.069	0.092	0.107	0.107	0.135	0.147
3. Mining	0.049	0.091	0.129	0.056	0.089	0.109	0.052	0.080	0.099	0.015	0.036	0.050
4. Manufacturing	0.040	0.077	0.125	0.039	0.092	0.119	0.038	0.079	0.112	0.029	0.059	0.082
5. Electricity, gas, water	0.031	0.050	0.094	0.032	0.049	0.077	0.062	0.076	0.106	0.042	0.059	0.082
6. Building & construction	0.061	0.106	0.170	0.076	0.106	0.140	0.076	0.103	0.143	0.058	0.085	0.114
7. Trade	0.126	0.148	0.213	0.168	0.190	0.231	0.123	0.143	0.190	0.121	0.144	0.178
8. Transport & communication	0.074	0.101	0.161	0.092	0.114	0.152	0.092	0.111	0.154	0.180	0.205	0.240
9. Finance	0.049	0.070	0.132	0.054	0.072	0.111	0.055	0.071	0.117	0.066	0.082	0.115
10. Public admin. & defence	0.112	0.141	0.236	0.137	0.158	0.220	0.137	0.156	0.223	0.134	0.153	0.205
11. Community services, entertainment	0.175	0.194	0.274	0.210	0.225	0.276	0.193	0.207	0.266	0.152	0.165	0.209

a — employees per $1000 output.

Table 7.15 (continued)[a]

Sector	Mackay			Northern			Far North			North West		
	Direct	Direct & Indirect	Total	Direct	Direct & Indirect	Total	Direct	Direct & Indirect	Total	Direct	Direct & Indirect	Total
1. Animal ind.	0.046	0.075	0.085	0.047	0.065	0.080	0.078	0.104	0.115	0.029	0.041	0.045
2. Other primary	0.075	0.104	0.120	0.060	0.078	0.103	0.067	0.093	0.109	0.115	0.124	0.130
3. Mining	0.009	0.031	0.045	0.051	0.072	0.096	0.024	0.056	0.077	0.015	0.024	0.033
4. Manufacturing	0.030	0.087	0.106	0.039	0.071	0.102	0.031	0.082	0.105	0.029	0.039	0.047
5. Electricity, gas, water	0.027	0.043	0.068	0.031	0.043	0.076	0.030	0.044	0.070	0.055	0.062	0.070
6. Building & construction	0.058	0.085	0.115	0.031	0.056	0.099	0.076	0.106	0.139	0.076	0.084	0.095
7. Trade	0.160	0.183	0.219	0.094	0.110	0.160	0.148	0.170	0.209	0.138	0.147	0.160
8. Transport & communication	0.180	0.202	0.236	0.038	0.057	0.106	0.092	0.115	0.151	0.092	0.104	0.117
9. Finance	0.066	0.084	0.120	0.039	0.052	0.100	0.054	0.072	0.110	0.054	0.061	0.075
10. Public admin. & defence	0.134	0.152	0.210	0.078	0.091	0.153	0.137	0.159	0.218	0.137	0.152	0.174
11. Community services, entertainment	0.162	0.176	0.221	0.119	0.129	0.190	0.198	0.212	0.262	0.159	0.164	0.181

a — employees per $1000 output.

Table 7.15 (continued)[a]

Sector	Central West			South West			Queensland		
	Direct	Direct & Indirect	Total	Direct	Direct & Indirect	Total	Direct	Direct & Indirect	Total
1. Animal ind.	0.020	0.050	0.059	0.029	0.055	0.067	0.054	0.085	0.105
2. Other primary	0.187	0.210	0.226	0.120	0.143	0.161	0.080	0.113	0.141
3. Mining	0.397	0.417	0.426	0.031	0.055	0.068	0.020	0.056	0.090
4. Manufacturing	0.037	0.055	0.066	0.028	0.067	0.088	0.040	0.089	0.134
5. Electricity, gas, water	0.061	0.071	0.087	0.044	0.056	0.078	0.033	0.052	0.094
6. Building & construction	0.076	0.090	0.108	0.076	0.092	0.119	0.061	0.106	0.165
7. Trade	0.104	0.116	0.139	0.122	0.138	0.171	0.126	0.147	0.207
8. Transport & communication	0.092	0.105	0.127	0.092	0.108	0.139	0.074	0.100	0.159
9. Finance	0.054	0.064	0.090	0.055	0.067	0.102	0.050	0.069	0.128
10. Public admin. & defence	0.137	0.153	0.191	0.137	0.153	0.206	0.112	0.140	0.229
11. Community services, entertainment	0.168	0.178	0.207	0.181	0.191	0.231	0.175	0.192	0.269

The tables of multipliers provide a large volume of information with respect to output, income and employment characteristics of Queensland regions; to our knowledge such information has not been available previously for any economy and its constituent regions. The input–output tables and multipliers provide a sufficient empirical base for a detailed study of the spatial structure of the Queensland economy, and this is planned as a topic of future research. However, this section has more modest aims, namely the identification from the multipliers of the most significant features or regularities; detailed comment is not provided.

Output Multipliers

Two types of output multipliers were calculated, namely the simple output multiplier as a summation of the columns of the inverse of the open model, and the total output multiplier as the summation of the non-household rows of the inverse of the closed model. The simple output multiplier for sector *j* indicates the direct and indirect industrial support requirements from all sectors required for each increase of one dollar[2] in sales of the output of sector *j* to final demand. For example, each increase in the sale of the output of the animal industries sector to final demand in the Moreton region requires an increase of \$1.368 from all sectors in the region. The additional \$0.368 required is in the form of industrial support from other local sectors; the disaggregation of these requirements by sector can be gained from the inverse of the open model, in this case the first column of Table IX.1.

The total output multiplier for sector *j* measures direct, indirect and induced requirements from all sectors for each dollar increase in sales of sector *j* to final demand. In addition to the components of the simple output multiplier, it therefore includes the induced effect, or that increase in output from the local sector occasioned by increased household income as a result of the increase in sales to final demand. For example, each increase in the sale of the output of the animal industries sector in the Moreton region produces a total increase in output of \$1.600. The induced effect of the increased sales will therefore be \$1.600 – \$1.368 = \$0.232.

An examination of Table 7.13 provides some important information with respect to the expected output response of each sector on a regional basis. This may be summarised by three main points. *First*, we would expect that the regions of Queensland, ranked in size from the metropolitan to rural regions, would display an overall pattern in the size of output multipliers which reflects this ranking. The 'larger' economies would be expected to be more diversified and therefore to contain stronger linkages which would contribute to higher output multipliers. In general terms the output multipliers show the expected rankings with the Moreton region showing consistently the highest regional multipliers and the rural regions showing the lowest. When the 'size' of the region is measured in terms of the total output of all sectors in the region there is some correspondence between the ranking of the regions and the size of the output multipliers for each sector; this correspondence does not, however, follow for all regions, particularly the Northern and Far North regions, which show larger output multipliers than would be expected according to their rank. Evidence suggests that this is explained in terms of their relative isolation in terms of distance from the metropolitan area, and the consequent tendency for this distance to act as a buffer zone (Moore and Petersen, 1955). These regions support locally, under a degree of protection conferred by distance, some industries which would otherwise not exist.

Second, it is noticeable that the output multipliers relating to each sector in the state table tend to be larger than those of the regions of these sectors in the regions. As outlined in section 7.2, the state table incorporates all of the linkages of the regional tables. From another point of view, the regional multipliers for each sector should be seen as the disaggregation of the spatial incidence of the state multiplier effects.

Third, some similarities occur in the rankings of multipliers across the regions. For instance, the manufacturing sector shows the highest simple output multiplier in those regions which have rural or mineral processing industries, an indication of the importance of these industries in the regional economies. In the Moreton region the largest simple output multiplier is that of the building and construction sector, with the manufacturing sector in third place. On the other hand, when the induced effect is included, the total output multiplier of the public administration and defence sector is the largest in virtually all regions. This draws attention to the importance of this sector as a leading component of all regional economies. The smallest simple output multiplier in all regions is the community services sector multiplier; as expected, this sector purchases little in the form of industrial inputs. It does, however, require a relatively large number of employees, which contributes significantly to the total output multiplier. The smallest total output multiplier amongst all regions is that for the animal industries sector.

Income Multipliers

Table 7.14 provides the GRIT income multipliers for the uniform tables for the regions and state of Queensland and Tables VIII.3 and VIII.4 provide income multipliers for non-uniform tables. These are provided in three forms namely: (i) the *direct* income multiplier or household coefficient, indicating the first round effect on household income of an increase in output of each sector. For instance, an increase of one dollar in output of the animal industries sector in the Moreton region would increase household income in that sector within the region by $0.045; (ii) the direct and indirect income multiplier, including the income increases occasioned in all sectors in the region by an increase in sales of one dollar to final demand by each sector. For instance, the direct and indirect income effect of the animal industries sector in the Moreton region would be $0.141 as a result of industrial support requirements. Finally, (iii) the direct, indirect and induced effect is listed, including the increase in income due to increased consumer expenditure in the region; this figure is $0.216 for the example quoted. The indirect effect may be calculated in this case as $0.141 – $0.045 = $0.096, and the induced effect as $0.216 – $0.141 = $0.075, per dollar of increased sales of the animal industries sector to the final demand of the Moreton region.

The direct income multipliers indicate, in effect, the labour intensity of each sector in each region. These show, as expected, a high degree of similarity between regions with slight variations reflecting the efficiency of labour use in particular sectors. There is, however, within each region a wide disparity in this coefficient between sectors, reflecting the differences in labour intensity. This ranges, for example, from $0.045 to $0.596 per dollar of output in the animal industries and public administration and defence sectors in the Moreton region. These differences have an important effect on the calculation of both direct and indirect, and total income multipliers.

The total (i.e. direct, indirect and induced) income multipliers show a consistency in the upper and lower rankings between regions. Those sectors with the highest direct coefficients, namely the public administration and defence and community services sectors, show variable, but consistently the highest, total income multipliers over all regions. This is further evidence of the contribution made by these sectors to the personal income of Queensland regions. Each increase of one dollar in the value of output of the public administration sector destined for final demand in the Moreton region adds an additional $1.123 to regional household income; the same dollar increase in the same sector in the Far North region would increase this income by only \$0.899. On the other hand, the rural sectors show the smallest total income multipliers.

Employment Multipliers

Table 7.15 presents the GRIT employment multipliers for the uniform tables for the state and regions of Queensland and Tables VIII.5 and VIII.6 provide employment multipliers for the non-uniform tables. These are provided in three forms, parallel to those described above for income multipliers. In general terms, if the wage rate between sectors is constant, employment multipliers would be expected to reflect income multipliers in terms of ranking between sectors and between regions. The extent to which the income multipliers and employment multipliers vary in ranking highlights difference in personal income levels between sectors. For example, while the animal industries sector consistently showed in Table 7.14 the lowest requirements for the direct income component, its direct requirement in terms of employment (Table 7.15) is relatively high. On the other hand, the mining sectors show low labour usage in terms of employment, but higher contributions to household income, reflecting higher levels of wages and salaries in this sector.

The columns of direct employment requirements show variations both between regions for the same sector and between sectors in the same region. The former is an indication of the differences in technology which exist between regions in the same sector. For example, in the animal industries sector, which varies considerably in enterprise mix throughout the state, the sector in the Moreton region requires 0.122 units of labour per unit[3] of output – the same sector in the North West region requires only 0.029 employees to produce the same level of output. These differences in technology, both between sectors and between regions, produce several changes in the rankings of total employment multipliers when compared overall with the regions of the state. These sectors, namely the community services, public administration and defence, and the trade sectors show the highest-ranked employment multipliers, but the ranking of these three sectors changes between regions. For instance, the community services sector shows the highest total employment multiplier in the Moreton, Wide Bay–Burnett and Darling Downs regions, but is replaced in the first rank by the trade sector in the Fitzroy region.

General Comment on Regional Multipliers

The multipliers assembled in Tables 7.13, 7.14 and 7.15 provide a wealth of information relating to the response which can be expected within the regions and state of Queensland to a change in economic circumstances. Several important points need to be established at this stage. First, although the uniform tables presented in this chapter enable comparisons of multipliers between regions without difficulty, it should be remembered that the industry content of some sectors will vary substantially between regions in a state like Queensland which encompasses several climatic and physical zones. This is so particularly with respect to the rural industries which vary from dairying to sheep to beef, with different combinations and technologies between regions. This variation is accompanied by variations in the manufacturing sector, which is dominated in various regions by meat processing, sugar milling, or the production of dairy products, or simply by highly developed industrial complexes. Although the industry content of other sectors, for example the trade, public administration and finance sectors could be expected to be reasonably constant between regions, it may be necessary to consult the non-uniform tables and multipliers to obtain a sufficient understanding of the response of a particular region to a change in economic circumstances. The analysis of this response should be interpreted in the knowledge of the nature of the industries which comprise the regional economy.

Second, the multipliers offer significant advantages and improvements in the regional planning process or in the formation of regional policy. They provide an opportunity to isolate those sectors which will contribute the highest additional output income and employment in each region and thereby indicate those sectors which might receive special attention if regional economic growth is to be encouraged. They provide also a basis of estimating the likely decrease in economic activity associated with the closure or contraction of an industry.

Comparisons of sector multipliers between regions provide measures of the response which can be expected in each region to the establishment of a new industry or the expansion of any sector, and thereby provide guidance to location policy. For instance, if it was desired to locate an industry to maximise the increase in regional output resulting from the establishment of that industry, the regions showing the highest relevant output multipliers would be considered as the appropriate location.

Third, although the tables of multipliers offer a convenient method of selecting regional economic growth strategies, it should be remembered that the multipliers are relevant only in the context of the transactions table from which they are derived and should be interpreted in this light. It often transpires, for example, that the ranking of multipliers suggests that one or two sectors offer the most promising avenues of regional expansion, but that the linkages shown in the transactions tables suggest that expansion of these sectors is not feasible. The manufacturing sector in many Queensland regions illustrates this point; it shows consistently high output multipliers throughout the regions and appears as a promising sector for expansion of regional output levels. This sector is dominated in many regions by rural processing factories. The transactions tables indicate strong linkages between the manufacturing sector and the rural industries, suggesting that the output of this sector cannot be increased without concurrent increases in rural production.

Fourth, it is an advantage to consider all of the multipliers for a region in determining regional development strategies, and to consider these multipliers in terms of criteria for regional development. It is possible that the multipliers can indicate different directions of development according to the development criteria, i.e. that sectors with the highest output multipliers are not necessarily those which would contribute the highest additional employment or income. Also, by considering separately the magnitudes of the direct and indirect effects and the induced effects, it is possible to determine whether the expansion of any sector in a region will confer advantages on the local sectors primarily through increased demand for industrial support requirements or through increased household expenditures.

7.4 Summary

This chapter, with accompanying appendices, has provided the empirical results of the GRIT system for the state and the regions of Queensland. The large volume of results has allowed only a highly selective discussion of the input–output tables and multipliers. This discussion has been cast only in explanatory terms; the potential contribution in understanding the structure and spatial response pattern of the Queensland economy is enormous, but has not been considered in this chapter.

Notes

1. Of greater importance in more recent years.
2. Or decrease in industrial support requirements for a *decrease* in sales to final demand.
3. That is, per thousand dollars of output.

8 A REVIEW OF THE SYSTEM

The empirical results presented in Chapter 7 and in the Appendices provide a wealth of information relating to the Queensland economy. They provide details of the economy of the state as a whole, the regional economies of the state, of economic reaction paths within each region, and through the multipliers provide expected patterns of responses to economic impacting agents. Information of such detail has not, to the knowledge of the authors, previously been prepared for any group of regions comprising a state or nation. GRIT makes possible the application of the input–output technique and its potential analytical power to the analysis of the regional structure of a state or nation with a facility which is necessary for current operational application. More importantly, it provides substance for a realistic application of the spatial structure of an economy in a consistent framework – a goal not satisfactorily achieved by other methods of analysis.

This was achieved for Queensland through the development and application of the GRIT system, described in some detail in Chapter 6. The appropriateness or acceptability of the input–output tables and multipliers reported must therefore reflect that of the GRIT system. This chapter provides some discussion on the limitations which should be borne in mind when applying the results of the study, and some retrospective comment on the GRIT system.

8.1 Limitations of the Results

Two types of limitations which apply to the GRIT results in this study are identifiable, namely as those which would apply in any input–output analysis irrespective of the method of derivation of the table, and those which may be specifically attributed to the characteristics of the GRIT system. It is not the purpose of this chapter to discuss the former; these have been discussed in detail in the input–output literature. One important point, however, deserves mention, namely the effect of the linearity assumptions on the range of economies represented by the GRIT tables in this study. Although analysts have observed the difficulties associated with this assumption in input–output, there has been a tendency not to take those difficulties too seriously in tables representing diverse and advanced economies. Application of tables of the smaller and simpler economies, such as that for the North West region of Queensland, appear to be more prone to distortion through the linearity assumption. Most sectors in these tables refer to the lower-order activities of the industries comprising the sector; any expansion of these sectors would involve more a development of medium-order activities than an expansion of lower-order activities, with a consequent change in the production function and coefficients of the sectors in the input–output tables.

Some limitations, specifically associated with the GRIT system, should be mentioned. As outlined in Chapter 6, GRIT provides tables which are derived from a sequence of mechanical procedures, supplemented by superior data insertions and by survey or other exogenous data as required to ensure freedom from substantial error. The authors do not claim accuracy in detail in that individual cells are accurate, but merely that the tables as a whole reflect the appropriate economies without errors which are significant in analytical uses or which are noticeable to experienced observers.[1] Application of the tables reported in this study which depend on the use of individual or small groups of coefficients, particularly the smaller coefficients, should be approached with caution.[2] Most of the larger coefficients in the tables, and certainly the dominant coefficients, both of which exert the major influences on multiplier calculation, have been accepted by the GRIT team as substantially accurate. This suggests however that the multipliers can be freely interpreted in 'order-of-magnitude' terms only.

The prototype tables received the attention of experienced economists to ensure their general representativeness; some subjective judgement was of necessity exercised in this regard. While this subjectivity can be reasonably expected to ensure the absence of significant error, it probably ensures the existence of some error. Analysts who feel that they are able to improve on the tables by further subjective assessment, or by the introduction of data from reliable sources, are encouraged to do so.

8.2 Some Retrospective Comment and Evaluation

The GRIT sequence described in Chapter 6 is the methodology finally resolved after several modifications of an original version.[3] Modifications were introduced to improve the progressive conversion of national to regional tables, to provide for insertion of superior data at the stage which maximised the benefit of the data, and to deal with computational difficulties as they occurred. The authors were satisfied that the final GRIT sequence provided a satisfactory method for calculation of regional tables in the Queensland data context.

It must always remain possible, even probable, that a more appropriate combination of steps could be devised to achieve the objectives of this study, particularly in applications to other states or countries. In retrospect, the authors feel that improvements to the GRIT sequence are desirable in some areas, notably in adjustments for price levels and the adjustment for international trade. The methods used for the calculation of regional imports (Phase II) are conventional non-survey methods, and while subject to some criticism in the literature, probably remain the most appropriate available at this stage.

A desirable extension of this work would be the application of sensitivity analysis to determine the effect on the multipliers of different methods within each step or module. In particular the effect of different forms of the location quotient within Step 5 would be informative. We have at present no indication of the sensitivity of the GRIT tables multipliers to such changes. We assume, however, that the larger the degree of interference by the operator in the mechanical aspects of the sequence, the less will be the importance of the sensitivity question.

Nevertheless the GRIT sequence will be subject to professional criticism, evaluation, improvement and ultimately replacement. In the meantime, the authors have been encouraged by the number of enquiries for possible application of the system.

Notes

1. This is a relatively modest claim. We are tempted to suggest, however, that most input–output analysts would claim no more for their tables, irrespective of the method of compilation.
2. We would suggest the same caution with all input–output tables.
3. Modifications to the original version are outlined in Mandeville, Jensen and Karunaratne (1977).

APPENDIX I: FLOWCHART OF METHODOLOGY

PHASE I: ADJUSTMENTS TO NATIONAL TABLE

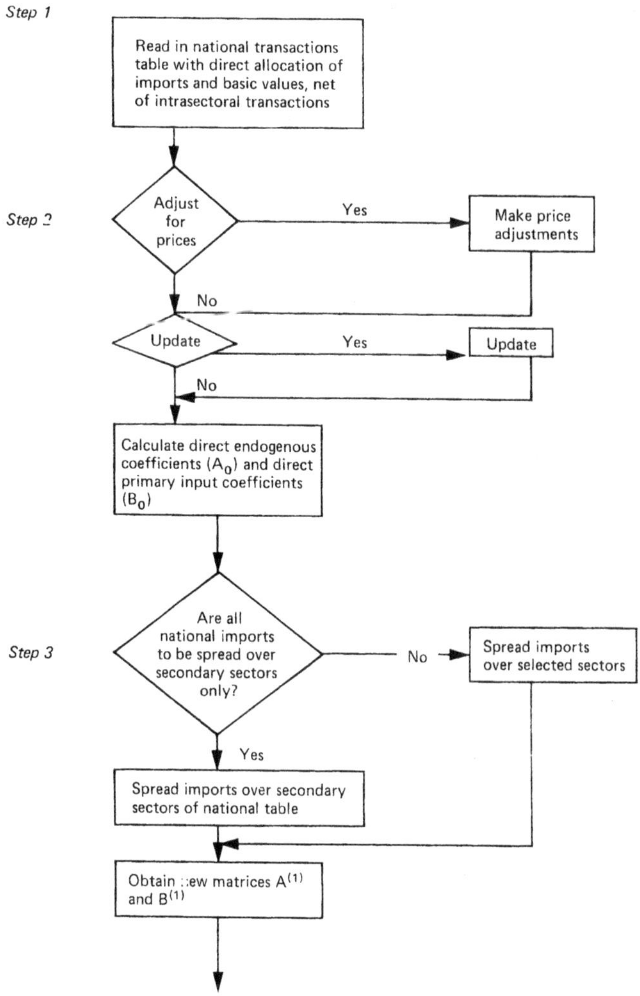

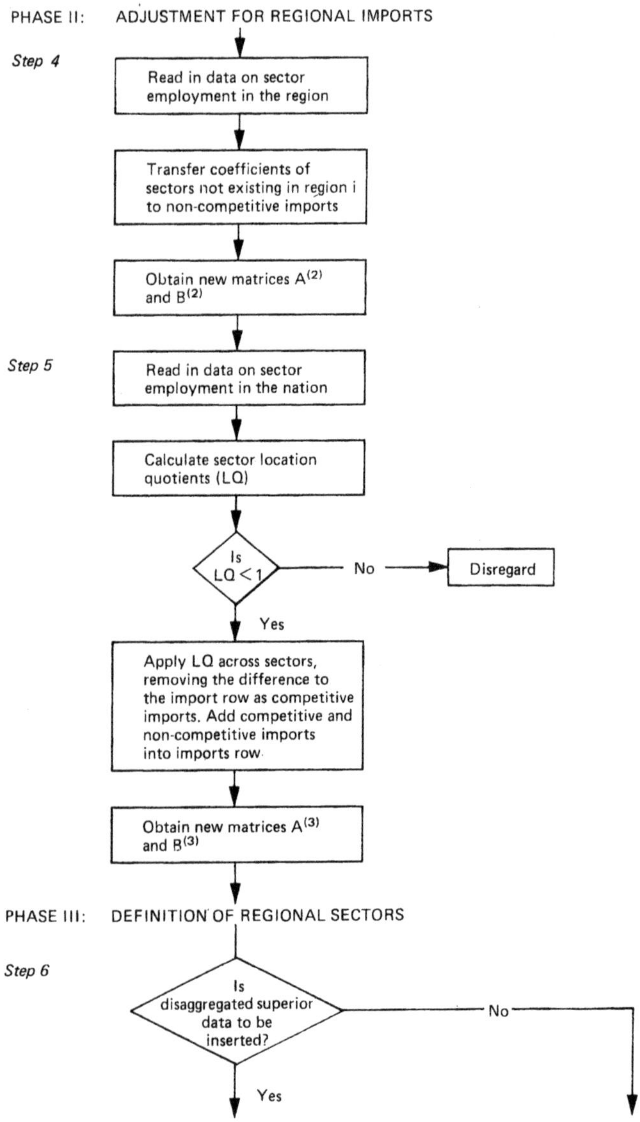
PHASE II: ADJUSTMENT FOR REGIONAL IMPORTS
Step 4
Read in data on sector employment in the region
Transfer coefficients of sectors not existing in region i to non-competitive imports
Obtain new matrices A(2) and B(2)
Step 5
Read in data on sector employment in the nation
Calculate sector location quotients (LQ)
Is LQ < 1
No
Disregard
Yes
Apply LQ across sectors, removing the difference to the import row as competitive imports. Add competitive and non-competitive imports into imports row
Obtain new matrices A(3) and B(3)
PHASE III: DEFINITION OF REGIONAL SECTORS
Step 6
Is disaggregated superior data to be inserted?
No
Yes

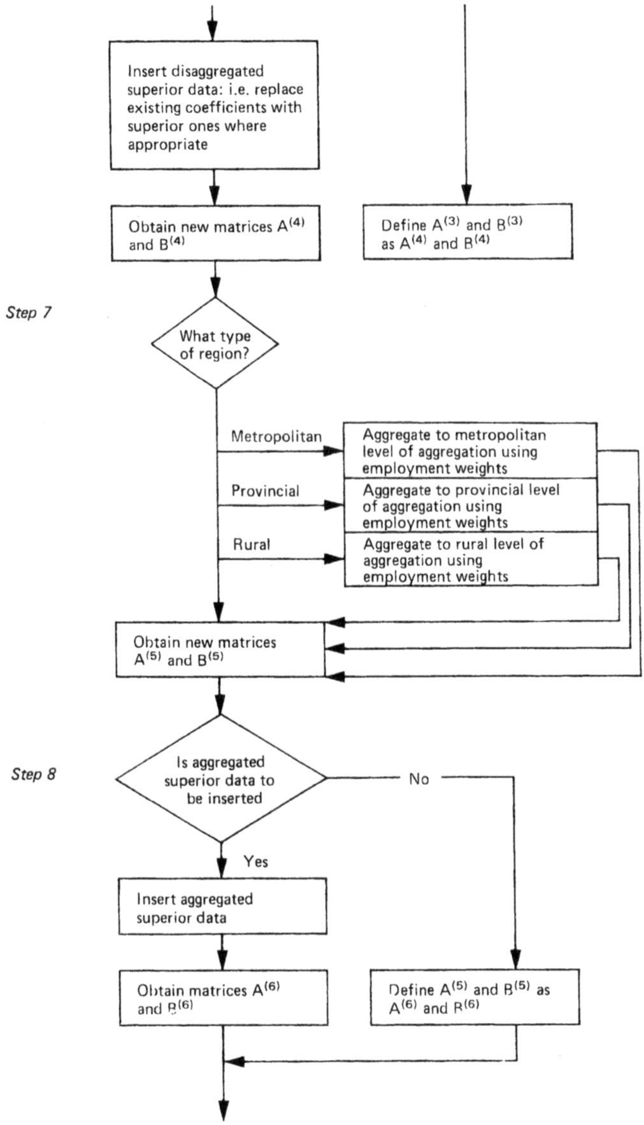
Insert disaggregated superior data: i.e. replace existing coefficients with superior ones where appropriate
Obtain new matrices A(4) and B(4)
Define A(3) and B(3) as A(4) and B(4)
Step 7
What type of region?
Metropolitan
Aggregate to metropolitan level of aggregation using employment weights
Provincial
Aggregate to provincial level of aggregation using employment weights
Rural
Aggregate to rural level of aggregation using employment weights
Obtain new matrices A(5) and B(5)
Step 8
Is aggregated superior data to be inserted
No
Yes
Insert aggregated superior data
Obtain matrices A(6) and B(6)
Define A(5) and B(5) as A(6) and B(6)

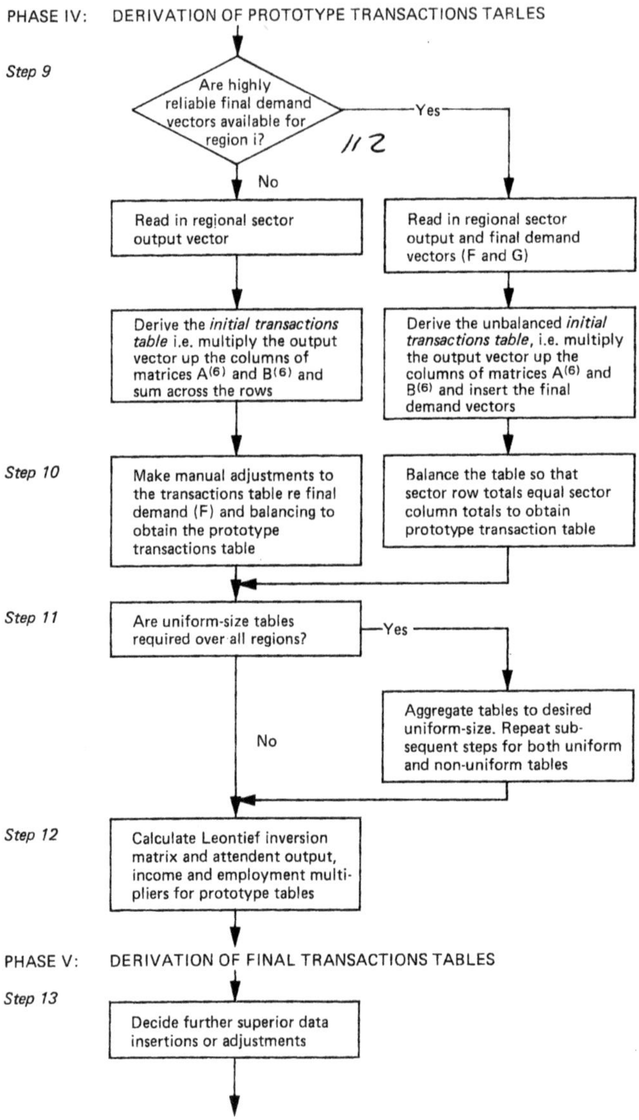
PHASE IV: DERIVATION OF PROTOTYPE TRANSACTIONS TABLES
Step 9
Are highly reliable final demand vectors available for region i?
Yes
No
Read in regional sector output vector
Read in regional sector output and final demand vectors (F and G)
Derive the initial transactions table i.e. multiply the output vector up the columns of matrices A(6) and B(6) and sum across the rows
Derive the unbalanced initial transactions table, i.e. multiply the output vector up the columns of matrices A(6) and B(6) and insert the final demand vectors
Step 10
Make manual adjustments to the transactions table re final demand (F) and balancing to obtain the prototype transactions table
Balance the table so that sector row totals equal sector column totals to obtain prototype transaction table
Step 11
Are uniform-size tables required over all regions?
Yes
No
Aggregate tables to desired uniform-size. Repeat subsequent steps for both uniform and non-uniform tables
Step 12
Calculate Leontief inversion matrix and attendent output, income and employment multipliers for prototype tables
PHASE V: DERIVATION OF FINAL TRANSACTIONS TABLES
Step 13
Decide further superior data insertions or adjustments

Step 14

Step 15

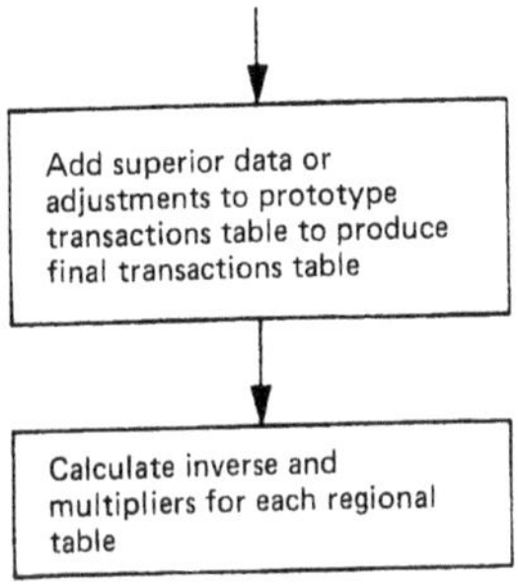

APPENDIX II: AUSTRALIAN NATIONAL INPUT–OUTPUT CLASSIFICATION

00	Agriculture, Forestry and Fishing		ASIC Code
	01.01	Sheep	0111, 0113 (part)
	01.02	Cereal grains	0112, 0113 (part)
	01.03	Meat cattle	0121
	01.04	Milk cattle and pigs	0122, 0123
	01.05	Poultry	013
	01.06	Other farming	014, 015, 016, 017
	02.00	Services to agriculture	020
	03.00	Forestry and logging	030
	04.00	Fishing, trapping and hunting	041, 042
10	Mining		
	11.01	Iron	1104
	11.02	Other metallic minerals	110 (excl. 1104)
	12.00	Coal and crude petroleum	120, 130
	14.00	Non-metallic n.e.c.	140, 150
	16.00	Services to mining	160
21–22	Food, Tobacco		
	21.01	Meat products	211
	21.02	Milk products	212
	21.03	Fruit and vegetable products	213
	21.04	Margarine, oils and fats	214
	21.05	Flour mill and cereal food products	215
	21.06	Bread, cakes, and biscuits	216
	21.07	Confectionery and cocoa products	2181
	21.08	Food products n.e.c. (including fish and sugar)	2182, 2183, 2184, 217
	21.09	Soft drinks, cordials and syrups	2191
	21.10	Beer and malt	2192, 2193
	21.11	Alcoholic beverages n.e.c.	2194, 2195
	22.01	Tobacco products	2210
23–24	Textile and Clothing		
	23.01	Prepared fibres (cotton ginning, wool scouring, top-making)	2311 to 2313
	23.02	Man-made fibres, yarns and fabrics	2314, 2315
	23.03	Cotton, silk and flax yarns, fabrics and household textiles	2316, 2319, 2322
	23.04	Wool and worsted yarns and fabrics	2317, 2318
	23.05	Textile finishing	2321
	23.06	Textile floor covering, felt and felt products	2331, 2332

			ASIC Code
23–24	Textile and Clothing (continued)		
	23.07	Textile products n.e.c. (incl. canvas, rope, etc.)	2333–2335
	24.01	Knitting mills	241
	24.02	Clothing	242
	24.03	Footwear	243
25	Wood		
	25.01	Sawmill products	2511, 2512, 2515
	25.02	Plywood, veneers and manufactured boards	2513
	25.03	Joinery and wood products n.e.c.	2514, 2516
	25.04	Furniture, mattresses, brooms and brushes	252, 3443
26	Paper		
	26.01	Pulp, paper and paperboard	2611
	26.02	Fibreboard and paper containers	2612–2614
	26.03	Paper products n.e.c.	2615
	26.04	Newspapers and books	2621
	26.05	Commercial and job printing and printing trade services	2622, 2623
27	Chemicals		
	27.01	Chemical fertilisers	2711
	27.02	Industrial chemicals n.e.c. (plastic materials, synthetic resins, industrial gases, synthetic rubber, other basic chemicals)	2712–2715
	27.03	Paints, varnishes and lacquers	2722
	27.04	Pharmaceutical and veterinary products, agricultural chemicals	2723, 2724
	27.05	Soap and other detergents	2725
	27.06	Cosmetic and toilet preparations	2726
	27.07	Chemical products n.e.c. (incl. ammunition, explosives and fireworks)	2721, 2727, 2728
	27.08	Petroleum and coal products	273, 274
28	Non-metallic Mineral Products		
	28.01	Glass and glass products	281
	28.02	Clay products	282
	28.03	Cement	2831
	28.04	Ready-mixed concrete	2832
	28.05	Concrete products	2833, 2834, 2835
	28.06	Gypsum, plaster and other non-metallic mineral products	2841–2843
29, 31	Metals, Metal Products		
	29.01	Basic iron and steel	291
	29.02	Non-ferrous metal basic products	292–295

			ASIC Code
29, 31	Metals, Metal Products (continued)		
	31.01	Fabricated structural metal products	311
	31.02	Metal containers, sheet metal products	312
	31.03	Cutlery and hand tools, metal coating and finishing and metal products n.e.c.	313
32	Transport Equipment		
	32.01	Motor vehicles and parts and transport equipment n.e.c.	321, 3225
	32.02	Ship and boat building and repair	3221, 3222
	32.03	Locomotives, rolling stock and repair	3223
	32.04	Aircraft building and repair	3224
33	Machinery and Household Appliances		
	33.01	Photographic, scientific equipment etc.	331
	33.02	Television sets, radios, communication and electronic equipment n.e.c.	3321
	33.03	Household appliances n.e.c.	3322, 3323
	33.04	Electrical machinery and equipment n.e.c.	3324–3326
	33.05	Agricultural machinery and equipment	3331
	33.06	Construction, earthmoving and materials handling machinery and equipment	3332, 3333
	33.07	Other machinery and equipment	3334–3339
34	Leather, Rubber and Plastic Products		
	34.01	Leather tanning, leather and leather substitute products n.e.c.	341
	34.02	Rubber products	342
	34.03	Plastic and related products	343
	34.04	Signs, advertising displays, writing, and marking equipment	3444, 3446
	34.05	Ophthalmic articles, jewellery, silverware and other manufacturing	3441, 3442, 3445, 3447
36, 37	Electricity, Gas and Water		
	36.01	Electricity generation and distribution	361
	36.02	Gas production and distribution	362
	37.01	Water, sewerage and drainage	370

			ASIC Code
41, 42	Building and Construction		
	41.01	Residential buildings	411 (part), 42 (part)
	41.02	Other building and construction	411 (part), 412, 42 (part)
45–46	Trade, Transport, Storage and Communication		
	46.01	Wholesale trade	46–47 (excl. repairs)
	48.01	Retail trade	48 (excl. repairs)
	48.02	Motor vehicle repairs	Re-definitions
	48.03	Other repairs	Re-definitions
	51.01	Road transport	51
	52.01	Railway transport, other transport and storage	52, 55
	53.01	Water transport	53
	54.01	Air transport	54
	55.01	Communication	56
61–63	Finance etc.		
	61.01	Banking	611
	61.02	Finance and life insurance	612, 621
	61.03	Other insurance	622
	61.04	Investment, real estate and leasing	613, 631, 632 (part), 636
	61.05	Technical and other business services	633–635
	61.06	Ownership of dwellings	632 (part) and imputed rent
71–94	Public Administration, Community Services, Entertainment etc.		
	71.01	Public administration	71, 8451–3
	72.01	Defence	72
	81.01	Health	81
	82.01	Education, libraries, etc.	82
	83.01	Welfare services, religious and community organisations	83, 841 (part), 842, 843, 844, 8454
	91.01	Entertainment and recreational services	91
	92.01	Restaurants, hotels and clubs	921, 922
	93.01	Personal services	93, 94
99	Business Expenses		
	99.01	Business expenses	Dummy industry, No ASIC equivalent

APPENDIX III: SECTOR CLASSIFICATION

Rural Regions	Provincial Regions	Metropolitan Region & State	National Sectors Included
1. Animal industries	1. Animal industries	1. Animal industries	01.01 Sheep
			01.03 Meat cattle
			01.04 Milk cattle and pigs
2. Other primary industries	2A. Other agriculture	2A. Other agriculture	01.02 Cereal grains
			01.05 Poultry
			01.06 Other farming
			02.00 Services to agriculture
	2B. Forestry, fishing	2B. Forestry, fishing	03.00 Forestry and logging
			04.00 Fishing, trapping and hunting
3. Mining	3A. Coal and crude petroleum mining	3A. Coal and crude petroleum mining	12.00 Coal and crude petroleum mining
	3B. Other mining	3B. Other mining	11.01 Iron
			11.02 Other metallic minerals
			14.00 Non-metallic n.e.c.
			16.00 Services to mining
4. Manufacturing	4A. Food manufacturing	4A1. Meat and milk products	21.01 Meat products
			21.02 Milk products
		4A2. Fruit and vegetable products, oils and fats	21.03 Fruit and vegetable products
			21.04 Margarines, oils and fats
		4A3. Flour, cereals, bread	21.05 Flour mill and cereal food products
			21.06 Bread, cakes and biscuits
		4A4. Confectionery and other food n.e.c.	21.07 Confectionery and cocoa products
			21.08 Food products n.e.c. (including fish and sugar)
		4A5. Beverages and tobacco	21.09 Soft drinks, cordials and syrups
			21.10 Beer and malt
			21.11 Alcoholic beverages n.e.c.
			22.01 Tobacco products

Rural Regions	Provincial Regions	Metropolitan Region & State	National Sectors Included
	4B. Wood and paper manufacturing	4B1. Sawmills, plywoods	25.01 Sawmill products
			25.02 Plywood, veneers and manufactured boards
		4B2. Joinery, furniture	25.03 Joinery and wood products n.e.c.
			25.04 Furniture, mattresses, brooms and brushes
		4B3. Paper products	26.01 Pulp, paper and paperboard
			26.02 Fibreboard and paper containers
			26.03 Paper products n.e.c.
		4B4. Newspapers, printing	26.04 Newspapers and books
			26.05 Commercial and job printing and printing trade services
	4C. Machinery, appliances, equipment	4C1. Household appliances, machinery and equipment	33.01 Photographic, scientific equipment etc.
			33.02 Television sets, radios, communication and electronic equipment n.e.c.
			33.03 Household appliances n.e.c.
			33.04 Electrical machinery and equipment n.e.c.
			33.05 Agricultural machinery and equipment
			33.06 Construction, earthmoving and materials handling machinery and equipment
			33.07 Other machinery and equipment
		4C2. Motor vehicles, ships, locomotives and aircraft	32.01 Motor vehicles and parts and transport equipment n.e.c.
			32.02 Ship and boat building and repair
			32.03 Locomotives, rolling stock and repair
			32.04 Aircraft building and repair
	4D. Metals, metal products	4D1. Basic iron and steel	29.01 Basic iron and steel
		4D2. Non-ferrous metal basic products	29.02 Non-ferrous metal basic products
		4D3. Fabricated and other metal products	31.01 Fabricated structural metal products
			31.02 Metal containers, sheet metal products
			31.03 Cutlery and hand tools, metal coating and finishing and metal products n.e.c.

Rural Regions	Provincial Regions	Metropolitan Region & State	National Sectors Included
	4E. Non-metallic mineral products	4E. Non-metallic mineral products	28.01 Glass and glass products
			28.02 Clay products
			28.03 Cement
			28.04 Ready-mixed concrete
			28.05 Concrete products
			28.06 Gypsum, plaster and other non-metallic mineral products
	4F. Other manufacturing	4F1. Chemicals, petroleum products	27.01 Chemical fertilisers
			27.02 Industrial chemicals n.e.c. (plastic materials, synthetic resins, industrial gases, synthetic rubber, other basic chemicals)
			27.03 Paints, varnishes and lacquers
			27.04 Pharmaceutical and veterinary products, agricultural chemicals
			27.05 Soap and other detergents
			27.06 Cosmetic and toilet preparations
			27.07 Chemical products n.e.c. (incl. ammunition, explosives and fireworks)
			27.08 Petroleum and coal products
		4F2. Textiles	23.01 Prepared fibres (cotton ginning, wool scouring, top-making)
			23.02 Man-made fibres, yarns and fabrics
			23.03 Cotton, silk and flax yarns, fabrics and household textiles
			23.04 Wool and worsted yarns and fabrics
			23.05 Textile finishing
			23.06 Textile floor covering, felt and felt products
			23.07 Textile products n.e.c. (incl. canvas, rope, etc)
		4F3. Knitting mills, clothing, footwear	24.01 Knitting mills
			24.02 Clothing
			24.03 Footwear

Rural Regions	Provincial Regions	Metropolitan Region & State	National Sectors Included
		4F4. Leather, rubber and plastic products	34.01 Leather tanning, leather and leather substitute products n.e.c.
			34.02 Rubber products
			34.03 Plastic and related products
		4F5. Other manufacturing	34.04 Signs, advertising displays, writing and marking equipment
			34.05 Ophthalmic articles, jewellery, silverware and other manufacturing
5. Electricity, gas, and water	5. Electricity, gas and water	5A1. Electricity	36.01 Electricity generation and distribution
		5A2. Gas	36.02 Gas production and distribution
		5A3. Water, sewerage	27.01 Water, sewerage and drainage
6. Building and construction	6. Building and construction	6. Building and construction	41.01 Residential buildings
			41.02 Other building and construction
7. Trade	7. Trade	7. Trade	46.01 Wholesale trade
			48.01 Retail trade
			48.02 Motor vehicle repairs
			48.03 Other repairs
8. Transport and communication	8. Transport and communication	8A1. Transport	51.01 Road transport
			52.01 Railway transport, other transport and storage
			53.01 Water transport
			54.01 Air transport
		8A2. Communication	55.01 Communication
9. Finance	9. Finance	9A1. Finance	61.01 Banking
			61.02 Finance and life insurance
			61.03 Other insurance

Rural Regions	Provincial Regions	Metropolitan Region & State	National Sectors Included
9. Finance (continued)	9. Finance	9A1. Finance	61.04 Investment, real estate and leasing 61.05 Technical and other business services 61.06 Ownership of dwellings
10. Public administration and defence	10. Public administration and defence	10. Public administration and defence	71.01 Public administration 72.01 Defence
11. Community services, entertainment	11A. Community services	11A. Community services	81.01 Health 82.01 Education, libraries, etc. 83.01 Welfare services, religious and community organisations
	11B. Entertainment etc.	11B. Entertainment etc.	91.01 Entertainment and recreational services 92.01 Restaurants, hotels and clubs 93.01 Personal services

APPENDIX IV: GRIT COMPUTER PROGRAM

```
C        GRIT COMPUTER PROGRAM
C        AUTHOR: M. BENJAMIN
C
C        PARAMETERS–
C        MNAT,NNAT – DIMENSIONS OF NATIONAL TABLE
C        MB – NO. OF ROWS IN B QUADRANT
C        NFD – NO. OF COLS IN FINAL DEMAND
C        ISEC1,ISECN – UPPER & LOWER LIMITS OF SECONDARY
C              SECTOR
C        ICI – COMPETITIVE IMPORTS ROW
C        INCI – NON–"             "        "
C        MAXS – MAX. NO. OF SECTORS
C        LPT,CDR,DSK – I/O CHANNELS
C
C        INPUTS–
C        THIS SYSTEM WAS IMPLEMENTED ON AN ONLINE
C        ENVIRONMENT & SO MAKES EXTENSIVE USE OF DISK FILES.
C        ALSO MUCH USE IS MADE OF FREE FORMAT I/P. OTHER USERS
C        WILL PROBABLY WISH TO USE THEIR OWN INPUT SCHEME.
C        NECESSARY INPUTS ARE–
C        (1) NATIONAL TABLE
C        (2) REGIONAL EMPLOYMENTS
C        (3) NATIONAL         "
C        (4) SUPERIOR DISAGG'D DATA
C        (5) AGG'N INFORMATION
C        (6) SUPERIOR ROW AGG'D,COL DISAGG'D DATA
C        (7) SUPERIOR AGG'D DATA
C        (8) OUTPUT & FINAL DEMAND DATA
C        (9) VARIOUS CONTROL FLAGS
C
C        CONTROL FLAGS–
C        (1) FDFLG – IF FALSE,FINAL DEMAND DATA IS NOT
C              AVAILABLE SO PRINT TRANSACTION TABLES WITHOUT
C              FINAL DEMAND & DO NOT FIND MULTIPLIERS.
C              OTHERWISE,PRINT TRANSACTION TABLES WITH FINAL
C              DEMAND & FIND MULTIPLIERS
C        (2) BALFLG – IF FALSE, DO NOT BALANCE.THIS WILL BE
C              NECESSARY WHEN DERIVING FINAL TABLES
C        (3) FASFLG – IF TRUE, USE RAS ROUTINE TO BALANCE
C              OTHERWISE SIMPLY ADJUST ENTRIES TO ADD
C              TO OUTPUTS
C
C        AGGREGATION SCHEME–
C        THERE ARE 3 MAIN TABLES INVOLVED–SLIST, DEFN1 &
C        DEFN2. EACH ENTRY IN SLIST POINTS TO A NATIONAL
C        SECTOR.CONTIGOUS SEQUENCES OF ENTRIES IN SLIST
C        DEFINE THE SETS OF SECTORS TO BE AGG'D. EACH ENTRY IN
```

```
C         DEFN1(I) POINTS TO THE SEQ. IN SLIST WHICH REPRESENTS
C         THE NAT'L SECTORS TO BE AGG'D TO GIVE REG'L SECTOR I.
C         THE SEQ'S IN SLIST ARE ARRANGED SO THAT THE SEQ. FOR
C         SECTOR I PRECEDES THAT FOR SECTOR I+1.
C         E.G. REG'L SEC. 1 CONSISTS OF NAT'L SEC'S 1, 3, 4
C                         2                         2, 5, 6
C         DEFN1= 1,4, . . . ETC.
C         SLIST= 1, 3, 4, 2, 5, 6, . . . ETC.
C         NOTE: SINCE THE AGG'N IS DONE "IN SITU" REG'L SEC.
C         I MUST NOT CONTAIN ANY NAT'L SEC. LESS THAN I
C         DEFN1 DEFINES THE FIRST NON-UNIFORM AGG'N
C         DEFN2 DEFINES THE SECOND UNIFORM AGG'N
C         HOWEVER, IT IS ASSUMED THAT THE SECOND AGG'N IS
C         STRICTLY HIERARCHICAL. I.E. SEQ'S OF ADJACENT SEC'S ARE
C         AGG'D--E.G. SEC'S 1, 2 AGG'D TO NEW SEC. 1, SEC'S 3, 4, 5
C         AGG'D TO NEW SEC. 2, ETC. THEREFORE, THE 2ND AGG'N
C         USES AN IMPLICIT (NON-EXISTENT) SLIST WITH ENTRIES
C         1, 2, 3, 4, 5 . . . .
C
C
          REAL IOTAB(113, 109), RE(109), NE(109), LQ(109)
          REAL Z(50, 50), Z2(50, 50)
          REAL U(50), V(50), WORK1(50), WORK2(50), WORK3(50)
          REAL T1OM(50), T1IM(50), T1EM(50), T2OM(50), T2IM(50),
                T2EM(50)
          REAL DIIC(50), DIEC(50), DIIEC(50)
          INTEGER SLIST(109), DEFN1(51), DEFN2(50)
          INTEGER IDENT(2), AGGFIL
          INTEGER LPT, CDR, DSK
          LOGICAL FDFLG, BALFLG, RASFLG
          DATA MNAT, NNAT, MB, NFD, ICI, INCI, ISEC1, ISECN/113,
          1 109, 4, 3, 113, 112, 15, 80/
          DATA MAXS/50/
          DATA LPT, CDR, DSK/3, 2, 1/
          COMMON LPT, CDR, DSK
          EQUIVALENCE (Z(1, 1), IOTAB(1, 60))
C
          READ(CDR, 20010)IDENT
20010     FORMAT(2A5)
          WRITE(LPT, 30010)IDENT
30010     FORMAT('*****RUN I.D.=', 2A5)
C
C         ***********************************************
C         PHASE 1 -- ADJUSTMENTS TO NATIONAL TABLE
C
C         STEP 1-- INPUT NATIONAL TRANSACTIONS TABLE
C
          CALL IFILE(DSK, 'BNTAB')
          READ(DSK)((IOTAB(I, J), J=1, NNAT), I=1, MNAT)
          END FILE DSK
C
C         STEP 2 -- PRICE ADJUSTMENTS & UPDATE NOT IMPLEMENTED
C                   CALCULATE COEFFICIENTS --> A.0, B.0
C
```

```
      DO 1030 J=1, NNAT
         SUM=0.0
         DO 1010 I=1, MNAT
            SUM=SUM+IOTAB(I,J)
 1010    CONTINUE
         DO 1020 I=1,MNAT
            IOTAB(I,J)=IOTAB(I,J)/SUM
 1020    CONTINUE
 1030 CONTINUE
C
C     STEP 3 – ADJUSTMENT FOR INTERNATIONAL TRADE –>
C              A.1,B.1
C              NOTE: THERE ARE NO OPTIONS IMPLEMENTED –
C                    IMPORTS ARE SPREAD OVER SECONDARY
C                    SECTORS
      DO 1070 J=1, NNAT
         SUM1=IOTAB(ICI,J)+IOTAB(INCI,J)
         IOTAB(ICI,J)=0.0
         IOTAB(INCI,J)=0.0
         SUM=0.0
         DO 1050 I=ISEC1,ISECN
         SUM=SUM+IOTAB(I,J)
 1050 CONTINUE
      C=(SUM1/SUM)+1
      DO 1060 I=ISEC1,ISECN
         IOTAB(I,J)=IOTAB(I,J)*C
 1060    CONTINUE
 1070 CONTINUE
C
C     SPECIAL STEP – SPREAD BUSINESS EXPENSES OVER
C           TERTIARY SECTORS
C           BUSINESS EXPENSES IS ROW & COL NNAT
C           TERTIARY SECTOR IS ISECN+1 . . . NNAT–1
C
      DO 1110 J=1, NNAT–1
         SUM=0.0
         DO 1090 I=ISECN+1, NNAT–1
            SUM=SUM+IOTAB(I,J)
 1090    CONTINUE
         C=(IOTAB(NNAT,J)/SUM)+1
         IOTAB(NNAT,J)=0.0
         DO 1100 I=ISECN+1,NNAT–1
            IOTAB(I,J)=IOTAB(I,J)*C
 1100    CONTINUE
 1110 CONTINUE
      DO 1120 I=1, MNAT
         IOTAB(I,NNAT)=0.0
 1120 CONTINUE
C
C     END OF PHASE 1
C
C     ************************************************
C
C     PHASE 2 – ADJUSTMENT FOR REGIONAL IMPORTS
```

```
C
C        STEP 4 – CALC'N OF NON-COMPETITIVE IMPORTS –> A.2,B.2
C                 INPUT REGIONAL EMPLOYMENTS
C
         READ(CDR,20020)RE
20020    FORMAT(10F)
         WRITE(LPT,30030)
30030    FORMAT(//' *****REGIONAL EMPLOYMENTS'/)
         CALL MATOUT(RE,NNAT,1,NNAT,1)
C
         DO 2030 I=1,NNAT
            IF(RE(I).NE.0.0)GO TO 2030
            DO 2010 J=1,NNAT
               IOTAB(INCI,J)=IOTAB(INCI,J)+IOTAB(I,J)
               IOTAB(I,J)=0.0
 2010       CONTINUE
            DO 2020 II=1,MNAT
               IOTAB(II,I)=0.0
 2020       CONTINUE
 2030    CONTINUE
C
C        STEP 5 – CALC'N OF COMPETITIVE IMPORTS –> A.3,B.3
C                 INPUT NATIONAL EMPLOYMENTS
C
         CALL IFILE(DSK,'NATEM')
         READ(DSK,10010)NE
10010    FORMAT(10F)
         END FILE DSK
C
C        FIND RATIO OF TOTAL NATIONAL TO REGIONAL
C              EMPLOYMENTS
C
         TRE=0.0
         TNE=0.0
         DO 2050 I=1,NNAT
            TRE=TRE+RE(I)
            TNE=TNE+NE(I)
 2050    CONTINUE
         C=TNE/TRE
C
C        CALCULATE, SAVE & APPLY LOCATION QUOTIENTS
C
         DO 2080 I=1,NNAT
            IF(RE(I).EQ.0.0)GO TO 2080
            CLQ=RE(I)/NE(I)*C
            LQ(I)=CLQ
            IF(CLQ.GE.1.0)GO TO 2080
            DO 2070 J=1,NNAT
               A2=IOTAB(I,J)
               A3=A2*CLQ
               IOTAB(ICI,J)=IOTAB(ICI,J)+A2–A3
               IOTAB(I,J)=A3
 2070       CONTINUE
```

```
 2080   CONTINUE
C
        WRITE(LPT,30040)
30040   FORMAT(//'*****LOCATION QUOTIENTS'/)
        CALL MATOUT(LQ,NNAT,1,NNAT,1)
C
C       COMBINE IMPORTS ROWS
C
        DO 2090 J=1,NNAT
           IOTAB(ICI,J)=IOTAB(ICI,J)+IOTAB(INCI,J)
 2090   CONTINUE
        MB=MB=1
C
C       END OF PHASE 2
C
C       ************************************************
C
C       PHASE 3 – DEFINITION OF REGIONAL SECTORS
C
C       STEP 6– INSERTION OF DISAGG'D SUPERIOR DATA —> A.4,B.4
C
        WRITE(LPT,30050)
30050   FORMAT(//' *****SUPERIOR DISAGG"D DATA'/)
        CALL INSERT(IOTAB,MNAT,NNAT)
C
C       STEP 7 – AGGREGATION —> A.5,B.5
C               INPUT SELECTED AGGREGATION TABLES
C
        READ(CDR,20030)AGGFIL
20030   FORMAT(A5)
        CALL IFILE(DSK,AGGFIL)
        READ(DSK,10020)SLIST,NSECT1,DEFN1(J),J=1,NSECT1),
            NSECT2,1(DEFN2(J),J=1,NSECT2)
10020   FORMAT(20I)
        END FILE DSK
C
C
C       AGGREGATE ROWS & OBTAIN EMPLOYMENT WEIGHTS IN
C           WORK1
C
        WRITE(LPT,30070)
30070   FORMAT(1H1,' *****NON-UNIFORM AGG"N SYSTEM'//' NEW
            OLD'/)
C
        DEFN1(NSECT1+1)=NNAT+1
        DO 3060 I=1,NSECT1
           L1=DEFN1(I)
           L2=DEFN1(I+1)–1
           WRITE(LPT,30080)I,(SLIST(J),J=L1,L2)
30080      FORMAT(1X,I3,5X,50(I3,',')) 
           DO 3020 J=1,NNAT
              SUM=0.0
              DO 3010 II=L1,L2
                 SUM=SUM+IOTAB(SLIST(II),J)
```

```
 3010          CONTINUE
               IOTAB(I,J)=SUM
 3020       CONTINUE
            SUM=0.0
            DO 3030 II=L1,L2
               SUM=SUM+RE(SLIST(II))
 3030       CONTINUE
            IF(SUM.EQ.0.0)GO TO 3050
            DO 3040 II=L1,L2
               KII=SLIST(II)
               WORK1(KII)=RE(KII)/SUM
 3040       CONTINUE
 3050       RE(I)=SUM
 3060    CONTINUE
C
C        MOVE B-QUANDRANT ADJACENT TO A-QUANDRANT
C
         II=NSECT1
         DO 3160 I=NNAT+1,MNEW
            II=II+1
            DO 3150 J=1,NNAT
               IOTAB(II,J)=IOTAB(I,J)
 3150       CONTINUE
 3160    CONTINUE
C
C        INSERT SUPERIOR ROW AGG'D, COL DISAGG'D DATA
C
         WRITE(LPT,30090)
30090    FORMAT(//' *****SUPERIOR ROW AGG''D, COL DISAGG''D
               DATA'/)
         CALL INSERT(IOTAB,MNAT,NNAT)
C
C        MULTIPLY COLUMNS BY WEIGHTS
C
         DO 3090 J=1,NNAT
            C=WORK1(J)
            DO 3070 I=1,NSECT1+MB
               IOTAB(I,J)=IOTAB(I,J)*C
 3070       CONTINUE
 3090    CONTINUE
C
C        AGGREGATE COLUMNS
C
         DO 3140 J=1,NSECT1
            L1=DEFN1(J)
            L2=DEFN1(J+1)-1
            DO 3110 I=1,NSECT1+MB
               SUM=0.0
               DO 3100 JJ=L1,L2
                  SUM=SUM+IOTAB(I,SLIST(JJ))
 3100          CONTINUE
               IOTAB(I,J)=SUM
 3110       CONTINUE
 3140    CONTINUE
C
```

```
C        STEP 8 – INSERT SUPERIOR AGG'D DATA –> A.6,B.6
C
         WRITE(LPT,30100)
30100    FORMAT(//' *****SUPERIOR AGG''D DATA'/)
         CALL INSERT(IOTAB,MNAT,NNAT)
C
         MHH=NSECT1+1
         MAGG=NSECT1+MB
         NAGG=NSECT1
C
         WRITE(LPT,30105)
30105    FORMAT(//' *****AGG''D MATRIX (A6,B6)'/)
         CALL MATOUT(IOTAB,MNAT,NNAT,MAGG,NAGG)
         WRITE(LPT,30110)
30110    FORMAT(//' *****AGG''D EMPLOYMENTS'/)
         CALL MATOUT(RE,NNAT,1,NSECT1,1)
C
C        END OF PHASE 3
C
C        ***********************************************
C
C        PHASE 4/5 – DERIVATION OF TRANSACTION TABLES
C
C        INPUT THE OUTPUT VECTOR
C
         READ(CDR,20040)(V(J),J=1,NSECT1)
20040    FORMAT(10F)
C
C        DERIVE TRANSACTION TABLE
C
         DO 4020 J=1,NAGG
            C=V(J)
            DO 4010 I=1,MAGG
               IOTAB(I,J)=IOTAB(I,J)*C
 4010       CONTINUE
 4020    CONTINUE
C
C        ARE FINAL DEMAND VECTORS AVAILABLE?
C
         READ(CDR,20050)FDFLG
20050    FORMAT(L1)
         IF(.NOT.FDFLG)GO TO 4060
C
C        YES – INPUT F & C QUANDRANTS & ADJUST DIMENSION
C
         NAGG=NAGG+NFD
         READ(CDR,20040)((IOTAB(I,J),I=1,NSECT1),J=MHH,NAGG)
         READ(CDR,20040)((IOTAB(I,J),I=MHH,MAGG),J=MHH,NAGG)
C
C        DERIVE EXTRA OUTPUTS
C
         DO 4040 J=MHH,NAGG
            SUM=0.0
            DO 4030 I=1,MAGG
               SUM=SUM+IOTAB(I,J)
```

```
 4030       CONTINUE
            V(J)=SUM
 4040    CONTINUE
C
 4060    CONTINUE
C
C        DO WE WANT TO BALANCE?
C
         READ(CDR,20050)BALFLG
         IF(.NOT.BALFLG)GO TO 4180
C
C        DO WE WANT TO BALANCE USING RAS?
C
         READ(CDR,20050)RASFLG
         IF(RASFLG)GO TO 4110
C
C        NO – BALANCE COLUMNS TO AGREE WITH OUTPUT
C
         DO 4100 J=1,NSECT1
            IF(RE(J).EQ.0.0)GO TO 4100
            SUM=0.0
            DO 4080 I=1,MAGG
               SUM=SUM+IOTAB(I,J)
 4080       CONTINUE
            C=V(J)/SUM
            DO 4090 I=1,MAGG
               IOTAB(I,J)=IOTAB(I,J)*C
 4090       CONTINUE
 4100    CONTINUE
C
         GO TO 4170
C
C        BALANCE USING RAS
C
 4110    DO 4130 I=1,MAGG
            SUM=0.0
            DO 4120 J=1,NAGG
               SUM=SUM+IOTAB(I,J)
 4120       CONTINUE
            WORK1(I)=SUM
 4130    CONTINUE
C
         DO 4140 I=1,NSECT1
            U(I)=V(I)
 4140    CONTINUE
C
         SUM2=0.0
         DO 4150 I=MHH,MAGG
            U(I)=WORK1(I)
            SUM2=SUM2+U(I)
 4150    CONTINUE
C
```

```
      SUM=0.0
      DO 4155 I=1,MAGG
         SUM=SUM+IOTAB(I,J)
 4155 CONTINUE
      WORK2(J)=SUM
      SUM1=SUM1+SUM
 4160 CONTINUE
C
      DO 4165 J=MHH,NAGG
         V(J)=(WORK2(J)/SUM1)*SUM2
 4165 CONTINUE
      CALL MATOUT(V,NNAT,1,NAGG,1)
      CALL MATOUT(U,NNAT,1,MAGG,1)
      CALL MATOUT(WORK1,NNAT,1,MAGG,1)
C
      NIT=100
      CALL RAS(IOTAB,MNAT,NNAT,U,V,WORK1,WORK2,MAGG,
            NAGG,.01,NIT)
      IF(NIT.GT.100)STOP
C
 4170 CONTINUE
 4180 CONTINUE
C
      WRITE(LPT,30115)
30115 FORMAT(//' *****SUPERIOR TRANS''N TABLE DATA'/)
      CALL INSERT(IOTAB,MNAT,NNAT)
C
 4190 WRITE(LPT,30120)NSECT1
30120 FORMAT(//' *****NO. OF SECTORS= ',I3/
      1' TRANSACTION TABLE FOLLOWS')
      CALL TRNOUT(IOTAB,MNAT,NNAT,Z2,MAXS,MAGG,NAGG)
C
C     ARE WE DOING INITIAL TRANSACTION TABLES?
C
      IF(.NOT.FDFLG)GO TO 4390
C
C
C     CONVERT TRANSACTION TABLE TO DIRECT COEFFS
C     CONVERT EMPLOYMENTS TO EMPLOYMENT COEFFS
C
      RE(MHH)=TRE
      DO 4210 J=1,MHH
         IF(RE(J).EQ.0.0)GO TO 4210
         C=V(J)
         RE(J)=RE(J)/C
         DO 4200 I=1,MHH
            IOTAB(I,J)=IOTAB(I,J)/C
 4200    CONTINUE
 4210 CONTINUE
C
      WRITE(LPT,30130)
30130 FORMAT(//' *****ENDOG. COEFFS. MATRIX FOLLOWS')
      CALL COFOUT(IOTAB,MNAT,NNAT,Z2,MAXS,MAXS,MHH,MHH)
C
```

```
C          DERIVE EXOGENOUS LEONTIEF MATRIX
C
           DO 4230 I=1,NSECT1
              DO 4220 J=1,NSECT1
                 Z(I,J)=-IOTAB(I,J)
 4220         CONTINUE
 4230      CONTINUE
           DO 4240 I=1,NSECT1
              Z(I,I)=1+Z(I,I)
 4240      CONTINUE
C
           CALL INVERT(Z,MAXS,MAXS,NSECT1,WORK1,WORK2,
                 WORK3,.00001,D)
           WRITE(LPT,30140)D
30140      FORMAT(//'*****EXOG. INVERTED MATRIX FOLLOWS '/'
                 DET=',F15.8)
           CALL COFOUT(Z,MAXS,MAXS,Z2,MAXS,MAXS,NSECT1,
                 NSECT1)
C
C          DERIVE TYPE 1 MULTIPLIERS
C
           DO 4290 J=1,NSECT1
              SUM=0.0
              SUM1=0.0
              SUM2=0.0
              IF(RE(J).NE.0.0)GOTO 4260
              T1IM(J)=0.0
              T1EM(J)=0.0
              GO TO 4280
 4260         DO 4270 T=1,NSECT1
                 C=Z(I,J)
                 SUM=SUM+C
                 SUM1=SUM1+C*IOTAB(MHH,I)
                 SUM2=SUM2+C*RE(I)
 4270         CONTINUE
              T1IM(J)=SUM1/IOTAB(MHH,J)
              T1EM(J)=SUM2/RE(J)
 4280         T1OM(J)=SUM
              DIIC(J)=SUM1
              DIEC(J)=SUM2
 4290      CONTINUE
C
C          DERIVE ENDOGENOUS LEONTIEF MATRIX
C
           DO 4310 I=1,MHH
              DO 4300 J=1,MHH
                 Z(I,J)=-IOTAB(I,J)
 4300         CONTINUE
 4310      CONTINUE
           DO 4320 I=1,MHH
              Z(I,I)=1+Z(I,I)
 4320      CONTINUE
C
           CALL INVERT(Z,MAXS,MAXS,MHH,WORK1,WORK2,WORK3,
```

```
              .00001,D)
        WRITE(LPT,30150)D
30150   FORMAT(//' *****ENDOG. INVERTED MATRIX FOLLOWS'/'
                DET=',F15.8)
        CALL COFOUT(Z,MAXS,MAXS,Z2,MAXS,MAXS,MHH,MHH)
C
C       DERIVE TYPE 2 MULTIPLIERS
C
        DO 4380 J=1,NSECT1
          SUM=0.0
          SUM1=0.0
          IF(RE(J).NE.0.0)GO TO 4350
          T2IM(J)=0.0
          T2EM(J)=0.0
          GO TO 4370
 4350     DO 4360 I=1,NSECT1
            SUM=SUM+Z(I,J)
            SUM1=SUM1+Z(I,J)*RE(I)
 4360     CONTINUE
          T2IM(J)=Z(MHH,J)/IOTAB(MHH,J)
          T2EM(J)=SUM1/RE(J)
 4370     T2OM(J)=SUM
          DITEC(J)=SUM1
 4380   CONTINUE
C
        WRITE(LPT,30160)
30160   FORMAT(1H1,' *****MULTIPLIERS,ETC.'//' #',7X,'DIC',
        1 6X,'EC',6X,'DIIC',6X,'DIEC',6X,'TIOM',6X,'T1IM',6X,
        2 'T1EM',5X,'DIIIC',5X,'DIIEC',6X,'T2OM',6X,'T2IM',6X,'T2EM')
C
C       ABBREVIATIONS
C       T1,T2,– TYPE 1, TYPE 2
C       OM,IM,EM – OUTPUT, INCOME, EMPLOY. MULTIPLIERS
C       IC,EC – INCOME, EMPLOY. CHANGE
C       (((D)I)I) – (((DIRECT),INDIRECT) & INDUCED)
C
        WRITE(LPT,30170)(J,IOTAB(MHH,J),RE(J),DIIC(J),DIEC(J),
        1T1OM(J),T1IM(J),T1EM(J),Z(MHH,J),DIIEC(J),T2OM(J),
        2T2IM(J),T2EM(J),J=1,NSECT1)
30170   FORMAT(//(1X,I2,12(1X,F9.5)))
C
C       TEST  FOR TERMINATION
C
 4390   IF((NSECT1.EQ.NSECT2).OR.(NSECT2.EQ.0))STOP
C
C       NOW AGGREGATE NON-UNIFORM TABLE INTO UNIFORM
C       IF NECESSARY, CONVERT BACK TO TRANSACTION TABLE
C
        IF(.NOT.FDFLG)GO TO 4415
        DO 4410 J=1,MHH
          C=V(J)
          RE(J)=RE(J)*C
          DO 4400 I=1,MHH
            IOTAB(I,J)=IOTAB(I,J)*C
```

```
 4400       CONTINUE
 4410    CONTINUE
 4415    CONTINUE
C
C        REDEFINE DIMENSIONS
C
         MHH=NSECT2+1
         MAGG=NSECT2+MB
         NAGG=NSECT2
         IF(FDFLG)NAGG=NAGG+NFD
C
C        ADD EXTRA ENTRIES TO AGG'N TABLE FOR
C        FINAL DEMAND & PRIMARY INPUTS
C
         DO 4417 I=1,MB+1
            DEFN2(NSECT2+I)=NSECT1+I
 4417    CONTINUE
C
         WRITE(LPT,30180)
30180    FORMAT(1H1,' *****UNIFORM AGG''N SYSTEM'//' NEW OLD'/)
C
         DO 4470 I=1,MAGG
            L1=DEFN2(I)
            L2=DEFN2(I31)-1
            WRITE(LPT,30080)I,(J,J=L1,L2)
            DO 4450 J=1,NAGG
               SUM=0.0
               DO 4430 II=L1,L2
                  DO 4420 JJ=DEFN2(J),DEFN2(J+1)-1
                     SUM=SUM+IOTAB(II,JJ)
 4420             CONTINUE
 4430          CONTINUE
               IOTAB(I,J)=SUM
 4450       CONTINUE
            SUM=0.0
            SUM1=0.0
            DO 4460 II=L1,L2
               SUM=SUM+RE(II)
               SUM1=SUM1+V(II)
 4460       CONTINUE
            RE(I)=SUM
            V(I)=SUM1
 4470    CONTINUE
C
C        NOW DERIVE MULTIPLIERS FOR UNIFORM TABLE
C
         NSECT1=NSECT2
         GO TO 4190
C
         END
C
C
         SUBROUTINE INSERT(A,M,N)
         REAL A(M,N)
```

```
      INTEGER IR(8),IC(8)
      REAL SD(8)
      INTEGER LPT,CDR
      COMMON LPT,CDR
C
C     THIS SUBROUTINE INSERTS DATA INTO MATRIX A
C     IT EXPECTS 8 TRIPLETS OF DATA PER LINE
C     EACH TRIPLET CONTAINS ROW,COLUMN,DATA
C     THE LIST IS TERMINATED BY A ZERO TRIPLET
C     THE NUMBERS ARE IN FREE FORMAT
C
 10   READ(CDR,24010)(IR(I),IC(I),SD(I),I=1,8)
24010 FORMAT(8(2I,F))
      I=1
C
 20   IF(IR(I).EQ.0)GO TO 30
      A(IR(I),IC(I))=SD(I)
      I=I+1
      IF(I.LE.8)GO TO 20
C
      WRITE(LPT,34010)(IR(I),IC(I),SD(I),I=1,8)
34010 FORMAT((1X,4(' (',I3,',',I3,')=',F)))
      GO TO 10
C
 30   IF(I.GT.1)WRITE(LPT,34010)(IR(J),IC(J),SD(J),J=1,I-1)
C
      RETURN
      END
C
C
      SUBROUTINE MATOUT(A,MA,NA,M2,N2)
C
C     THIS ROUTINE PRINTS OUT LARGE VECTORS & ARRAYS
C     BY COLUMNS. EACH COLUMN TAKES A NO. OF LINES.
C     7 ITEMS ARE PRINTED PER LINE IN F15.8 FORMAT.
C
C     ARGUMENTS-
C     A(MA,NA) - THE REAL VECTOR OR ARRAY CONTAINING THE
C           DATA
C     M2,N2 - THE DIMENSIONS OF THE SUB-MATRIX/VECTOR OF A
C           TO BE PRINTED
C
      REAL A(MA,NA)
      COMMON LPT
C
      DO 20 J=1,N2
         WRITE(LPT,32010)J
32010    FORMAT(/' COLUMN ',I3)
C
         L2=0
 10      L1=L2+1
         L2=L2+7
         IF(L2.GT.M2)L2=M2
```

```
            WRITE(LPT,32020)L1,(A(I,J),I=L1,L2)
32020       FORMAT(1X,I3,': ',7F15.8)
            IF(L2.LT.2)GO TO 10
 20       CONTINUE
C
          RETURN
          END
C
C
          SUBROUTINE TRNOUT(A,MA,NA,IA,MI,NI,M1,N1)
C
C         THIS ROUTINE PRINTS OUT A TRANSACTION TABLE IN
C         PROPER TABLE FORM OVER A NO. OF PAGES. THE TABLE IS
C         SUPPLIED AS A REAL ARRAY & IS TRANSFORMED INTO
C         ROUNDED INTEGER FORM.
C         ALSO INTEGER ROW & COL TOTALS ARE OBTAINED FOR
C         DISPLAY. (THE LOWER LEFT CORNER ENTRY SHOULD BE
C         IGNORED)
C
C         ARGUMENTS–
C         A(MA,NA) – REAL ARRAY CONTAINING TRANSACTION TABLE
C         IA(MI,NI) – WORK ARRAY SUPPLIED BY CALLER
C         M1,N1 – DIMENSIONS OF SUBMATRIX OF A TO BE PRINTED
C
          REAL A(MA,NA)
          INTEGER IA(MI,NI)
          COMMON LP1
C
          M2=M1+1
          N2=N1+1
C
C         CONVERT & OBTAIN TOTALS
C
          DO 20 I=1,M1
             K=0
             DO 10 J=1,N1
                IA(I,J)=IFIX(A(I,J)+6.5)
                K=K+IA(I,J)
 10          CONTINUE
             IA(I,N2)=K
 20       CONTINUE
C
          DO 40 J=1,N1
             K=0
             DO 30 I=1,M1
                K=K+IA(I,J)
 30          CONTINUE
             IA(M2,J)=K
 40       CONTINUE
C
          L2=0
 50       L1=L2+1
          L2=L2+14
          IF(L2.GT.N2)L2=N2
```

```
C
        WRITE(LPT,31010)(J,J=L1,L2)
31010   FORMAT(1H1,5X,14I8)
C
        DO 60 I=1,M2
           WRITE(LPT,31020)I,(IA(I,J),J=L1,L2)
31020      FORMAT(/1X,I3,': ',14I8)
 60     CONTINUE
C
        IF(L2.LT.N2) GO TO 50
C
        RETURN
        END
C
C
        SUBROUTINE COFOUT(A,MA,NA,Z,MZ,NZ,M1,N1)
C
C       THIS ROUTINE IS FOR PRINTING OUT COEFFICIENT-TYPE
C       TABLES. THE DATA WILL BE ROUNDED TO 3 DECIMAL PLACES.
C
C       ARGUMENTS–
C       A(MA,NA) – THE REAL ARRAY CONTAINING THE DATA
C       Z(MZ,NZ) – A WORK ARRAY SUPPLIED BY CALLER
C       M1,N1 – THE DIMENSIONS OF THE SUB-MATRIX OF A TO BE
C       PRINTED
C
        REAL A(MA,NA),Z(MZ,NZ)
        COMMON LPT
C
        DO 20 I=1,M1
           DO 10 J=1,N1
              IF(A(I,J).GT.0.00040)GO TO 5
              Z(I,J)=0.0
              GO TO 10
 5            Z(I,J)=(FLOAT(IFIX(A(I,J)*1000.+0.5)))/1000.
 10        CONTINUE
 20     CONTINUE
C
        L2=0
 30     L1=L2+1
        L2=L2+20
        IF(L2.GT.N1)L2=N1
C
        WRITE(LPT,33010)(J,J=L1,L2)
33010   FORMAT(1H1,5X,20I6)
C
        DO 40 I=1,M1
           WRITE(LPT,33020)I,(Z(I,J),J=L1,L2)
33020   FORMAT(/1X,I3,': ',20F6.3)
 40     CONTINUE
C
        IF(L2.LT.N1)GO TO 30
        RETURN
        END
```

```
C
C
      SUBROUTINE RAS(B,M,N,AROW,ACOL,BROW,BCOL,IR,IC,EPS,
     1   NO)
C
C
C        ARGUMENTS—
C        B(M,N) — CONTAINS TABLE TO BE BALANCED
C        AROW,ACOL — ROW & COL TOTAL CONSTRAINT VECTORS
C        BROW,BCOL — ACTUAL ROW & COL TOTALS
C        IR,IC — DIMENSIONS OF TABLE
C        EPS — TOLERANCE VALUE
C        NO — THE NO. OF ITERATIONS
C              =NO+1 ON ERROR RETURN
C
      REAL B(M,N),AROW(IR),ACOL(IC),BROW(IR),BCOL(IC)
      LOGICAL CONVRG
      ISTORE = NO
      DO 50 NO=1,ISTORE
      CONVRG = .TRUE.
      DO 10 J=1,IC
 10   BCOL(J) = 0
      DO 21 I=1,IR
      AB = AROW(I) / BROW(I)
      DO 20 J=1,IC
      B(I,J) = B(I,J) * AB
 20   BCOL(J) = BCOL(J) + B(I,J)
      IF(ABS(BROW(I) — AROW(I)).GT.EPS) CONVRG = .FALSE.
 21   CONTINUE
      DO 30 I=1,IR
 30   BROW(I) = 0
      DO 41 J=1,IC
      AB = ACOL(J) / BCOL(J)
      DO 40 I=1,IR
      B(I,J) = B(I,J) * AB
 40   BROW(I) = BROW(I) + B(I,J)
      IF(ABS(BCOL(J) — ACOL(J)).GT.EPS) CONVRG = .FALSE.
 41   CONTINUE
      IF(CONVRG) RETURN
 50   CONTINUE
      TYPE 60,ISTORE
 60   FORMAT(1H0,'% '' RAS '' HAS NOT CONVERGED AFTER ',I4,
     1 ' ITERATIONS')
      NO = ISTORE +1
      RETURN
      END
C
C
      SUBROUTINE INVERT(A,MA,NA,N,B,C,Z,EPS,D)
C
C     ADAPTED FROM C.A.C.M. ALGORITHM 120
C        BY M. BENJAMIN FEB, '77
C
C        ARGUMENTS—
```

```
C           A(MA,NA) – CONTAINS THE MATRIX TO BE INVERTED
C           N – THE ORDER OF THE MATRIX
C           B,C,Z – WORK VECTORS SUPPLIED BY CALLER
C           EPS – TOLERANCE VALUE
C           D – = DETERMINANT ON NORMAL RETURN
C                = 0 OR SMALL NO. ON ERROR RETURN
C
            REAL A(MA,NA),B(N),C(N)
            INTEGER Z(N),P
C
            N1=N–1
C
            D=1.0
            DO 10 J=1,N
 10         Z(J)=J
C
            DO 60 I=1,N
            K=I
            Y=A(I,I)
            L=I–1
            P=I+1
C
            IF(P.GT.N)GO TO 25
            DO 20 J=P,N
            W=A(I,J)
            IF(ABS(W).LE.ABS(Y))GO TO 20
            K=J
            Y=W
 20         CONTINUE
C
 25         D=D*Y
            IF(ABS(Y).LT.EPS)GO TO 90
            Y=1.0/Y
C
            DO 30 J=1,N
            C(J)=A(J,K)
            A(J,K)=A(J,I)
            A(J,I)=–C(J)*Y
            A(I,J)=A(I,J)*Y
 30         B(J)=A(I,J)
C
            A(I,I)=Y
            J=Z(I)
            Z(I)=Z(K)
            Z(K)=J
C
            IF(L.LT.1)GO TO 57
            K1=1
            K2=L
 40         DO 55 K=K1,K2
            CC=C(K)
            IF(L.LT.1)GO TO 52
            J1=1
            J2=L
```

```
 45         DO 50 J=J1,J2
 50         A(K,J)=A(K,J)-B(J)*CC
            IF(J2.GE.N1)GO TO 55
 52         J1=P
            J2=N
            GO TO 45
 55         CONTINUE
            IF(K2.GE.N1)GO TO 60
 57         K1=P
            K2=N
            GO TO 40
C
 60         CONTINUE
C
            DO 80 I=1,N
 65         K=Z(I)
            IF(K.EQ.1)GO TO 80
            DO 70 J=1,N
            W=A(I,J)
            A(I,J)=A(K,J)
 70         A(K,J)=W
C
            P=Z(I)
            Z(I)=Z(K)
            Z(K)=P
            D=-D
            GO TO 65
 80         CONTINUE
            RETURN
C
 90         D=0.0


            RETURN
            END
```

APPENDIX V: MATHEMATICAL EXPOSITION OF THE GRIT SEQUENCE

Phase I Adjustments to National Tables

Step 1

The national 109 x 109 input–output technical coefficient matrix and matrix of primary inputs are taken as initial data:

$$\begin{bmatrix} \underset{n\times n}{A^{(0)}} \\ \cdots\cdots \\ \underset{l\times n}{B^{(0)}} \end{bmatrix}$$

Superscript '0' denotes initial datum.
A is a matrix of technical coefficients.
B is a matrix of primary inputs.

Step 2

Adjustment for prices and updating at the discretion of the analyst.

Step 3.1

Identification of primary, secondary and tertiary sub-matrices denoted by P, S, T respectively by partitioning A thus:

$$\begin{bmatrix} \underset{p\times n}{P^{(0)}} \\ \cdots\cdots \\ \underset{s\times n}{S^{(0)}} \\ \cdots\cdots \\ \underset{t\times n}{T^{(0)}} \\ \cdots\cdots \\ \underset{l\times n}{B^{(0)}} \end{bmatrix}$$

Note that: $n = p + s + t$.

Step 3.2

Define a row vector of imports $\underset{1\times n}{m}$ which is the sum of competitive and non-competitive imports vectors in B.

Reallocate m proportionally over secondary sectors, $S^{(0)}$, by the following matrix operation:

$$\underset{1\times s}{i^T}\ \underset{s\times n}{S^{(0)}} = \underset{1\times n}{d_1},$$

i is a unit column vector and d_1 is sum of column elements of $S^{(0)}$.

Define sum, $\underset{1\times n}{d_1} + \underset{1\times n}{m} = \underset{1\times n}{d_2}$.

$$S^{(1)} = \underset{n\times n}{\hat{d}_2}\ \underset{n\times n}{\hat{d}_1^{-1}}\ \underset{n\times n}{S^{(0)}}$$

Superscript symbols: ˆ refers to diagonal matrices obtained from vectors and −1 refers to inverse.

The results after above steps could be written as:

$$\begin{bmatrix} \underset{p\times n}{P^{(1)}} \\ \cdots\cdots \\ \underset{s\times n}{S^{(1)}} \\ \cdots\cdots \\ \underset{t\times n}{T^{(1)}} \\ \cdots\cdots \\ \underset{l\times n}{B^{(1)}} \end{bmatrix} = \begin{bmatrix} \underset{n\times n}{A^{(1)}} \\ \cdots\cdots \\ \underset{l\times n}{B^{(1)}} \end{bmatrix}$$

It should be noted that an analogous procedure to operations contained in Step 3.2 could be affected to allocate imports proportionally over other sub-matrices P, T or any combination of them.

Phase II Adjustment for Regional Imports

Step 4

Regionalisation of the above $A^{(1)}$ national matrix by zeroising sectors non-existent in the regions results in $A^{(2)}$. The intermediate input coefficients of these zeroised sectors are summed up column-wise and included in the empty import row of $B^{(1)}$, thus obtaining $B^{(2)}$. The end result is:

$$\begin{bmatrix} \underset{n\times n}{A^{(2)}} \\ \cdots\cdots \\ \underset{l\times n}{B^{(2)}} \end{bmatrix}$$

Step 5

Regionalisation of national matrix by the application of location quotient reduction technique. Location quotients q_i which are defined such that $0 \leqslant q_i \leqslant 1$ for all i, comprise elements in a vector $\underset{1\times n}{q}$.

$$A^{(3)} = \underset{n\times n}{\hat{q}}\ \underset{n\times n}{A^{(2)}}$$

$\underset{l \times n}{B^{(3)}}$ is obtained by adding to the import row of $\underset{l \times n}{B^{(2)}}$

the column sums of the difference matrix $A^{(2)}$ and $A^{(3)}$ i.e. $1^T[A^{(2)} - A^{(3)}]$.

Therefore, we get

$$\begin{bmatrix} \underset{n \times n}{A^{(3)}} \\ \cdots\cdots\cdots \\ \underset{l \times n}{B^{(3)}} \end{bmatrix}$$

Phase III Definition of Regional Sectors

Step 6

Insertion of superior data in A and B matrices to obtain:

$$\begin{bmatrix} \underset{n \times n}{A^{(4)}} \\ \cdots\cdots\cdots \\ \underset{l \times n}{B^{(4)}} \end{bmatrix}$$

Step 7

Aggregation of sectors using regional (employment) weights.

Here, the mathematical exposition is in terms of a 6 x 6 matrix which is to be weighted by regional employment and aggregated as formalised below:

Given $A^{(4)}$ and $B^{(4)}$, partition it appropriately according to sectors to be aggregated thus:

$$\begin{bmatrix} \underset{6 \times 6}{A^{(4)}} \\ \cdots\cdots\cdots \\ \underset{2 \times 6}{B^{(4)}} \end{bmatrix} = \left[\begin{array}{cc:cc:cc} a_{11} & a_{12} & a_{13} & a_{14} & a_{15} & a_{16} \\ a_{21} & a_{22} & a_{23} & a_{24} & a_{25} & a_{26} \\ \hdashline a_{31} & a_{32} & a_{33} & a_{34} & a_{35} & a_{36} \\ a_{41} & a_{42} & a_{43} & a_{44} & a_{45} & a_{46} \\ \hdashline a_{51} & a_{51} & a_{52} & a_{53} & a_{54} & a_{55} \\ a_{61} & a_{62} & a_{63} & a_{64} & a_{64} & a_{65} \\ \hdashline b_{11} & b_{12} & b_{13} & b_{14} & b_{15} & b_{16} \\ b_{21} & b_{22} & b_{23} & b_{24} & b_{25} & b_{26} \end{array}\right]^{(4)} \begin{array}{l} \\ \\ \\ \\ \\ \\ \text{(imports row)} \\ \text{(value-added row)} \end{array}$$

The given regional employment figures are $\underset{1 \times 6}{r} = [r_1 \ \ r_2 \ \ r_3 \ \ r_4 \ \ r_5 \ \ r_6]$

The regional weights are $\underset{1\times 6}{w} = [w_1 \;\; w_2 \;\; w_3 \;\; w_4 \;\; w_5 \;\; w_6]$ where

$$w_j = \frac{r_j}{r_j + r_{j+1}} \text{ (when } j \text{ is odd) and } w_j = \frac{r_j}{r_{j-1} + r_j} \text{ (when } j \text{ is even).}$$

The regional weighted elements of the given matrix are:

$$\underset{6\times 6}{A^{(4)}} \; \underset{6\times 6}{\hat{w}} = \underset{6\times 6}{A^{(5)}} \qquad (\hat{\ }: \text{indicates a diagonalised row vector})$$

$$\underset{2\times 6}{B^{(4)}} \; \underset{6\times 6}{\hat{w}} = \underset{2\times 6}{B^{(5)}}$$

Therefore,

$$\begin{bmatrix} \underset{6\times 6}{A^{(5)}} \\ \underset{2\times 6}{B^{(6)}} \end{bmatrix} = \left[\begin{array}{cc|cc|cc} a_{11} & a_{12} & a_{13} & a_{14} & a_{15} & a_{16} \\ a_{21} & a_{22} & a_{23} & a_{24} & a_{25} & a_{26} \\ \hline a_{31} & a_{32} & a_{33} & a_{34} & a_{35} & a_{36} \\ a_{41} & a_{42} & a_{43} & a_{44} & a_{45} & a_{46} \\ \hline a_{51} & a_{52} & a_{53} & a_{54} & a_{55} & a_{56} \\ a_{61} & a_{62} & a_{63} & a_{64} & a_{65} & a_{66} \\ \hline b_{11} & b_{12} & b_{13} & b_{14} & b_{15} & b_{16} \\ \hline b_{21} & b_{22} & b_{23} & b_{24} & b_{25} & b_{26} \end{array}\right]^{(5)}$$

Note that superscript (5) is put at top of the matrix and refers to all elements.

Now aggregating the weighted elements given in each partitioned submatrix above we obtain the matrices $A^{(6)}$ and $B^{(6)}$ which are the regional matrices formed by adding up employment weighted elements thus:

$$\begin{bmatrix} \underset{3\times 3}{A^{(6)}} \\ \underset{1\times 3}{B^{(6)}} \end{bmatrix} =$$

$$\left[\begin{array}{ccc} a_{11}+a_{12}+a_{21}+a_{22} & a_{13}+a_{14}+a_{23}+a_{24} & a_{15}+a_{16}+a_{25}+a_{26} \\ a_{31}+a_{32}+a_{41}+a_{42} & a_{33}+a_{34}+a_{43}+a_{44} & a_{35}+a_{36}+a_{45}+a_{46} \\ a_{51}+a_{52}+a_{61}+a_{62} & a_{53}+a_{54}+a_{63}+a_{64} & a_{55}+a_{56}+a_{65}+a_{66} \\ \hline b_{11}+b_{12}+b_{21}+b_{22} & b_{13}+b_{14}+b_{23}+b_{24} & b_{15}+b_{16}+b_{25}+b_{26} \end{array}\right]^{(6)}$$

Note that superscript (6) refers to all elements in the above matrix.

Step 8

Insert aggregated superior data into matrix $A^{(6)}$, $B^{(6)}$, if available.

Phase IV Derivation of Prototype Transactions Tables

Step 9

Converting regional coefficient matrices to flow matrices by using given regional gross output estimates $\underset{3\times 1}{x}$.

$$\underset{3\times 3}{A^{(6)}} \; \underset{3\times 3}{\hat{x}} = \underset{3\times 3}{x}$$

$$\underset{1\times 3}{B^{(6)}} \; \underset{3\times 3}{\hat{x}} = \underset{1\times 3}{y}$$

Furthermore, estimated final demand matrix $\underset{3\times 1}{F}$ and an estimated matrix of primary inputs in final demand is given as $\underset{1\times 1}{G}$. The available data could now be arranged in transactions form compactly as $\bar{X}$ thus:

$$\underset{4\times 4}{\bar{X}} = \left[\begin{array}{c|c} \underset{3\times 3}{X} & \underset{3\times 1}{F} \\ \hline \underset{1\times 3}{y} & \underset{1\times 1}{G} \end{array}\right]$$

N.B. In the study, $\underset{3\times 1}{F}$ was derived as a residual.

Step 10

In the study, manual balancing of the table was achieved by using final demand (F). The following is a mathematical outline of the alternative, iterative procedure which can be used in GRIT if reliable final demand vectors are available for region i.

In general, given regional data $\underset{m\times m}{\bar{X}}$ (where $m = 4$ is the specific example) and row and column regional control totals u, v, respectively, a matrix $\underset{m\times m}{\bar{X}^*}$ could be found that meets the row and column constraints. (See Bacharach, 1970, p. 44.) The matrix $\underset{m\times m}{\bar{X}^*}$ is biproportional to $\underset{m\times m}{\bar{X}}$ and it is non-negative.

I. $\underset{m\times 1}{u_1} = \underset{m\times m}{\bar{X}} \; i$ First row estimate for the region.

$\underset{m\times m}{\bar{X}^{(1)}} = \underset{m\times m}{\hat{u}} \; \hat{u}_1^{-1} \bar{X}$ Row consistent regional matrix obtained by distributing row errors proportionally among all elements of $\bar{X}$.

$$\underset{1\times m}{V_1} = \underset{1\times m}{i^T} \; \underset{m\times m}{\bar{X}^{(1)}}$$ First column estimate for the region.

II. $$\underset{m\times m}{\bar{X}^{(2)}} = \underset{m\times m}{\bar{X}^{(1)}} \; \underset{m\times m}{\hat{V}_1^{-1}} \; \underset{m\times m}{\hat{V}}$$ Column consistent regional matrix obtained by distributing column errors proportionally among all elements of $\bar{X}^{(1)}$.

By performing operations I and II alternatively we could eventually obtain the row and column matrix $\underset{m\times m}{\bar{X}^*}$ i.e.

$$\underset{t\to\infty}{\text{Limit}}(\hat{u}\hat{u}_t^{-1})\bar{X}(\hat{V}_1^{-1}\hat{V}) = \underset{t\to\infty}{\text{Limit}}\;\hat{R}\bar{X}\hat{S}$$

The above iterative procedure to establish row and column consistent matrix $\bar{X}^*$ which is biproportional to given $\bar{X}$ is analogous to McMenamin and Harings' (1974) application of Stone's RAS technique. However, McMenamin and Harings' claim that the $\hat{R}$ and $\hat{S}$ multipliers are estimates of substitution and fabrication effects must be accepted with circumspection.

Step 11

Aggregation procedure as per Step 7 without weights.

Steps 12–15

Further adjustments at the analyst's discretion plus derivation of inverses and multipliers using standard procedures.

APPENDIX VI: TECHNICAL APPENDIX

Use of Australian Bureau of Statistics Data

After consultations with the Australian Bureau of Statistics (ABS), 1973–4 was chosen as the year for which the GRIT application to Queensland regions would apply. This was the latest year for which the data required were available from the ABS. The application of GRIT required data for the regions in the 109 national input–output sector format for 1973/4 for employment, number of establishments, turnover, wages and salaries, and value added.

Employment data were required primarily for the calculation of location quotients. Data relating to number of establishments provide a check on the existence of sectors within each region, while turnover figures were required in deriving sector outputs in the regional transactions tables. Wages and salaries and value added were considered as possible candidates for insertion as superior data. The methodology required the 1968–9 national table in basic values and with direct allocation of imports. Other ABS data utilised was information from the Australian National Accounts on Queensland household consumption.

Most of the data required were available from the ABS for the primary and secondary sectors and the wholesale–retail sector. For the tertiary sectors the only data available were on employment by sector from the 1971 Population Census. At the Australian level, employment was available on the 109-sector basis from the 1971 Population Census, and an unpublished version of the national table required was released for use on this project.

Processing contingencies which arose in the handling of the ABS data basically revolved around the problems of:

(1) all ABS data was based on ASIC at the 4-digit level – it was necessary to reconcile these data to the 109-sector format in which the national tables were prepared;
(2) confidentiality restrictions necessitated data disaggregation by indirect estimation;
(3) some data were not available for 1973/4, notably for the wholesale–retail sector. This was adjusted to 1973/4 levels using the Consumer Price Index. More appropriate allocations may

need to be considered in future applications of GRIT;

(4) data relating to the manufacturing and wholesale–retail sectors were available only on the basis of statistical divisions defined on an earlier and different basis. It was, however, possible to reconcile this data with the regions defined in terms of the recent statistical division definitions.

Calculation of Final Demand and Tertiary Sector Outputs

(1) Final Demand

The aggregate sales to final demand of each sector was estimated as the residual calculated by subtracting total endogenous sales from the column total. For most sectors in most regions the residual was positive and the problem remained to estimate the household, other final demand and export components of total final demand.

The proportions of each sector's output sold to the various final demand components were calculated from other Australian national, regional and state input–output tables. For each region, allocators were chosen from the above tables to estimate the final demand components. The final demand component estimates were then proportionally constrained upwards or downwards to sum to each sector's total final demand, calculated originally as a residual.

In some instances, total final demand calculated as a residual was found to be negative. This was due to the adjusted national coefficients overstating the endogenous sales for individual sectors. Final demand components were estimated as above, and the difference between the row and column totals was reconciled by removing proportions of row elements to imports. This procedure is similar in concept to the commodity balance non-survey technique.

For the Queensland state table, exports posed a problem since no reliable benchmark allocator could be calculated. This necessitated the calculation of each sector's state exports as the residual found by subtracting total final demand from the household and other final demand components.

The figure for private final consumption expenditure for Queensland from the *Australian National Accounts* (Australian Bureau of Statistics, 1976) was allocated over the regions on a population basis. This provided a household column control total and enabled the calculation of household imports as the residual between the control and household purchases from the endogenous sectors.

(2) Tertiary Sector Outputs

Outputs of the electricity and gas sectors were calculated from information in the annual reports of the State Electricity Commission of Queensland (1975) and the Government Gas Engineer (1975). For the remaining tertiary sectors, output was indirectly estimated by applying employment/output ratios calculated from the national table to the regional sector employment figures. The study team considers that in cases where GRIT is applied to a single region, it would be more appropriate to utilise employment/output ratios calculated from an existing input–output table for a similar region. However, for the Queensland state table, the national employment/output ratios were considered as most appropriate and thus the regional tables required use of the same ratios for consistency.

Details of Superior Data Use

Superior data utilised in GRIT can be classified into four general categories: (1) direct survey data, (2) ABS data, (3) other secondary data and (4) miscellaneous. These will be discussed in turn, but first it is necessary to further classify superior data in the methodological sequence sense:

(1) disaggregated superior data – these are information available at the disaggregated 109-sector level;
(2) aggregated superior data – these refer to coefficients available at the various levels of aggregation used in GRIT, i.e. 11, 19 and 36 sectors;
(3) disaggregated/aggregated – this term was defined, and the programme adjusted accordingly, to describe superior data available in a form disaggregated by column and aggregated by row in the input–output matrix format;
(4) transactions – this refers to information available in transactions form plus adjustments to transactions for balancing purposes.

Superior data may be inserted into the methodological sequence during Phases III and V. The research team used both. Some superior data were inserted at Phase III, while the remainder of the superior data were added at Phase V after a thorough examination of the prototype transactions tables and multipliers for anomalies.

Each of the four general categories of superior data mentioned at the beginning of this section could consist of any or all of the four methodological sequence categories. Details on the four general categories of superior data follow:

(1) Direct Survey Data

Consistent with the 'low level of interference' approach adopted by the study team, the direct inquiry method was utilised mainly in one instance; to obtain cost coefficients for the alumina refinery in the Fitzroy region.

(2) ABS Data

The use of ABS data was discussed in the first section of this Appendix. ABS data used in the superior data sense were (a) wages and salaries coefficients for the manufacturing sectors; (b) household consumption figures for Queensland from the Australian National Accounts.

(3) Other Secondary Data

Superior data obtained from other published sources were mainly representative coefficients taken from previously completed regional input–output tables. The Central Queensland (Jensen, 1976a), Northern (Dickinson, 1977) and Queensland Interregional Trade Flows (Huxley, 1973) studies featured prominently. Other regional input–output tables investigated for comparative purposes were Toowoomba (McGaurr, 1976a), Central Macquarie (Mandeville and Powell, 1976), Bourke (Harvey, 1976) and Tasmania (Edwards, 1977).

Statistics were also supplied by two Queensland government departments involved with the project, namely the Co-ordinator General's Department and the Department of Commercial and Industrial Development.

(4) Miscellaneous

These include data and/or manual adjustments estimated subjectively to be superior to the adjusted national coefficients.

Anomalies in the Prototype Transactions Tables

The need for some superior data insertions was highlighted during examination of prototype tables for anomalies. Knowledge of where superior data should be applied is a function of the analyst's knowledge of the region under consideration. The research team were fortunate in having access to a Steering Committee which had been set up to co-ordinate the project. The steering committee included: the research team, and representatives from the Co-ordinator General's

Department, Department of Commercial and Industrial Development, Department of Primary Industries, Department of Mines, Department of Health and the Australian Bureau of Statistics. Taken together, the Steering Committee possessed a considerable knowledge of the economies of Queensland and its constituent regions. The prototype tables were distributed to the Steering Committee and members were asked to report any discrepancies to the research team. Anomalies discovered by the research team and other members of the Steering Committee are discussed below.

(1) Sugar is a major primary industry in the Far North, Northern, Mackay and Wide Bay–Burnett regions. All the sugar cane grown in the regions is sold to local sugar mills which are included in the food manufacturing sector. However, the prototype tables showed a high proportion of the output of the other primary sector sold to exports and to households, thus understating sales to the local food manufacturing sector. The problem was rectified by inserting a column of representative coefficients for the food processing sector taken from the Northern (Dickinson, 1977) survey based input–output table.

(2) The Metals and Metal Products sector (which includes the alumina refinery at Gladstone) in the Fitzroy prototype table showed an inordinately high purchase from the other mining sector. This represented purchases of bauxite which the national coefficients showed erroneously as purchases within the region. Since bauxite is not produced in the Bowen Basin, superior data to override the national coefficients were clearly desired. Further, the location quotient import calculating procedure failed to isolate this error, as the location quotient was always greater than unity at the regional level for the primary sectors. The problem was rectified by inserting cost coefficients obtained from trade sources into the alumina refining subsector of the Metals and Metal Products sector.

(3) Another problem with the Fitzroy prototype table was that transactions based on national coefficients underestimated the purchases of the electricity sector from the coal and crude petroleum sector. The national coefficients include different technologies for generating electricity, whereas in the Fitzroy region, electricity is generated exclusively from locally produced coal. Thus the national coefficient for this element was overruled by figures provided by the Department of Commercial

and Industrial Development.

(4) An anomaly existing in all of the prototype tables was the excessively high national coefficients for wages and salaries of the mining sectors. At least two reasons could be put forward why this would be so. First, in the case of the Coal and Crude Petroleum Mining sector, the national coefficient may include oil company overheads. Second, most Queensland mining operations are highly capital-intensive open-cut mining, while the national average includes a large component of labour-intensive underground mining.

Footnotes to the Final Transactions Tables

1. North West region re: classification of output of M.I.M. Holdings Ltd.

   The entire output of this firm appears in the table as mining. However, in addition to mining and ore treatment, smelting of lead and copper is undertaken at Mt Isa before being exported from the region for refining. Technically, smelting operations should be included in the manufacturing sector, but for operational reasons this output appears in the mining sector.
2. All regions re: intrasectoral transactions of animal industries, and building and construction appearing as zero entries.

   This situation arises from the use of the national table net of intrasectoral transactions discussed in section 5.4 of the text. In all regions a significant number of cattle are sold as 'stores', i.e. for breeding or fattening purposes, and considerable subcontracting occurs within the building and construction sector. However, the decision was taken not to allocate research resources to the estimation of these intrasectoral transactions.
3. All regions re: classification of the value of home-building.

   Home-building is considered an investment item and thus is included in building and construction's sales to other final demand.
4. Fitzroy region re: alumina exports and bauxite imports.

   For accounting purposes, the alumina refinery at Gladstone acts as a processor for parent companies. Thus purchases of bauxite do not appear as inputs, nor does the value of bauxite appear in the output (export) distribution of the alumina refinery.
5. All regions re: services to agriculture.

   Attention needs to be drawn to this sector being classified with the other agriculture sector.
6. All regions re: dwelling rent.

The household consumption columns of the regional transactions tables do not include dwelling rent. This is classified in ASIC as part of the finance sector; the study team considered it inappropriate to inflate the finance sector artificially with dwelling rent and lacked the data to develop dwelling rent sectors for each table. For Queensland in 1973–4, dwelling rent has been estimated by the ABS (1976) as $523 million.

7. Queensland re: exports by mining and manufacturing.

   Following the production of the final transactions tables, overseas and interstate trade statistics supplied by the ABS indicate that exports of mining may be overstated and manufacturing exports may be understated.

APPENDIX VII: NON-UNIFORM (19- AND 36-SECTOR) TRANSACTIONS TABLES FOR THE REGIONS AND STATE OF QUEENSLAND

Table VII.1: 36-Sector Transactions Table: Moreton Region, 1973–4 (thousands)

	1	2A	2B	3A	3B	4A1	4A2	4A3	4A4	4A5	4B1	4B2	4B3	4B4	4C1	4C2	4D1	4D2	4D3	4E
1	0	0	0	0	0	43416	0	0	0	0	0	0	0	0	0	0	0	0	0	2
2A	1250	2243	0	0	0	9867	8574	1356	9514	1380	0	47	0	0	0	0	0	0	0	0
2B	0	0	0	771	78	364	94	1	356	3	6170	44	629	0	17	1	10	0	5	33
3A	0	0	0	0	3	659	51	8	52	34	69	0	303	1	4	51	1688	50	5	1329
3B	0	6	13	767	347	0	0	0	75	1	0	0	45	2	31	42	390	1752	27	6482
4A1	429	67	46	0	0	30	5357	2747	2999	49	1	352	1	0	3	4	0	0	1	10
4A2	5	6	1	0	1	173	245	1348	384	1980	12	2	5	1	11	11	541	0	10	10
4A3	626	413	59	0	1	184	392	12793	1482	64	4	3	530	1	0	2	10	7	1	31
4A4	1386	3368	43	1	0	608	3360	2029	601	6327	3	5	5	2	49	2	3	0	3	3
4A5	38	0	0	0	0	123	27	8	63	60	0	0	0	0	0	0	20	0	0	2
4B1	0	590	39	124	13	10	0	0	9	323	3802	15251	319	1	203	2492	152	12	341	152
4B2	2	48	35	3	0	39	10	2	5	92	1492	1273	7	8	334	1186	29	1	275	27
4B3	4	2802	1	1	386	347	952	989	472	1430	187	449	10763	9256	755	330	7	15	513	2107
4B4	0	91	0	0	18	93	263	126	27	2197	3	14	1204	2256	290	6	0	3	204	39
4C1	295	424	242	501	4117	301	175	93	170	166	449	176	393	305	4947	10986	688	79	2789	1217
4C2	15	54	247	238	266	296	228	75	184	239	670	219	644	239	985	1286	273	35	908	1139
4D1	5	36	3	122	953	1	71	3	9	8	91	1079	23	63	4505	11535	0	84	18216	1919
4D2	0	0	0	2	39	3	6	0	23	0	11	216	40	78	2334	1548	576	0	2972	58
4D3	8	61	55	469	313	5567	8945	304	2000	7009	551	3351	452	238	6549	22254	1028	109	8730	1286

4E	0	1	1	640	1609	683	953	3	152	3669	80	925	11	6	508	944	1192	142	757	10836
4F1	3050	6099	802	234	2641	725	650	570	376	856	1731	1341	1381	742	2007	5812	1301	187	2189	2872
4F2	35	181	50	0	6	34	609	49	46	93	150	1321	119	12	53	293	127	12	247	51
4F3	1	4	7	0	32	1	1	1	37	4	1	117	121	5	43	238	69	0	30	15
4F4	2	37	171	16	1585	544	1445	563	700	695	51	1633	307	426	1522	5087	25	9	746	143
4F5	1	4	13	1	13	18	26	22	15	8	23	82	118	84	71	80	19	0	72	28
5A1	429	1187	51	1301	599	2104	917	810	436	1157	1712	656	1129	693	1720	3191	2404	410	2689	3379
5A2	2	8	0	0	1	34	14	281	25	14	9	18	11	37	238	298	169	18	519	476
5A3	264	641	0	52	180	159	128	71	62	463	57	20	95	16	54	73	97	3	161	288
6	696	1334	57	499	241	1068	1182	508	604	1289	1343	575	1185	789	715	1112	238	54	1800	2769
7	2137	4823	1049	961	5317	11065	5034	4545	2671	6943	1444	4400	2136	9208	8112	13325	1702	416	8695	6991
8A1	1014	3420	232	931	2336	14630	6205	3507	3607	4271	3496	3216	1874	1479	4552	6084	6608	856	7082	13183
8A2	0	0	0	0	0	0	0	0	0	0	0	0	0	0	0	0	0	0	0	0
9	25	141	0	158	4052	1688	1112	866	561	1003	2736	1937	1024	2269	2810	2775	486	71	3865	2134
10	0	0	0	1	0	1	0	0	0	0	0	0	0	0	0	0	1	0	0	1
11A	135	13	1	17	25	0	0	0	0	0	0	0	0	0	0	0	0	0	0	0
11B	1	0	0	0	10	0	0	0	0	0	0	0	0	6	6	5	1	0	0	29
Households	2173	9069	2501	2540	5034	38746	12881	16273	6694	12511	14540	23700	11503	31118	33760	60614	12342	1557	57970	31570
Other Value Added	29633	52469	4177	11455	7700	15655	8354	8730	6509	17474	9341	10279	9348	13931	14918	43325	16781	3126	32315	31419
Imports	4937	13012	844	2095	10228	131435	11313	8894	13112	9255	8533	11220	13273	10660	28944	48044	11010	2858	60384	12487
Total	48598	102652	10740	23900	48144	280671	79574	67575	54032	81067	58762	83921	59048	83932	121050	243036	59987	11866	214521	134517

Table VII.1 (continued)

	4F1	4F2	4F3	4F4	4F5	5A1	5A2	5A3	6	7	8A1	8A2	9	10	11A	11B	House-holds	Other Final Demand	Exports	Total
1	0	118	0	19	0	0	0	0	1	0	0	0	0	0	0	0	491	0	4551	48598
2A	12	828	3	0	1	0	0	0	0	0	0	0	0	3	0	51	22584	0	44939	102652
2B	16	0	93	141	0	61	0	0	10	1	535	34	0	0	14	0	1259	0	0	10740
3A	1736	20	2	19	44	5456	611	52	176	716	750	0	0	29	192	211	0	0	9589	23900
3B	372	0	0	10	89	0	0	2	4645	19	66	0	13	0	16	30	0	0	32903	48144
4A1	2422	478	60	5957	2	1	0	3	1	809	8	1	13	185	2085	13	147098	0	109439	280671
4A2	1178	2	2	94	1	0	0	5	110	112	9	1	7	14	666	1	41644	0	30982	79574
4A3	817	2	0	26	0	0	0	1	0	8	3	0	2	11	135	0	28651	0	21316	67575
4A4	269	1	1	6	2	1	0	4	21	67	11	1	12	42	33	13	20500	0	15250	54032
4A5	114	0	0	0	0	0	0	1	0	15	28	0	1	7	3	1130	45539	0	33888	81067
4B1	198	3	1	281	49	0	0	1	23354	604	660	1	1	28	7	0	1856	1675	6210	58762
4B2	261	9	28	125	23	1	0	7	16226	2309	80	13	7	1996	782	40	10880	9823	36443	83921
4B3	3033	211	816	512	291	1	0	17	122	9572	1961	175	63	463	173	476	1788	1615	5993	59048
4B4	1731	83	48	154	9	0	0	2	1	1166	42	3	92	9192	2845	8	37000	0	24722	83932
4C1	2260	44	69	318	150	33	130	162	25841	2769	358	7043	425	5325	823	2540	13155	0	31092	121050
4C2	3576	79	91	233	49	3427	6	40	793	1770	22193	39	64	8567	41	30	48450	30953	114495	243036
4D1	621	2	10	51	141	29	0	5	3789	64	15	9	3	116	6	2	0	3481	12917	59987
4D2	1039	22	6	121	254	0	0	5	1422	2	0	2	0	14	2	3	0	226	842	11866
4D3	8570	90	184	1744	616	1	110	1657	54743	2313	265	2755	51	4264	1287	570	2489	13488	50045	214521

4E	1351	17	72	207	12	38	0	9	67563	26	12	675	7	57	178	224	0	8696	32261	134517
4F1	14599	283	265	4012	388	668	75	405	14641	5124	13778	139	2696	4533	2493	2356	21740	10700	39710	174171
4F2	145	3374	4101	1256	27	0	0	1	36	432	771	5	2	184	624	511	3758	0	6866	25581
4F3	8	15	507	215	5	0	0	2	49	460	61	3	1	1464	36	31	18354	0	33520	55458
4F4	3870	60	3742	642	644	4	18	32	1925	2286	2954	485	13	1296	576	542	10483	0	19143	64423
4F5	123	2	80	295	38	4	0	9	117	1166	4	15	1	92	410	34	3983	1962	7274	16307
5A1	3652	277	478	1171	164	0	674	3446	1797	5621	1814	1063	17972	3850	6159	6437	37199	16422	0	135170
5A2	229	7	24	30	32	168	0	6	233	475	158	1	39	188	726	91	2975	2802	0	10257
5A3	358	52	43	57	10	24	4	0	568	15	262	64	6994	95	3457	2059	12490	13634	0	43070
6	2550	259	451	757	149	2628	350	5796	0	9495	18994	1159	20539	28896	8839	494	13671	467318	0	600403
7	13484	975	1532	4816	1143	1533	569	987	55466	28118	16730	5327	32226	2454	11568	6014	390940	0	34182	709087
8A1	5878	870	1040	1206	384	6991	1170	203	21881	24752	4489	4367	3889	3373	2173	831	76111	29155	27094	304440
8A2	0	0	0	0	0	0	0	0	0	0	0	0	2817	462	0	66	29845	86190	0	119380
9	3131	267	1918	1532	532	565	153	0	1817	78685	4572	386	52833	8222	597	6563	237157	139907	55545	624095
10	0	0	0	0	0	5	1	0	0	1	10	0	0	0	0	0	5585	273629	0	279235
11A	0	0	0	0	0	0	0	0	0	0	499	0	684	2876	74	0	74044	146479	21970	246817
11B	1	0	0	0	0	77	0	0	51	1347	535	0	244	53	35	419	111429	0	12562	126811
Households	21785	6360	19434	15772	4898	33431	3332	11634	176947	271165	102757	44096	233587	166391	152165	46076	0	0	0	1696926
Other Value Added	35223	2158	3947	9247	2644	77021	2486	17692	74760	223171	85252	35536	237966	3600	36876	39336	0	0	0	1233854
Imports	39559	8613	16410	13397	3516	3002	568	884	51297	34432	23804	15983	10831	20833	10820	9609	479139	0	0	1155295
Total	174171	25581	55458	64423	16307	135170	10257	43070	600403	709087	304440	119380	624095	279235	246817	126811	1952287	1258055	875735	

Table VII.2: 19-Sector Transactions Table: Wide-Bay—Burnett Region, 1973-4 (thousands)

	1	2A	2B	3A	3B	4A	4B	4C	4D	4E	4F	5	6	7	8	9	10	11A	11B	Households	Other Final Demand	Exports	Total
1	0	0	0	0	0	13326	0	0	0	0	0	0	0	0	0	0	0	0	0	607	0	41864	55797
2A	3724	9472	0	0	0	37716	2	0	0	0	0	0	0	0	0	0	0	0	6	16597	0	18438	85955
2B	0	0	0	37	37	37	2712	0	0	2	2	9	2	0	152	0	0	2	0	1857	371	1486	6706
3A	0	0	0	0	0	36	0	0	11	21	0	257	11	25	30	0	0	8	8	0	0	263	670
3B	0	4	8	13	55	29	0	4	5	160	0	0	396	1	5	0	0	1	1	0	0	5962	6644
4A	2943	198	27	0	0	2792	8	1	0	2	23	1	3	56	4	1	9	174	2	41242	0	61249	108735
4B	2	760	20	5	5	38	1136	221	8	6	5	1	3935	173	63	2	258	207	1	6329	9585	0	22760
4C	438	537	191	6	279	72	222	454	22	66	3	327	657	62	139	14	208	14	18	9055	13711	0	26495
4D	3	18	5	3	42	120	46	644	55	24	4	17	869	22	25	0	33	14	5	274	414	0	2637
4E	0	0	0	8	22	12	21	18	13	22	0	2	3624	1	31	0	1	4	3	471	713	0	4966
4F	20	60	16	0	2	29	18	6	2	1	3	0	19	50	32	0	7	32	21	277	418	0	1013
5	541	986	17	29	123	615	218	259	52	99	9	273	246	341	199	852	201	640	514	3815	6360	0	16389
6	826	1106	53	14	40	317	293	172	18	107	9	694	0	662	3084	1154	1837	831	29	1820	52531	0	65597
7	2649	3833	816	26	675	2248	817	1005	68	170	34	245	4333	3615	1723	1543	124	772	337	25691	1749	0	52473
8	983	2569	124	22	231	3765	920	1228	101	404	13	758	1870	1162	274	337	76	156	56	11417	1801	5415	33682
9	12	52	0	2	192	716	207	195	17	32	13	33	85	3214	70	1355	336	24	244	16842	6842	3684	34167
10	0	0	0	0	0	24	0	0	0	0	0	1	0	0	0	0	0	0	0	722	15428	0	16175
11A	136	0	0	0	2	59	0	0	0	0	0	0	0	0	6	29	152	5	0	2709	19261	0	22359
11B	2	0	0	0	2	176	0	1	0	1	0	5	7	127	10	14	2	3	26	7527	0	1705	9608
Households	2526	8554	1848	71	892	15014	7361	10043	729	1482	334	4248	20112	20254	12550	13346	10176	13803	3643	0	0	0	146986
Other value Added	33999	46332	2393	322	1364	10734	3853	3192	511	1052	124	8336	8182	16017	8271	13105	248	3328	2877	0	0	0	164240
Imports	6993	11474	1188	112	2681	20860	4926	9052	1025	1315	437	1182	21246	6691	7014	2415	2507	2341	1817	112748	0	0	218024
Total	55797	85955	6706	670	6644	108735	22760	26495	2637	4966	1013	16389	65597	52473	33682	34167	16175	22359	9608	260000	129184	140066	

Table VII.3: 19-Sector Transactions Table: Darling Downs Region, 1973–4 (thousands)

	1	2A	2B	3A	3B	4A	4B	4C	4D	4E	4F	5	6	7	8	9	10	11A	11B	Households	Other Final Demand	Exports	Total
1	0	0	0	0	0	34823	0	0	0	0	376	0	0	0	0	0	0	0	0	913	0	62912	99024
2A	8295	12547	0	0	0	6368	1	0	0	0	122	0	0	0	0	0	0	0	8	56053	0	62278	145672
2B	0	0	0	70	0	30	1570	0	0	2	7	3	2	0	159	0	0	1	0	155	31	1069	3099
3A	0	0	0	0	0	25	0	0	3	4	2	30	3	14	10	0	0	4	4	0	0	1155	1254
3B	0	4	3	31	1	3	0	2	2	116	4	0	262	1	3	0	0	1	1	0	0	1295	1729
4A	3760	1012	4	0	0	3693	5	1	0	3	200	0	1	101	6	1	17	276	83	28818	0	42797	80778
4B	3	918	2	9	0	64	810	37	22	5	26	0	3951	245	58	3	274	291	1	4005	6067	0	16791
4C	620	984	29	5	45	22	21	126	23	7	10	2	345	64	93	9	87	13	20	5595	8476	0	16596
4D	6	39	2	5	6	102	31	205	83	9	23	12	1134	39	20	1	51	20	9	2742	1811	0	6350
4E	0	0	0	12	4	3	11	3	5	16	0	1	2532	1	26	0	1	3	1	511	772	0	3902
4F	16	71	4	0	0	10	10	4	14	27	1098	0	3	48	21	0	46	43	38	6458	9783	0	17694
5	675	1091	4	36	5	410	100	107	50	42	116	66	135	329	145	784	135	602	468	290	480	0	6070
6	1450	2043	28	27	6	483	208	141	47	73	158	314	0	1069	3251	1213	2021	1143	40	1967	43159	0	58841
7	5247	7918	426	56	260	3398	933	693	216	163	464	83	4666	5987	2746	2103	186	1215	517	42533	2896	0	82706
8	1825	4038	67	47	63	4802	720	1147	157	397	254	243	1888	1946	264	472	155	247	82	14184	2240	6719	41957
9	26	79	0	3	68	212	129	89	37	20	182	6	93	4919	31	1711	419	19	239	20890	8487	4571	42230
10	0	0	0	0	0	0	0	0	0	0	0	0	0	0	0	0	0	0	0	864	18432	0	19296
11A	276	5	0	1	1	0	0	0	0	0	0	0	0	0	3	43	140	7	0	3614	25696	0	29786
11B	3	0	0	0	0	0	1	0	0	1	0	2	5	160	6	14	4	4	34	10063	0	2280	12577
Households	5323	10986	910	133	124	12369	5034	5747	1884	1125	5107	1539	17776	31841	15142	16717	11380	18343	4702	0	0	0	166182
Other value Added	59645	82962	1064	601	189	6230	2946	2001	996	752	1934	3200	7335	25463	11372	15840	240	4459	3788	0	0	0	231017
Imports	11854	20975	556	218	957	7731	4261	6293	2811	1140	7611	569	18710	10479	8601	3319	4140	3095	2542	81345	0	0	197207
Total	99024	145672	3099	1254	1729	80778	16791	16596	6350	3902	17694	6070	58841	82706	41957	42230	19296	29786	12577	281000	128330	185076	

Table VII.4: 19-Sector Transactions Table: Fitzroy Region, 1973–4 (thousands)

	1	2A	2B	3A	3B	4A	4B	4C	4D	4E	4F	5	6	7	8	9	10	11A	11B	Households	Other Final Demand	Exports	Total
1	0	0	0	0	0	24214	0	0	0	1	38	0	0	0	0	0	0	0	0	451	0	31097	55801
2A	4436	3005	0	0	0	3313	1	0	0	0	63	0	0	0	0	0	0	0	7	9234	0	10259	30318
2B	0	0	0	1632	41	25	111	0	1	1	1	3	1	0	25	0	0	1	0	18	4	10	1874
3A	0	0	0	0	6	150	0	17	2600	234	17	2000	49	90	95	0	2	29	30	0	0	149183	154502
3B	0	2	3	972	545	3	0	15	502	1096	32	0	1093	2	5	1	0	3	3	0	0	26638	30915
4A	1824	129	19	5	1	2699	6	1	233	2	137	1	1	74	4	1	7	236	94	23443	0	34816	63733
4B	3	404	11	918	67	90	472	286	188	54	26	1	5342	365	90	1	198	235	7	715	1082	0	10555
4C	171	75	22	1486	651	29	22	565	376	28	15	96	741	47	1750	6	83	12	20	9640	14600	0	30435
4D	9	21	6	2366	465	505	181	3720	6917	69	363	71	8296	115	45	1	128	87	32	25108	38026	0	86531
4E	0	0	0	1552	482	1	3	3	33	526	1	1	2920	1	7	0	1	1	1	1735	2628	0	9896
4F	68	51	4	35	210	43	23	59	504	18	83	3	45	45	14	13	21	111	33	1146	1732	0	4261
5	460	297	6	6265	667	422	76	331	2301	232	89	192	309	370	137	658	152	682	548	2938	3696	1203	22031
6	852	400	11	3310	239	324	112	163	370	191	70	732	0	793	2625	881	1488	1071	38	1526	81622	0	96818
7	2834	1474	222	6427	2970	2511	525	1550	1507	419	225	288	6998	4312	972	1309	107	1007	415	23724	1618	0	61484
8	811	671	27	4051	941	2116	261	624	1361	887	79	768	2355	1346	211	196	75	148	53	3224	509	1528	22242
9	15	20	0	483	754	219	113	226	547	55	49	43	153	4073	108	1199	290	41	295	11155	4532	2437	26807
10	0	0	0	6	0	0	0	0	375	0	0	1	0	0	0	0	0	0	0	569	12139	0	13090
11A	129	1	0	111	10	0	0	0	289	0	0	0	0	0	10	24	163	8	0	3367	23936	0	28048
11B	4	0	0	0	12	0	0	1	57	3	0	10	10	148	13	11	1	4	30	8943	0	2027	11274
Households	3094	2856	452	16421	4852	10470	3274	8300	22599	1571	775	5571	29436	23674	8637	10315	8243	17534	4249	0	0	0	182323
Other Value Added	33546	16577	718	74047	7421	4740	1747	3700	23906	2418	859	11036	12072	18915	4572	10231	201	4018	3418	0	0	0	234142
Imports	7545	4335	373	34415	10581	11859	3558	10874	21865	2091	1339	1214	26997	7114	2922	1960	1930	2820	2001	91064	0	0	246857
Total	55801	30318	1874	154502	30915	63733	10555	30435	86531	9896	4261	22031	96818	61484	22242	26807	13090	28048	11274	218000	186120	259198	

Table VII.5: 19-Sector Transactions Table: Mackay Region, 1973–4 (thousands)

	1	2A	2B	3A	3B	4A	4B	4C	4D	4E	4F	5	6	7	8	9	10	11A	11B	Households	Other Final Demand	Exports	Total
1	0	0	0	0	0	5604	0	0	0	0	0	0	0	0	0	0	0	0	0	222	0	15308	21134
2A	1423	6177	0	0	0	43575	1	0	0	0	1	0	0	0	0	0	0	0	5	3563	0	3957	58702
2B	0	0	0	974	0	9	151	0	0	1	1	2	1	0	13	0	0	0	0	22	4	19	1197
3A	0	0	0	0	0	38	0	0	0	52	14	517	35	43	31	0	1	13	25	0	0	47555	48324
3B	0	2	1	689	0	15	0	0	0	86	6	0	340	0	1	0	0	0	1	0	0	444	1585
4A	795	86	14	2	0	881	4	1	0	0	77	1	2	34	1	1	3	91	1	36823	0	54687	93504
4B	1	480	10	328	0	13	234	16	1	8	6	0	3226	78	25	0	88	134	1	405	614	0	5668
4C	136	275	24	455	89	15	22	36	4	30	36	75	600	34	138	5	38	10	15	366	554	0	2957
4D	0	1	0	43	0	12	2	6	1	1	3	3	350	2	1	0	3	2	1	58	85	0	574
4E	0	0	0	414	0	7	2	2	0	4	0	0	1743	0	5	0	0	1	1	620	939	0	3738
4F	851	1997	12	5	38	33	13	12	2	21	246	1	26	15	4	1	4	46	16	533	807	0	4683
5	194	669	5	2059	8	421	44	32	6	78	170	180	252	193	59	436	87	352	481	1721	2868	0	10315
6	327	715	5	1035	8	130	63	16	4	85	100	440	0	376	722	387	773	483	22	868	58240	0	64799
7	1128	2839	141	2124	230	1591	332	129	21	183	217	179	5011	2093	564	778	55	478	299	10020	680	0	29092
8	275	1164	15	1160	48	2004	135	73	11	237	69	326	1462	544	108	88	37	62	36	1162	184	551	9751
9	6	48	0	89	53	687	34	18	2	20	22	13	118	1296	34	424	123	10	138	6561	2664	1434	13794
10	0	0	0	2	0	28	0	0	0	0	0	0	0	0	0	0	0	0	0	295	6297	0	6622
11A	37	0	0	24	1	69	0	0	0	0	0	0	0	0	7	9	60	3	0	1502	10693	0	12405
11B	2	0	0	0	0	207	0	0	0	1	0	3	7	72	13	5	0	2	18	6574	0	1490	8398
Households	1209	7184	259	5136	127	9193	1869	1100	166	794	810	2683	19952	11198	3493	5360	4260	7748	3264	0	0	0	85805
Other value Added	12675	31138	479	23159	195	9623	949	378	79	875	1159	5205	8085	8961	2517	5089	108	1780	2479	0	0	0	114933
Imports	2075	5927	232	10626	788	19349	1813	1138	277	1262	1746	687	23589	4153	2015	1211	982	1190	1595	52685	0	0	133340
Total	21134	58702	1197	48324	1585	93504	5668	2957	574	3738	4683	10315	64799	29092	9751	13794	6622	12405	8398	124000	84629	125449	

Table VII.6: 19-Sector Transactions Table: Northern Region, 1973–4 (thousands)

	1	2A	2B	3A	3B	4A	4B	4C	4D	4E	4F	5	6	7	8	9	10	11A	11B	Households	Other Final Demand	Exports	Total
1	0	0	0	0	0	13079	0	0	0	1	0	0	0	0	0	0	0	0	0	109	0	7520	20709
2A	1389	7482	0	0	0	37471	1	0	0	0	0	0	0	0	0	0	1	0	18	15147	0	16828	79337
2B	0	0	0	165	6	135	262	1	0	2	4	9	2	0	215	0	0	4	0	354	70	282	1511
3A	0	0	0	0	0	161	5	5	87	326	8	1487	63	137	398	0	10	36	64	0	0	3892	6679
3B	0	3	1	92	15	17	0	2	645	616	7	0	811	2	12	1	0	2	4	0	0	1264	3494
4A	848	342	29	0	0	2503	5	1	3	2	66	1	7	115	12	3	86	253	6	50502	0	75002	129786
4B	1	980	6	14	11	97	387	53	17	110	29	1	3189	610	348	2	249	135	24	1628	2463	0	10354
4C	60	154	38	50	65	51	39	138	48	69	15	424	443	54	6947	11	1837	18	21	862	1305	0	12649
4D	3	32	4	86	56	183	128	966	921	155	197	64	9355	103	93	2	399	67	50	1134	1713	0	15711
4E	0	0	0	167	106	12	8	3	37	1010	1	3	9462	1	115	0	6	4	4	1250	1894	0	14083
4F	55	101	6	0	27	45	37	10	76	19	59	1	34	109	159	10	116	225	100	1185	1794	0	4168
5	253	1226	10	426	79	873	173	158	409	524	104	346	612	878	955	2434	719	1293	1812	5954	9923	0	29161
6	325	873	5	143	26	338	139	51	78	273	55	980	0	1279	9866	1685	5333	1534	96	1680	115035	0	139794
7	1263	4207	198	344	481	4226	708	678	523	663	250	440	13484	7214	6085	3415	768	1613	1195	44453	3029	0	95237
8	415	2245	27	247	160	5149	361	290	785	1364	87	1340	4732	3169	1664	565	1103	264	167	19838	3132	57304	104408
9	8	69	0	19	117	738	135	63	64	88	49	48	299	6282	554	2967	1060	46	568	28076	11406	6140	58796
10	0	0	0	0	0	23	0	0	0	0	0	1	0	0	2	0	0	0	0	2673	56970	0	59669
11A	51	1	0	5	2	58	0	0	0	0	0	0	0	0	90	54	377	11	0	3281	23332	9195	36457
11B	3	0	0	0	1	173	0	0	0	3	0	14	13	209	107	24	17	5	78	20066	0	4552	25265
Households	1320	12416	303	710	441	15812	2915	5624	4919	3222	1085	7320	41680	36510	38940	22528	31073	23074	9324	0	0	0	259216
Other Value Added	12312	40336	625	3201	675	11357	1639	1223	2918	3548	771	15951	17416	29732	24159	21816	443	5011	7778	0	0	0	200911
Imports	2403	7870	259	1010	1226	37285	3412	3383	4181	2088	1381	731	38192	8833	13687	3279	16072	2862	3956	41808	0	0	193918
Total	20709	78337	1511	6679	3494	129786	10354	12649	15711	14083	4168	29161	139794	95237	104408	58796	59669	36457	25265	240000	232066	181979	

Table VII.7: 19-Sector Transactions Table: Far North Region, 1973–4 (thousands)

	1	2A	2B	3A	3B	4A	4B	4C	4D	4E	4F	5	6	7	8	9	10	11A	11B	Households	Other Final Demand	Exports	Total
1	0	0	0	0	0	14156	0	0	0	1	0	0	0	0	0	0	0	0	0	89	0	6161	20407
2A	1436	9620	0	0	0	55995	1	0	0	0	1	0	0	0	0	0	0	0	7	11384	0	12646	91090
2B	0	0	0	0	407	64	3127	1	1	3	2	11	2	0	76	0	0	3	0	47	38	9	3791
3A	0	0	0	0	0	0	0	0	0	0	0	0	0	0	0	0	0	0	0	0	0	0	0
3B	0	8	4	0	1034	44	0	2	143	395	24	0	514	2	6	1	0	3	3	0	0	55991	58174
4A	818	450	50	0	1	2037	6	2	1	1	125	1	2	60	4	1	10	152	123	47147	0	91878	142869
4B	1	761	41	0	57	126	2234	192	18	10	11	1	3487	141	81	1	197	136	1	6282	9511	0	23289
4C	71	248	138	0	1390	82	215	111	27	36	34	362	327	52	1342	7	251	19	43	1670	2528	0	8953
4D	2	25	6	0	486	41	71	371	130	46	44	27	927	30	10	1	52	20	10	767	1161	0	4230
4E	0	0	0	0	165	18	10	1	6	23	0	1	2157	1	27	0	1	1	1	1081	1637	0	5130
4F	430	1634	18	0	18	3	4	1	1	0	3	0	3	14	3	0	1	7	7	577	878	0	3602
5	238	1327	22	0	1638	948	498	114	116	91	70	270	200	419	237	1079	241	689	730	906	1510	5861	17204
6	314	1137	15	0	288	412	407	39	29	87	49	660	0	646	1578	936	1660	735	33	1456	38684	0	49165
7	1125	4645	456	0	6563	3369	926	537	140	266	152	253	4096	3596	1636	1519	134	832	404	17453	1190	0	49292
8	358	2466	62	0	2265	4840	884	224	217	519	88	672	1430	1370	528	296	150	131	60	7420	1172	3513	28665
9	6	68	0	0	1608	1004	343	57	30	41	24	30	80	2676	196	1078	276	43	254	12890	5237	2819	28760
10	0	0	0	0	0	35	0	0	0	0	0	1	0	0	1	0	0	0	0	659	14042	0	14738
11A	50	1	0	0	22	87	0	0	0	0	0	0	0	0	47	23	181	6	0	2520	17921	0	20858
11B	2	0	0	0	20	261	0	0	0	2	0	7	5	120	57	12	1	3	26	7979	0	1809	10304
Households	1147	10317	785	0	8237	15072	7075	3143	1017	1154	795	4363	14668	18947	10079	11122	9210	13158	3920	0	0	0	134209
Other Value Added	12255	48498	1547	0	12599	15793	3703	1160	885	970	603	9182	6125	15252	7659	10825	221	2911	3106	0	0	0	153294
Imports	2154	9885	647	0	21376	28482	3785	2998	1469	1485	1577	1363	15142	5966	5098	1859	2152	2009	1578	80130	0	0	189155
TOTAL	20407	91090	3791	0	58174	142869	23289	8953	4230	5130	3602	17204	49165	49292	28665	28760	14738	20858	10306	200457	95512	180687	

Table VII.8: 19-Sector Transactions Table: North West Region, 1973–4 (thousands)

	1	2A	2B	3A	3B	4A	4B	4C	4D	4E	4F	5	6	7	8	9	10	11A	11B	Households	Other Final Demand	Exports	Total
1	0	0	0	0	0	742	0	0	0	0	2	0	0	0	0	0	0	0	0	471	0	45885	47100
2A	2404	205	0	0	0	24	0	0	0	0	0	0	0	0	0	0	0	0	4	418	0	464	3519
2B	0	0	0	0	0	3	0	0	0	0	1	0	0	0	0	0	0	1	0	270	0	5124	5399
3A	0	0	0	0	0	0	0	0	0	0	0	0	0	0	0	0	0	0	0	0	0	0	0
3B	0	0	0	0	7779	0	0	0	0	71	0	0	342	1	3	0	0	1	2	0	0	259750	267949
4A	59	0	10	0	1	20	0	0	0	0	3	0	0	3	0	0	0	7	0	1409	0	2758	4270
4B	0	0	0	0	2	0	2	0	0	0	0	0	0	2	0	0	25	43	0	339	514	0	927
4C	27	1	2	0	845	0	0	3	5	0	0	0	81	6	5	0	3	1	4	280	429	0	1692
4D	1	0	2	0	77	1	0	11	17	1	0	1	631	2	1	0	3	4	2	1081	1641	0	3476
4E	0	0	0	0	305	0	0	0	0	1	0	0	322	0	3	0	0	0	0	182	277	0	1090
4F	0	0	0	0	0	0	0	0	0	0	0	0	0	0	0	0	0	0	0	25	38	0	63
5	80	9	9	0	2388	10	1	5	9	3	0	4	25	25	17	61	13	31	87	143	237	0	3157
6	704	36	0	0	1584	34	8	8	27	16	1	89	0	185	1010	214	418	234	17	525	26552	0	31662
7	1045	65	208	0	7397	108	33	29	54	22	1	14	897	463	267	162	11	76	80	3216	221	0	14369
8	560	63	46	0	6827	88	9	30	59	79	1	103	658	234	100	62	18	27	27	1531	242	723	11487
9	10	2	0	0	1162	7	3	6	8	3	0	2	39	375	8	150	55	6	51	3889	1580	848	8204
10	0	0	0	0	0	0	0	0	0	0	0	0	0	0	0	0	0	0	0	158	3370	0	3528
11A	69	0	0	0	37	0	0	0	0	0	0	0	0	0	18	4	49	2	0	734	5219	0	6132
11B	3	0	0	0	101	0	0	0	0	0	0	1	3	36	22	3	0	1	14	4749	1082	0	6015
Households	3434	682	738	0	65435	848	370	567	619	220	14	786	9519	5532	4136	3345	2298	3979	2318	0	0	0	104840
Other Value Added	27634	1771	2489	0	77225	519	161	231	520	200	8	1765	3946	4421	2791	2997	60	776	1788	0	0	0	129302
Imports	11070	685	1895	0	96784	1866	340	802	2158	474	32	392	15199	3084	3106	1206	575	943	1621	55580	0	0	197812
Total	47100	3519	5399	0	267949	4270	927	1692	3476	1090	63	3157	31662	14369	11487	8204	3528	6132	6015	75000	41391	315559	

Table VII.9: 36-Sector Transactions Table: Queensland, 1973–4 (thousands)

	1	2A	2B	3A	3B	4A1	4A2	4A3	4A4	4A5	4B1	4B2	4B3	4B4	4C1	4C2	4D1	4D2	4D3	4E
1	0	0	0	0	0	309819	0	0	0	0	0	0	0	0	0	0	0	0	0	12
2A	41501	61381	0	0	0	18355	15229	8818	247785	2802	0	82	0	0	0	0	0	0	0	0
2B	0	1	0	9356	1966	771	110	1	0	2	16287	88	777	0	24	1	13	1	7	55
3A	0	0	0	0	80	1697	72	18	5	29	120	0	431	2	9	97	2530	752	7	2575
3B	1	48	63	7636	7089	0	0	0	197	1	0	1	58	3	83	73	634	43166	36	11566
4A1	4448	154	126	3	1	55	5451	4223	284	43	2	340	1	0	4	4	0	0	1	14
4A2	51	28	4	1	10	311	248	2043	65	1676	18	2	6	1	14	10	575	1	11	12
4A3	5760	724	158	2	7	336	391	19387	209	39	5	4	540	1	1	2	11	72	1	40
4A4	16217	8041	158	7	5	1457	4601	4116	839	6945	7	7	7	2	83	3	5	2	4	6
4A5	294	2	0	0	1	201	30	12	0	50	1	0	0	0	0	0	19	0	0	3
4B1	1	4360	130	1589	357	20	0	0	13	253	6461	22100	417	1	371	3671	205	164	418	246
4B2	22	300	103	32	4	74	9	3	14	71	3036	1376	7	10	414	1423	32	9	319	33
4B3	207	13937	3	9	2154	530	801	1284	123	899	187	477	7019	6623	785	267	5	117	473	2319
4B4	1	339	0	2	78	113	180	132	16	670	3	10	875	2036	230	3	0	23	151	31
4C1	4227	3952	664	3409	19478	370	122	98	14	82	691	146	291	244	4888	10723	529	568	2173	1073
4C2	158	300	658	1824	1707	500	212	105	17	159	1313	212	615	265	1213	1204	255	349	815	1345
4D1	43	148	8	842	4463	1	49	3	40	4	97	772	17	48	5292	9317	0	622	13214	1709
4D2	3	3	2	102	2972	31	37	1	57	0	85	1764	236	488	16641	9433	3519	0	17984	407
4D3	111	364	125	3578	1678	6768	5827	310	152	3397	900	2384	355	207	6776	18262	799	844	6614	1178
4E	4	4	2	6203	14563	719	564	3	80	1561	83	908	9	4	443	524	949	1117	495	14251

4F1	28967	34902	1849	1459	12549	861	419	536	17	406	2039	1300	1103	579	1883	4001	1033	1540	1634	2390
4F2	253	655	118	4	25	45	214	53	6	30	167	972	150	16	121	221	102	97	424	343
4F3	7	15	14	0	162	1	1	1	0	1	1	68	81	4	37	209	48	1	21	10
4F4	11	145	291	93	6352	567	852	502	123	335	44	977	193	276	1229	2729	18	57	481	96
4F5	5	17	24	4	61	21	18	23	4	4	21	54	88	67	60	55	13	1	52	26
5A1	4080	6665	157	13250	10158	3956	941	1260	576	814	2926	798	1138	822	2552	3655	2622	4490	2896	4543
5A2	13	38	0	4	8	47	11	324	505	7	10	15	9	32	242	242	136	146	410	401
5A3	2059	2881	0	424	1920	239	105	88	520	257	57	19	79	16	66	65	84	28	139	326
6	7461	7885	217	5082	2458	2002	1210	790	138	967	2469	699	1261	965	1177	1259	260	588	1919	3648
7	21512	26388	3311	9291	38686	20383	5010	6775	4086	5207	2246	5429	2311	11270	11347	15860	1802	4425	9058	8900
8A1	10485	19871	799	9466	19802	27154	6234	5549	11967	2827	7061	4070	2013	1814	8719	6871	7163	9431	7470	18041
8A2	0	0	0	0	0	0	0	0	2014	0	0	0	0	0	0	0	0	0	0	0
9	221	660	0	1158	18765	2284	819	968	3714	515	3035	1702	803	1987	2966	2277	389	563	2994	2017
10	0	0	0	11	0	1	0	0	158	0	0	0	0	0	0	0	1	0	0	1
11A	1422	23	2	168	154	0	0	0	395	0	0	0	0	0	0	0	0	0	0	0
11B	25	3	1	0	154	0	0	0	1185	0	0	0	0	9	10	5	1	0	0	38
Households	28669	68866	8648	25216	60175	71166	13638	24870	50788	9758	29956	28759	11973	38426	54824	79250	12915	18473	60012	43456
Other Value Added	303288	331894	13387	113709	92037	28764	8331	13233	46278	11791	19783	12685	9945	16977	22098	44918	17841	33340	33855	40754
Imports	24005	27251	4245	23323	99536	16651	8473	7144	24151	6599	14394	13197	19769	18942	37192	63853	9063	7445	59749	15851
Total	505532	622245	35267	237257	419615	516270	80209	102673	96535	58201	113505	101417	62643	102137	181794	280487	63571	18432	223837	177716

Table VII.9 (continued)

	4F1	4F2	4F3	4F4	4F5	5A1	5A2	5A3	6	7	8A1	8A2	9	10	11A	11B	Households	Other Final Demand	Exports	Total
1	0	1487	0	777	0	0	0	0	3	0	1	0	0	0	0	0	10111	0	183322	505532
2A	23	309	6	0	30	0	0	0	0	0	0	0	0	9	0	148	136894	0	88873	622245
2B	25	1	110	166	0	120	0	0	23	1	1521	67	0	0	26	1	3746	0	0	35267
3A	2323	43	3	28	68	12482	1172	109	491	1604	2023	0	0	61	427	538	0	0	207461	237257
3B	819	0	0	14	126	0	0	4	11394	41	173	0	21	1	33	65	0	0	336269	419615
4A1	2602	100	62	6164	2	1	0	4	2	1279	18	1	18	282	3301	20	278785	0	208475	516270
4A2	1216	2	2	96	1	0	0	8	217	172	18	2	10	20	1039	2	43313	0	29004	80209
4A3	1118	52	0	26	0	0	0	1	0	12	6	0	2	16	211	0	55445	0	18094	102673
4A4	488	1	1	8	2	2	0	9	46	132	33	2	22	85	72	28	214131	0	138961	396535
4A5	153	0	0	0	0	0	0	1	1	19	51	0	1	0	5	1944	31428	0	23976	58201
4B1	200	6	1	317	70	0	0	1	49492	1111	1488	1	2	52	12	0	11546	8429	0	113505
4B2	289	16	27	137	27	2	0	10	30093	3733	153	20	10	2911	1234	61	12170	8884	34349	101417
4B3	2671	265	730	421	259	2	0	23	193	13013	3026	245	58	613	232	647	2026	0	0	62643
4B4	1175	92	33	108	7	1	0	2	1	1239	49	4	87	9765	4102	9	65000	0	15570	102137
4C1	1607	54	49	219	116	40	134	193	30080	2907	509	6961	495	5474	870	2519	30905	0	44920	181794
4C2	3467	115	85	217	47	5561	8	51	1210	1757	40692	41	59	11430	58	36	47683	24571	130173	280487
4D1	520	3	7	36	114	33	0	5	4941	64	21	10	3	123	7	3	0	5565	15423	63571
4D2	6203	213	32	708	1605	0	0	44	15161	17	5	22	2	122	16	30	0	0	50487	128432
4D3	5870	109	130	1290	466	1	124	1777	81159	2539	326	2874	49	4514	1492	680	4477	19608	35723	223837
4E	1008	40	45	129	8	45	0	10	101351	28	20	1057	7	72	189	259	0	15568	15394	177716

4F1	12981	427	191	3562	364	662	62	368	18082	4802	13448	134	2290	4314	2834	2588	14018	5582	0	186176
4F2	90	3184	3871	796	106	0	0	2	48	503	1041	6	2	323	893	1025	7239	0	9760	32905
4F3	5	32	334	149	4	0	0	2	56	447	73	3	1	1493	40	36	12361	0	40465	56183
4F4	2556	83	3134	397	434	3	14	28	2124	2078	2760	448	10	1162	582	563	14390	0	19273	65410
4F5	93	2	48	201	30	5	0	9	143	1279	5	12	1	95	458	37	3940	1569	9360	17908
5A1	4393	578	496	1218	187	0	940	5222	3570	9052	3410	1709	25226	5904	9968	11869	64000	3319	0	219420
5A2	207	10	18	23	27	208	0	6	327	564	200	1	42	213	758	129	5000	3614	0	13947
5A3	339	60	36	48	9	31	4	0	896	18	390	83	7530	118	4656	2839	18446	18737	0	63614
6	2925	422	462	792	170	4375	488	8780	0	15024	44502	1864	28008	44375	14889	794	24136	857360	0	1091821
7	13984	753	1462	4879	1288	2449	767	1458	99505	41522	26371	8222	43209	3606	18304	9800	625541	0	0	1116417
8A1	6165	745	1057	1234	436	11757	1647	304	40517	38181	7517	6715	5286	5023	3481	1462	133713	41403	41403	534853
8A2	0	0	0	0	0	0	0	0	0	0	0	0	4256	702	0	98	46801	133331	0	187202
9	2453	415	1432	1148	440	676	153	0	2750	105563	5298	447	59842	11708	775	8540	324634	0	280210	854301
10	0	0	0	0	0	8	1	0	0	2	14	0	0	0	0	0	8381	410464	0	419042
11A	0	0	0	0	0	0	0	0	0	0	704	0	913	4330	119	0	119622	270889	0	398741
11B	1	0	0	0	0	124	0	0	103	2360	810	0	348	74	59	675	170778	0	39412	216175
Households	24359	7826	19785	15905	5113	54269	4530	17183	325614	427912	187563	69148	323647	249265	247053	79829	0	0	0	2798845
Other Value Added	38804	4653	3992	9395	2970	125029	3381	26131	136021	348767	138248	55724	324300	5371	58698	66291	0	0	0	2562683
Imports	45044	10807	18542	14802	3382	1534	522	1869	136209	88674	52367	31374	28543	45410	21847	22628	908881	0	0	1933268
Total	186176	32905	56183	65410	17908	219420	13947	63614	1091823	1116416	534854	187200	854300	419045	398740	216173	3449546	1828897	2016357	

APPENDIX VIII: MULTIPLIERS: NON-UNIFORM TABLES FOR THE REGIONS AND STATE OF QUEENSLAND

Table VIII.1: 36-Sector Output Multipliers: Moreton Region and State of Queensland

	Moreton Region		State of Queensland	
Sector	Direct & Indirect	Total	Direct & Indirect	Total
1	1.381	1.600	1.469	1.727
2A	1.428	1.748	1.472	1.825
2B	1.457	2.047	1.381	1.958
3A	1.489	1.886	1.460	1.841
3B	1.775	2.311	1.585	2.098
4A1	1.478	1.855	2.132	2.626
4A2	1.879	2.483	1.986	2.610
4A3	1.810	2.532	1.963	2.719
4A4	1.763	2.247	2.018	2.501
4A5	1.797	2.398	1.833	2.429
4B1	1.677	2.382	1.638	2.361
4B2	1.720	2.501	1.720	2.510
4B3	1.662	2.256	1.495	2.021
4B4	1.504	2.348	1.382	2.190
4C1	1.528	2.224	1.575	2.316
4C2	1.556	2.210	1.500	2.184
4D1	1.492	2.043	1.566	2.137
4D2	1.577	2.018	1.821	2.369
4D3	1.438	2.072	1.489	2.130
4E	1.679	2.358	1.657	2.350
4F1	1.678	2.169	1.647	2.128
4F2	1.486	2.091	1.427	1.980
4F3	1.422	2.183	1.361	2.098
4F4	1.601	2.243	1.632	2.265
4F5	1.479	2.186	1.556	2.256
5A1	1.244	1.752	1.260	1.777
5A2	1.546	2.324	1.563	2.350
5A3	1.460	2.107	1.438	2.082
6	1.764	2.588	1.695	2.502
7	1.361	2.174	1.311	2.105
8A1	1.474	2.238	1.446	2.229
8A2	1.293	2.039	1.241	1.968
9	1.318	2.098	1.285	2.058
10	1.495	2.705	1.434	2.623
11A	1.285	2.423	1.266	2.406
11B	1.354	2.115	1.304	2.053

Table VIII.2: 19-Sector Output Multipliers: Provincial Regions of Queensland

	Wide Bay—Burnett		Darling Downs		Fitzroy		Mackay		Northern		Far North		North West	
Sector	Direct & Indirect	Total	Direct & Indirect	Total	Direct & Indirect	Total	Direct & Indirect	Total	Direct & Indirect	Total	Direct & Indirect	Total	Direct & Indirect	Total
1	1.302	1.414	1.303	1.454	1.283	1.404	1.326	1.465	1.308	1.551	1.322	1.468	1.118	1.151
2A	1.289	1.455	1.267	1.441	1.279	1.441	1.311	1.518	1.295	1.698	1.318	1.529	1.121	1.193
2B	1.235	1.589	1.226	1.690	1.230	1.550	1.234	1.546	1.283	1.785	1.274	1.606	1.057	1.107
3A	1.307	1.505	1.296	1.540	1.249	1.431	1.238	1.426	1.347	1.703	—	—	—	—
3B	1.313	1.553	1.322	1.558	1.337	1.602	1.358	1.578	1.430	1.893	1.340	1.624	1.118	1.208
4A	1.744	1.990	1.892	2.239	1.759	2.035	1.775	2.011	1.661	2.089	1.772	2.028	1.272	1.349
4B	1.365	1.797	1.337	1.845	1.238	1.628	1.223	1.648	1.300	1.938	1.494	1.990	1.068	1.202
4C	1.194	1.631	1.186	1.695	1.316	1.686	1.139	1.582	1.248	2.138	1.234	1.707	1.061	1.173
4D	1.173	1.499	1.126	1.546	1.268	1.604	1.110	1.454	1.313	1.998	1.256	1.607	1.057	1.119
4E	1.279	1.659	1.280	1.746	1.518	1.817	1.265	1.575	1.507	2.142	1.378	1.753	1.203	1.287
4F	1.156	1.524	1.219	1.648	1.404	1.692	1.262	1.519	1.296	1.889	1.236	1.552	1.165	1.245
5	1.200	1.516	1.158	1.533	1.247	1.562	1.207	1.541	1.236	1.775	1.169	1.512	1.076	1.162
6	1.310	1.712	1.320	1.824	1.378	1.797	1.247	1.658	1.409	2.131	1.359	1.813	1.105	1.210
7	1.221	1.679	1.220	1.795	1.241	1.714	1.198	1.679	1.272	2.082	1.230	1.747	1.102	1.236
8	1.220	1.657	1.207	1.739	1.364	1.867	1.216	1.670	1.349	2.183	1.258	1.745	1.140	1.268
9	1.191	1.638	1.184	1.753	1.203	1.659	1.187	1.664	1.243	2.028	1.214	1.722	1.089	1.227
10	1.256	1.956	1.234	2.058	1.273	1.994	1.236	1.997	1.270	2.302	1.280	2.073	1.186	1.412
11A	1.166	1.821	1.169	1.994	1.174	1.854	1.170	1.883	1.200	2.370	1.172	1.929	1.078	1.291
11B	1.160	1.583	1.151	1.673	1.182	1.616	1.152	1.612	1.210	1.943	1.206	1.695	1.052	1.180

Table VIII.3: 36-Sector Income Multipliers: Moreton Region and State of Queensland

	Moreton Region			State of Queensland		
Sector	Direct	Direct & Indirect	Total	Direct	Direct & Indirect	Total
1	0.045	0.134	0.202	0.057	0.158	0.230
2A	0.088	0.191	0.287	0.111	0.216	0.314
2B	2.233	0.357	0.536	0.245	0.352	0.514
3A	0.106	0.238	0.358	0.106	0.233	0.340
3B	0.105	0.329	0.496	0.143	0.314	0.458
4A1	0.138	0.231	0.348	0.138	0.302	0.440
4A2	0.162	0.371	0.558	0.170	0.381	0.556
4A3	0.241	0.444	0.667	0.242	0.462	0.674
4A4	0.124	0.292	0.439	0.128	0.295	0.430
4A5	0.154	0.363	0.546	0.168	0.364	0.531
4B1	0.247	0.433	0.652	0.264	0.442	0.645
4B2	0.282	0.480	0.721	0.284	0.483	0.704
4B3	0.195	0.364	0.548	0.191	0.322	0.469
4B4	0.371	0.518	0.779	0.376	0.494	0.720
4C1	0.279	0.427	0.643	0.301	0.453	0.660
4C2	0.249	0.402	0.604	0.283	0.418	0.610
4D1	0.206	0.338	0.505	0.203	0.349	0.509
4D2	0.131	0.271	0.407	0.144	0.335	0.488
4D3	0.270	0.389	0.585	0.268	0.392	0.571
4E	0.235	0.417	0.627	0.245	0.424	0.618
4F1	0.125	0.302	0.454	0.131	0.295	0.429
4F2	0.249	0.372	0.559	0.238	0.338	0.493
4F3	0.350	0.467	0.703	0.352	0.450	0.657
4F4	0.245	0.394	0.593	0.243	0.387	0.565
4F5	0.300	0.434	0.653	0.286	0.428	0.625
5A1	0.247	0.312	0.469	0.247	0.316	0.460
5A2	0.325	0.478	0.719	0.325	0.481	0.702
5A3	0.270	0.398	0.599	0.270	0.393	0.573
6	0.295	0.506	0.761	0.298	0.493	0.719
7	0.382	0.499	0.750	0.383	0.486	0.708
8A1	0.338	0.469	0.705	0.351	0.479	0.699
8A2	0.370	0.458	0.689	0.370	0.444	0.648
9	0.374	0.479	0.720	0.379	0.473	0.690
10	0.596	0.743	1.118	0.595	0.727	1.060
11A	0.617	0.699	1.051	0.620	0.697	1.016
11B	0.363	0.467	0.702	0.369	0.458	0.668

Table VIII.4: 19-Sector Income Multipliers: Provincial Regions of Queensland

	Wide Bay—Burnett			Darling Downs			Fitzroy			Mackay		
Sector	Direct	Direct & Indirect	Total	Direct	Direct & Indirect	Total	Direct	Direct & Indirect	Total	Direct	Direct & Indirect	Total
1	0.045	0.115	0.144	0.054	0.122	0.160	0.055	0.121	0.154	0.057	0.132	0.161
2A	0.100	0.169	0.213	0.075	0.141	0.185	0.094	0.161	0.205	0.122	0.196	0.240
2B	0.276	0.361	0.455	0.294	0.376	0.495	0.241	0.319	0.407	0.217	0.296	0.362
3A	0.106	0.202	0.254	0.106	0.197	0.259	0.106	0.182	0.232	0.106	0.178	0.218
3B	0.134	0.246	0.309	0.071	0.191	0.251	0.157	0.264	0.337	0.080	0.208	0.255
4A	0.138	0.251	0.316	0.153	0.281	0.369	0.164	0.275	0.351	0.098	0.224	0.274
4B	0.323	0.442	0.556	0.300	0.411	0.541	0.310	0.389	0.496	0.330	0.404	0.494
4C	0.379	0.447	0.562	0.346	0.412	0.541	0.273	0.368	0.470	0.372	0.420	0.514
4D	0.276	0.333	0.419	0.297	0.340	0.447	0.261	0.335	0.427	0.288	0.326	0.399
4E	0.299	0.388	0.489	0.288	0.377	0.496	0.159	0.297	0.379	0.212	0.293	0.359
4F	0.330	0.376	0.473	0.289	0.347	0.456	0.182	0.288	0.367	0.173	0.244	0.298
5	0.259	0.323	0.407	0.254	0.304	0.400	0.253	0.314	0.400	0.260	0.317	0.388
6	0.307	0.411	0.517	0.302	0.408	0.536	0.304	0.417	0.532	0.308	0.390	0.477
7	0.386	0.467	0.588	0.385	0.466	0.612	0.385	0.472	0.601	0.385	0.456	0.559
8	0.373	0.446	0.562	0.361	0.431	0.566	0.388	0.500	0.638	0.358	0.431	0.528
9	0.391	0.457	0.576	0.396	0.461	0.606	0.385	0.454	0.579	0.389	0.453	0.554
10	0.629	0.715	0.900	0.590	0.667	0.877	0.630	0.718	0.916	0.643	0.722	0.883
11A	0.617	0.669	0.842	0.616	0.668	0.878	0.625	0.677	0.864	0.625	0.677	0.828
11B	0.379	0.432	0.544	0.374	0.422	0.555	0.377	0.432	0.551	0.389	0.436	0.534

Table VIII.4 (continued)

	Northern			Far North			North West		
Sector	Direct	Direct & Indirect	Total	Direct	Direct & Indirect	Total	Direct	Direct & Indirect	Total
1	0.064	0.145	0.215	0.056	0.132	0.166	0.073	0.106	0.117
2A	0.159	0.239	0.355	0.113	0.190	0.240	0.194	0.226	0.251
2B	0.200	0.298	0.444	0.207	0.300	0.377	0.137	0.158	0.175
3A	0.106	0.211	0.314	—	—	—	—	—	—
3B	0.126	0.275	0.409	0.142	0.256	0.323	0.244	0.283	0.314
4A	0.122	0.254	0.378	0.106	0.231	0.291	0.199	0.243	0.269
4B	0.282	0.379	0.564	0.304	0.448	0.564	0.398	0.423	0.470
4C	0.445	0.529	0.786	0.351	0.427	0.538	0.335	0.356	0.395
4D	0.313	0.407	0.605	0.241	0.317	0.399	0.178	0.197	0.219
4E	0.229	0.337	0.561	0.225	0.338	0.426	0.202	0.266	0.296
4F	0.260	0.353	0.524	0.221	0.285	0.359	0.218	0.255	0.283
5	0.251	0.320	0.475	0.254	0.309	0.389	0.249	0.274	0.305
6	0.298	0.429	0.637	0.298	0.410	0.517	0.301	0.333	0.369
7	0.383	0.481	0.715	0.384	0.467	0.588	0.385	0.423	0.469
8	0.373	0.495	0.736	0.352	0.439	0.553	0.360	0.406	0.450
9	0.383	0.466	0.693	0.387	0.459	0.578	0.408	0.438	0.487
10	0.521	0.613	0.911	0.625	0.716	0.902	0.651	0.715	0.794
11A	0.633	0.695	1.033	0.631	0.684	0.861	0.649	0.674	0.749
11B	0.369	0.435	0.647	0.380	0.442	0.557	0.386	0.403	0.448

Table VIII.5: 36-Sector Employment Multipliers: Moreton Region and State of Queensland

Sector	Moreton Region			State of Queensland		
	Direct[a]	Direct & Indirect	Total	Direct	Direct & Indirect	Total
1	0.122	0.144	0.161	0.054	0.083	0.102
2A	0.089	0.113	0.137	0.078	0.107	0.134
2B	0.111	0.140	0.186	0.122	0.149	0.192
3A	0.046	0.077	0.107	0.014	0.043	0.072
3B	0.050	0.098	0.140	0.024	0.061	0.100
4A1	0.028	0.069	0.099	0.029	0.097	0.135
4A2	0.030	0.084	0.131	0.030	0.092	0.140
4A3	0.053	0.101	0.158	0.054	0.114	0.172
4A4	0.023	0.074	0.111	0.023	0.097	0.134
4A5	0.018	0.065	0.111	0.043	0.094	0.139
4B1	0.043	0.087	0.142	0.050	0.098	0.153
4B2	0.053	0.095	0.156	0.061	0.105	0.165
4B3	0.030	0.064	0.110	0.030	0.058	0.098
4B4	0.068	0.101	0.167	0.073	0.101	0.162
4C1	0.066	0.098	0.152	0.060	0.092	0.148
4C2	0.038	0.069	0.120	0.049	0.074	0.126
4D1	0.027	0.056	0.099	0.031	0.061	0.104
4D2	0.026	0.060	0.095	0.024	0.063	0.105
4D3	0.043	0.067	0.116	0.048	0.073	0.122
4E	0.033	0.073	0.126	0.033	0.069	0.122
4F1	0.015	0.053	0.091	0.017	0.053	0.089
4F2	0.068	0.101	0.148	0.059	0.085	0.127
4F3	0.100	0.125	0.185	0.112	0.134	0.190
4F4	0.042	0.077	0.127	0.043	0.079	0.127
4F5	0.103	0.132	0.187	0.111	0.142	0.196
5A1	0.030	0.044	0.084	0.033	0.047	0.086
5A2	0.048	0.083	0.143	0.047	0.080	0.140
5A3	0.032	0.057	0.108	0.031	0.056	0.104
6	0.061	0.106	0.170	0.061	0.103	0.164
7	0.126	0.148	0.212	0.126	0.146	0.207
8A1	0.074	0.102	0.162	0.074	0.102	0.161
8A2	0.074	0.094	0.152	0.074	0.091	0.146
9	0.049	0.070	0.131	0.050	0.069	0.127
10	0.112	0.142	0.236	0.112	0.139	0.229
11A	0.175	0.194	0.282	0.175	0.193	0.279
11B	0.175	0.196	0.255	0.175	0.199	0.250

[a]Direct employment requirement per $1,000 of output.

Table VIII.6: 19-Sector Employment Multipliers: Provincial Regions of Queensland

	Wide Bay—Burnett			Darling Downs			Fitzroy			Mackay		
Sector	Direct	Direct & Indirect	Total	Direct	Direct & Indirect	Total	Direct	Direct & Indirect	Total	Direct	Direct & Indirect	Total
1	0.089	0.115	0.125	0.051	0.075	0.087	0.051	0.077	0.086	0.046	0.073	0.084
2A	0.081	0.108	0.123	0.068	0.091	0.105	0.106	0.134	0.146	0.074	0.103	0.118
2B	0.198	0.228	0.259	0.134	0.158	0.196	0.129	0.152	0.175	0.104	0.133	0.157
3A	0.199	0.232	0.250	0.020	0.048	0.068	0.009	0.030	0.043	0.006	0.030	0.044
3B	0.042	0.074	0.096	0.075	0.107	0.126	0.043	0.071	0.091	0.080	0.123	0.140
4A	0.028	0.092	0.114	0.030	0.088	0.116	0.038	0.092	0.113	0.025	0.087	0.106
4B	0.078	0.126	0.165	0.071	0.106	0.147	0.063	0.085	0.113	0.072	0.097	0.130
4C	0.046	0.065	0.104	0.066	0.083	0.124	0.033	0.052	0.079	0.088	0.104	0.139
4D	0.070	0.086	0.115	0.032	0.043	0.077	0.016	0.030	0.055	0.120	0.133	0.160
4E	0.045	0.070	0.103	0.042	0.066	0.104	0.028	0.070	0.092	0.032	0.062	0.086
4F	0.117	0.132	0.165	0.020	0.033	0.067	0.041	0.067	0.089	0.030	0.050	0.070
5	0.032	0.051	0.079	0.062	0.076	0.106	0.042	0.058	0.081	0.027	0.043	0.069
6	0.076	0.106	0.142	0.076	0.103	0.144	0.058	0.084	0.115	0.058	0.086	0.117
7	0.168	0.191	0.232	0.123	0.142	0.189	0.121	0.144	0.179	0.160	0.183	0.220
8	0.092	0.115	0.154	0.092	0.111	0.154	0.180	0.204	0.242	0.180	0.203	0.238
9	0.054	0.072	0.112	0.055	0.071	0.117	0.066	0.082	0.116	0.066	0.084	0.121
10	0.137	0.158	0.221	0.137	0.156	0.223	0.134	0.153	0.206	0.134	0.152	0.211
11A	0.188	0.204	0.262	0.188	0.203	0.270	0.134	0.147	0.198	0.134	0.149	0.204
11B	0.261	0.275	0.313	0.203	0.216	0.258	0.196	0.209	0.241	0.203	0.216	0.251

Table VIII.6 (continued)

Sector	Northern			Far North			North West		
	Direct	Direct & Indirect	Total	Direct	Direct & Indirect	Total	Direct	Direct & Indirect	Total
1	0.047	0.065	0.080	0.078	0.103	0.114	0.029	0.050	0.053
2A	0.060	0.078	0.102	0.062	0.088	0.104	0.274	0.297	0.304
2B	0.085	0.105	0.135	0.181	0.211	0.236	0.012	0.018	0.023
3A	0.035	0.054	0.075	—	—	—	—	—	—
3B	0.083	0.110	0.137	0.024	0.057	0.078	0.015	0.024	0.032
4A	0.031	0.069	0.094	0.022	0.078	0.097	0.031	0.049	0.056
4B	0.078	0.098	0.136	0.066	0.122	0.159	0.078	0.085	0.098
4C	0.069	0.085	0.137	0.080	0.102	0.137	0.036	0.042	0.052
4D	0.064	0.082	0.122	0.050	0.069	0.096	0.012	0.018	0.023
4E	0.027	0.053	0.090	0.022	0.052	0.080	0.018	0.032	0.040
4F	0.050	0.068	0.103	0.039	0.057	0.081	0.048	0.057	0.065
5	0.031	0.042	0.074	0.030	0.045	0.071	0.055	0.062	0.070
6	0.031	0.056	0.099	0.076	0.108	0.142	0.076	0.084	0.094
7	0.094	0.110	0.158	0.148	0.171	0.209	0.138	0.147	0.160
8	0.038	0.058	0.107	0.092	0.117	0.153	0.092	0.104	0.116
9	0.039	0.052	0.098	0.054	0.072	0.110	0.054	0.061	0.074
10	0.078	0.091	0.152	0.137	0.160	0.220	0.137	0.153	0.174
11A	0.130	0.141	0.210	0.188	0.203	0.260	0.188	0.195	0.215
11B	0.102	0.113	0.156	0.217	0.232	0.269	0.129	0.134	0.146

APPENDIX IX: INVERSE MATRICES FOR THE ELEVEN-SECTOR TABLES (OPEN MODEL)

Table IX.1: Inverse Matrix, 11-Sector Open Model: Moreton Region

	1	2	3	4	5	6	7	8	9	10	11
1	1.004	0.005	0.006	0.028	0.002	0.010	0.002	0.004	0.001	0.005	0.002
2	0.030	1.025	0.018	0.027	0.003	0.010	0.002	0.006	0.001	0.005	0.002
3	0.002	0.003	1.020	0.012	0.035	0.013	0.003	0.005	0.002	0.004	0.004
4	0.178	0.205	0.289	1.289	0.091	0.470	0.078	0.199	0.036	0.230	0.098
5	0.020	0.023	0.042	0.027	1.028	0.016	0.017	0.014	0.047	0.023	0.056
6	0.020	0.020	0.023	0.020	0.053	1.012	0.022	0.054	0.041	0.111	0.031
7	0.063	0.073	0.122	0.086	0.035	0.132	1.058	0.076	0.067	0.039	0.062
8	0.035	0.048	0.070	0.068	0.056	0.067	0.045	1.037	0.020	0.032	0.020
9	0.012	0.015	0.086	0.036	0.013	0.030	0.131	0.027	1.102	0.042	0.031
10	0.000	0.000	0.000	0.000	0.000	0.000	0.000	0.000	0.000	1.000	0.000
11	0.003	0.000	0.001	0.001	0.001	0.001	0.002	0.003	0.002	0.011	1.002

Table IX.2: Inverse Matrix, 11-Sector Open Model: Wide Bay—Burnett Region

	1	2	3	4	5	6	7	8	9	10	11
1	1.006	0.002	0.005	0.084	0.003	0.012	0.001	0.002	0.001	0.004	0.002
2	0.094	1.122	0.028	0.292	0.010	0.041	0.003	0.012	0.002	0.014	0.006
3	0.001	0.001	1.010	0.002	0.017	0.007	0.001	0.002	0.001	0.001	0.001
4	0.070	0.027	0.058	1.053	0.031	0.148	0.011	0.024	0.007	0.051	0.022
5	0.012	0.013	0.024	0.013	1.018	0.007	0.009	0.007	0.027	0.015	0.038
6	0.020	0.019	0.016	0.017	0.049	1.007	0.019	0.095	0.039	0.117	0.031
7	0.062	0.065	0.113	0.055	0.026	0.082	1.081	0.064	0.055	0.021	0.043
8	0.026	0.037	0.043	0.054	0.052	0.039	0.026	1.014	0.014	0.012	0.012
9	0.005	0.005	0.036	0.012	0.005	0.008	0.069	0.007	1.045	0.024	0.012
10	0.000	0.000	0.000	0.000	0.000	0.000	0.000	0.000	0.000	1.000	0.000
11	0.003	0.000	0.001	0.002	0.000	0.001	0.003	0.001	0.001	0.010	1.001

Table IX.3: Inverse Matrix, 11-Sector Open Model: Darling Downs Region

	1	2	3	4	5	6	7	8	9	10	11
1	1.013	0.007	0.009	0.264	0.003	0.036	0.002	0.004	0.001	0.010	0.006
2	0.096	1.095	0.029	0.091	0.002	0.013	0.001	0.006	0.001	0.004	0.002
3	0.000	0.000	1.011	0.001	0.005	0.005	0.000	0.001	0.000	0.001	0.001
4	0.053	0.027	0.036	1.068	0.012	0.146	0.010	0.018	0.006	0.042	0.025
5	0.009	0.009	0.016	0.010	1.012	0.004	0.006	0.004	0.020	0.009	0.026
6	0.020	0.020	0.019	0.020	0.056	1.007	0.019	0.080	0.033	0.108	0.032
7	0.070	0.072	0.126	0.076	0.024	0.100	1.086	0.080	0.061	0.025	0.050
8	0.027	0.035	0.045	0.067	0.044	0.044	0.028	1.012	0.015	0.015	0.013
9	0.005	0.005	0.033	0.010	0.003	0.009	0.067	0.006	1.046	0.025	0.010
10	0.000	0.000	0.000	0.000	0.000	0.000	0.000	0.000	0.000	1.000	0.000
11	0.003	0.000	0.001	0.001	0.000	0.000	0.002	0.000	0.002	0.008	1.001

Table IX.4: Inverse Matrix, 11-Sector Open Model: Fitzroy Region

	1	2	3	4	5	6	7	8	9	10	11
1	1.006	0.004	0.007	0.131	0.003	0.024	0.002	0.014	0.001	0.007	0.004
2	0.089	1.104	0.012	0.033	0.002	0.006	0.001	0.005	0.000	0.002	0.001
3	0.003	0.003	1.014	0.028	0.094	0.018	0.003	0.010	0.003	0.004	0.006
4	0.050	0.036	0.059	1.113	0.026	0.205	0.019	0.122	0.011	0.062	0.033
5	0.011	0.012	0.040	0.022	1.014	0.009	0.009	0.010	0.027	0.015	0.033
6	0.021	0.019	0.027	0.016	0.041	1.008	0.020	0.123	0.038	0.118	0.032
7	0.065	0.067	0.063	0.054	0.026	0.090	1.083	0.064	0.060	0.023	0.045
8	0.020	0.028	0.033	0.035	0.041	0.033	0.026	1.018	0.011	0.012	0.009
9	0.005	0.006	0.012	0.011	0.005	0.010	0.075	0.011	1.051	0.026	0.012
10	0.000	0.000	0.000	0.002	0.000	0.000	0.000	0.000	0.000	1.000	0.000
11	0.003	0.000	0.001	0.002	0.001	0.001	0.003	0.002	0.002	0.013	1.001

Table IX.5: Inverse Matrix, 11-Sector Open Model: Mackay Region

	1	2	3	4	5	6	7	8	9	10	11
1	1.005	0.003	0.002	0.053	0.001	0.005	0.000	0.001	0.000	0.002	0.001
2	0.117	1.141	0.037	0.463	0.008	0.043	0.004	0.014	0.002	0.015	0.009
3	0.001	0.001	1.017	0.003	0.052	0.007	0.002	0.004	0.002	0.002	0.004
4	0.095	0.059	0.034	1.046	0.015	0.098	0.009	0.027	0.005	0.034	0.020
5	0.012	0.014	0.044	0.014	1.021	0.007	0.009	0.008	0.034	0.016	0.042
6	0.020	0.018	0.027	0.015	0.048	1.005	0.018	0.077	0.032	0.120	0.028
7	0.070	0.066	0.060	0.058	0.029	0.091	1.084	0.072	0.067	0.023	0.046
8	0.020	0.026	0.030	0.036	0.036	0.028	0.022	1.016	0.010	0.011	0.008
9	0.004	0.005	0.006	0.011	0.003	0.007	0.050	0.007	1.035	0.021	0.010
10	0.000	0.000	0.000	0.000	0.000	0.000	0.000	0.000	0.000	1.000	0.000
11	0.002	0.000	0.001	0.003	0.001	0.001	0.003	0.002	0.001	0.009	1.001

Table IX.6: Inverse Matrix, 11-Sector Open Model: Northern Region

	1	2	3	4	5	6	7	8	9	10	11
1	1.004	0.002	0.005	0.074	0.002	0.012	0.001	0.007	0.001	0.005	0.002
2	0.087	1.111	0.035	0.243	0.009	0.041	0.005	0.025	0.002	0.015	0.006
3	0.002	0.002	1.015	0.012	0.053	0.009	0.003	0.007	0.003	0.002	0.005
4	0.058	0.032	0.072	1.060	0.033	0.176	0.019	0.098	0.009	0.066	0.024
5	0.016	0.019	0.055	0.020	1.016	0.010	0.014	0.013	0.046	0.016	0.053
6	0.022	0.018	0.027	0.017	0.041	1.009	0.021	0.100	0.035	0.094	0.031
7	0.079	0.073	0.103	0.071	0.031	0.121	1.093	0.083	0.073	0.032	0.057
8	0.030	0.038	0.053	0.059	0.054	0.049	0.040	1.029	0.017	0.028	0.014
9	0.007	0.007	0.022	0.013	0.005	0.012	0.076	0.013	1.059	0.022	0.015
10	0.000	0.000	0.000	0.000	0.000	0.000	0.000	0.000	0.000	1.000	0.000
11	0.003	0.000	0.001	0.002	0.001	0.001	0.003	0.002	0.002	0.007	1.002

Table IX.7: Inverse Matrix, 11-Sector Open Model: Far North Region

	1	2	3	4	5	6	7	8	9	10	11
1	1.006	0.004	0.003	0.080	0.003	0.011	0.001	0.005	0.001	0.004	0.002
2	0.106	1.130	0.024	0.377	0.013	0.054	0.004	0.026	0.003	0.020	0.009
3	0.000	0.001	1.018	0.004	0.001	0.011	0.000	0.001	0.000	0.001	0.001
4	0.076	0.047	0.045	1.059	0.033	0.152	0.012	0.065	0.008	0.056	0.024
5	0.015	0.018	0.033	0.019	1.017	0.009	0.012	0.011	0.041	0.020	0.048
6	0.020	0.018	0.013	0.017	0.042	1.006	0.019	0.059	0.037	0.116	0.028
7	0.073	0.072	0.134	0.066	0.025	0.104	1.087	0.074	0.065	0.027	0.049
8	0.027	0.036	0.049	0.054	0.044	0.041	0.033	1.026	0.016	0.018	0.012
9	0.005	0.006	0.038	0.013	0.004	0.009	0.062	0.012	1.043	0.022	0.013
10	0.000	0.000	0.000	0.000	0.000	0.000	0.000	0.000	0.000	1.000	0.000
11	0.003	0.000	0.001	0.003	0.001	0.001	0.003	0.004	0.002	0.013	1.001

Table IX.8: Inverse Matrix, 11-Sector Open Model: North West Region

	1	2	3	4	5	6	7	8	9	10	11
1	1.000	0.000	0.000	0.065	0.000	0.002	0.000	0.000	0.000	0.001	0.000
2	0.052	1.024	0.000	0.006	0.000	0.000	0.000	0.000	0.000	0.000	0.000
3	0.000	0.000	1.030	0.007	0.000	0.011	0.000	0.001	0.000	0.001	0.001
4	0.003	0.002	0.005	1.006	0.001	0.033	0.002	0.004	0.001	0.013	0.006
5	0.002	0.002	0.009	0.003	1.001	0.001	0.002	0.002	0.008	0.004	0.010
6	0.017	0.006	0.009	0.012	0.031	1.003	0.016	0.090	0.028	0.120	0.022
7	0.026	0.033	0.031	0.025	0.006	0.031	1.035	0.027	0.022	0.008	0.014
8	0.014	0.013	0.028	0.025	0.034	0.023	0.018	1.011	0.009	0.008	0.006
9	0.001	0.001	0.005	0.003	0.001	0.002	0.028	0.002	1.019	0.016	0.005
10	0.000	0.000	0.000	0.000	0.000	0.000	0.000	0.000	0.000	1.000	0.000
11	0.002	0.000	0.001	0.000	0.001	0.000	0.003	0.004	0.001	0.014	1.001

Table IX.9: Inverse Matrix, 11-Sector Open Model: Central West Region

	1	2	3	4	5	6	7	8	9	10	11
1	1.000	0.000	0.001	0.070	0.000	0.001	0.000	0.000	0.000	0.000	0.000
2	0.112	1.081	0.000	0.023	0.000	0.000	0.000	0.000	0.000	0.000	0.000
3	0.000	0.000	1.001	0.001	0.000	0.007	0.000	0.001	0.000	0.001	0.000
4	0.001	0.002	0.008	1.006	0.001	0.012	0.001	0.001	0.000	0.005	0.004
5	0.009	0.017	0.015	0.016	1.016	0.007	0.010	0.009	0.031	0.021	0.056
6	0.017	0.012	0.015	0.015	0.043	1.003	0.015	0.067	0.025	0.122	0.026
7	0.049	0.038	0.108	0.058	0.014	0.053	1.068	0.054	0.033	0.014	0.029
8	0.020	0.028	0.050	0.039	0.048	0.036	0.024	1.017	0.021	0.012	0.012
9	0.000	0.000	0.003	0.000	0.000	0.001	0.002	0.000	1.003	0.011	0.000
10	0.000	0.000	0.000	0.000	0.000	0.000	0.000	0.000	0.000	1.000	0.000
11	0.002	0.000	0.001	0.000	0.001	0.000	0.003	0.002	0.001	0.010	1.002

Table IX.10: Inverse Matrix, 11-Sector Open Model: South West Region

	1	2	3	4	5	6	7	8	9	10	11
1	1.003	0.003	0.003	0.294	0.001	0.012	0.001	0.002	0.000	0.003	0.002
2	0.121	1.096	0.044	0.105	0.002	0.005	0.000	0.005	0.000	0.001	0.001
3	0.000	0.000	1.023	0.002	0.009	0.013	0.001	0.002	0.001	0.002	0.001
4	0.012	0.009	0.012	1.047	0.004	0.042	0.003	0.006	0.001	0.012	0.008
5	0.007	0.011	0.027	0.011	1.014	0.004	0.006	0.005	0.021	0.011	0.034
6	0.018	0.015	0.024	0.021	0.059	1.005	0.017	0.077	0.027	0.121	0.026
7	0.059	0.054	0.076	0.070	0.019	0.072	1.075	0.063	0.047	0.018	0.038
8	0.022	0.033	0.047	0.063	0.043	0.038	0.026	1.016	0.018	0.011	0.011
9	0.002	0.002	0.006	0.003	0.001	0.003	0.029	0.002	1.018	0.021	0.003
10	0.000	0.000	0.000	0.000	0.000	0.000	0.000	0.000	0.000	1.000	0.000
11	0.003	0.000	0.001	0.001	0.000	0.000	0.003	0.001	0.001	0.007	1.001

Table IX.11: Inverse Matrix, 11-Sector Open Model: Queensland

	1	2	3	4	5	6	7	8	9	10	11
1	1.018	0.018	0.020	0.130	0.008	0.041	0.006	0.017	0.003	0.018	0.008
2	0.113	1.124	0.043	0.156	0.011	0.050	0.007	0.023	0.004	0.022	0.010
3	0.005	0.006	1.030	0.031	0.051	0.022	0.004	0.009	0.003	0.007	0.007
4	0.174	0.165	0.188	1.231	0.075	0.391	0.057	0.162	0.027	0.173	0.075
5	0.019	0.022	0.049	0.027	1.027	0.015	0.015	0.014	0.044	0.022	0.054
6	0.022	0.021	0.023	0.022	0.053	1.012	0.022	0.071	0.040	0.113	0.032
7	0.064	0.067	0.099	0.082	0.034	0.125	1.053	0.070	0.064	0.035	0.059
8	0.038	0.049	0.065	0.073	0.058	0.066	0.043	1.035	0.020	0.031	0.019
9	0.010	0.011	0.047	0.025	0.010	0.022	0.108	0.018	1.083	0.037	0.024
10	0.000	0.000	0.000	0.000	0.000	0.000	0.000	0.000	0.000	1.000	0.000
11	0.003	0.000	0.001	0.001	0.001	0.001	0.003	0.003	0.002	0.011	1.002

APPENDIX X: INVERSE MATRICES FOR THE ELEVEN-SECTOR TABLES (CLOSED MODEL)

Table X.1: Inverse Matrix, 11-Sector Closed Model: Moreton Region

	1	2	3	4	5	6	7	8	9	10	11	House-holds
1	1.006	0.007	0.010	0.033	0.006	0.016	0.008	0.010	0.007	0.014	0.010	0.012
2	0.034	1.031	0.028	0.039	0.013	0.025	0.017	0.020	0.016	0.028	0.021	0.031
3	0.004	0.005	1.022	0.015	0.038	0.017	0.007	0.008	0.006	0.010	0.009	0.008
4	0.253	0.319	0.447	1.488	0.274	0.735	0.346	0.448	0.292	0.624	0.430	0.537
5	0.031	0.039	0.064	0.055	1.054	0.054	0.055	0.050	0.083	0.079	0.103	0.076
6	0.027	0.029	0.037	0.037	0.068	1.034	0.045	0.075	0.062	0.143	0.059	0.045
7	0.118	0.155	0.236	0.230	0.167	0.323	1.251	0.255	0.253	0.323	0.302	0.387
8	0.054	0.077	0.109	0.118	0.102	0.133	0.112	1.099	0.084	0.131	0.103	0.135
9	0.050	0.071	0.165	0.135	0.104	0.161	0.263	0.150	1.229	0.237	0.196	0.266
10	0.001	0.001	0.001	0.002	0.002	0.002	0.002	0.002	0.002	1.003	0.003	0.004
11	0.024	0.032	0.045	0.055	0.051	0.073	0.076	0.071	0.072	0.119	1.093	0.147
House-holds	0.216	0.325	0.451	0.569	0.523	0.756	0.763	0.711	0.732	1.123	0.948	1.531

Table X.2: Inverse Matrix, 11-Sector Closed Model: Wide Bay—Burnett Region

	1	2	3	4	5	6	7	8	9	10	11	Households
1	1.009	0.007	0.011	0.093	0.011	0.023	0.014	0.014	0.013	0.024	0.018	0.027
2	0.115	1.155	0.071	0.350	0.069	0.115	0.090	0.094	0.087	0.146	0.117	0.185
3	0.001	0.001	1.010	0.003	0.017	0.007	0.002	0.002	0.001	0.002	0.002	0.001
4	0.105	0.083	0.130	1.149	0.129	0.269	0.154	0.159	0.147	0.268	0.204	0.305
5	0.016	0.019	0.031	0.023	1.028	0.018	0.023	0.021	0.041	0.036	0.056	0.030
6	0.024	0.024	0.023	0.026	0.058	1.018	0.033	0.108	0.052	0.138	0.048	0.029
7	0.081	0.096	0.152	0.107	0.080	0.149	1.160	0.139	0.132	0.141	0.143	0.168
8	0.035	0.051	0.062	0.079	0.078	0.071	0.064	1.050	0.051	0.070	0.060	0.081
9	0.017	0.023	0.059	0.043	0.037	0.047	0.116	0.051	1.090	0.094	0.071	0.099
10	0.000	0.001	0.001	0.001	0.001	0.001	0.002	0.002	0.002	1.003	0.002	0.004
11	0.009	0.010	0.013	0.018	0.017	0.021	0.027	0.023	0.025	0.046	1.032	0.051
Households	0.148	0.231	0.296	0.397	0.406	0.503	0.591	0.562	0.578	0.898	0.756	1.267

Table X.3: Inverse Matrix, 11-Sector Closed Model: Darling Downs Region

	1	2	3	4	5	6	7	8	9	10	11	House-holds
1	1.021	0.017	0.021	0.286	0.023	0.063	0.034	0.034	0.033	0.056	0.047	0.068
2	0.134	1.140	0.087	0.192	0.097	0.137	0.146	0.140	0.144	0.211	0.188	0.312
3	0.000	0.000	1.011	0.002	0.006	0.005	0.001	0.001	0.001	0.001	0.001	0.001
4	0.084	0.065	0.083	1.151	0.089	0.249	0.129	0.128	0.124	0.213	0.178	0.257
5	0.010	0.011	0.018	0.013	1.015	0.009	0.011	0.009	0.025	0.016	0.033	0.011
6	0.024	0.025	0.025	0.032	0.067	1.021	0.035	0.095	0.049	0.131	0.052	0.034
7	0.103	0.112	0.176	0.163	0.106	0.207	1.212	0.196	0.185	0.205	0.211	0.270
8	0.039	0.049	0.064	0.100	0.075	0.084	0.075	1.055	0.062	0.082	0.073	0.101
9	0.020	0.023	0.056	0.049	0.040	0.057	0.124	0.058	1.102	0.105	0.082	0.122
10	0.000	0.001	0.001	0.001	0.001	0.002	0.002	0.002	0.002	1.003	0.002	0.004
11	0.011	0.010	0.013	0.022	0.020	0.027	0.033	0.028	0.032	0.051	1.040	0.065
House-holds	0.162	0.192	0.246	0.428	0.402	0.528	0.617	0.568	0.610	0.880	0.788	1.325

Table X.4: Inverse Matrix, 11-Sector Closed Model: Fitzroy Region

	1	2	3	4	5	6	7	8	9	10	11	House-holds
1	1.012	0.013	0.017	0.148	0.019	0.046	0.027	0.040	0.025	0.045	0.035	0.052
2	0.098	1.116	0.026	0.056	0.025	0.036	0.035	0.041	0.033	0.054	0.046	0.073
3	0.004	0.005	1.017	0.032	0.098	0.023	0.010	0.017	0.009	0.014	0.014	0.013
4	0.102	0.107	0.140	1.247	0.157	0.377	0.217	0.330	0.201	0.362	0.287	0.419
5	0.015	0.017	0.047	0.033	1.024	0.022	0.024	0.026	0.042	0.038	0.053	0.032
6	0.024	0.024	0.032	0.025	0.049	1.019	0.033	0.136	0.050	0.137	0.048	0.027
7	0.088	0.099	0.099	0.113	0.084	0.167	1.171	0.156	0.144	0.156	0.157	0.185
8	0.025	0.034	0.041	0.048	0.053	0.050	0.045	1.038	0.029	0.040	0.033	0.040
9	0.016	0.020	0.029	0.039	0.032	0.045	0.116	0.053	1.090	0.087	0.064	0.086
10	0.001	0.001	0.001	0.003	0.001	0.002	0.002	0.002	0.002	1.003	0.003	0.004
11	0.012	0.013	0.015	0.026	0.024	0.031	0.038	0.038	0.035	0.066	1.046	0.074
House-holds	0.158	0.219	0.248	0.412	0.404	0.530	0.607	0.638	0.585	0.921	0.781	1.288

Table X.5: Inverse Matrix, 11-Sector Closed Model: Mackay Region

	1	2	3	4	5	6	7	8	9	10	11	House-holds
1	1.008	0.007	0.006	0.058	0.008	0.014	0.011	0.011	0.011	0.018	0.014	0.023
2	0.146	1.185	0.076	0.517	0.078	0.128	0.105	0.109	0.103	0.174	0.138	0.223
3	0.001	0.002	1.017	0.004	0.053	0.008	0.004	0.006	0.003	0.004	0.006	0.003
4	0.148	0.140	0.105	1.145	0.145	0.253	0.196	0.203	0.191	0.329	0.258	0.412
5	0.016	0.020	0.050	0.022	1.030	0.018	0.023	0.021	0.048	0.037	0.060	0.030
6	0.023	0.022	0.031	0.020	0.055	1.014	0.028	0.087	0.043	0.136	0.041	0.023
7	0.089	0.095	0.085	0.092	0.074	0.146	1.150	0.133	0.132	0.126	0.129	0.144
8	0.024	0.032	0.035	0.044	0.046	0.040	0.036	1.029	0.024	0.033	0.026	0.031
9	0.015	0.020	0.020	0.030	0.028	0.037	0.086	0.041	1.070	0.077	0.055	0.078
10	0.000	0.001	0.001	0.001	0.001	0.001	0.001	0.001	0.001	1.002	0.002	0.003
11	0.013	0.017	0.015	0.023	0.026	0.032	0.040	0.038	0.039	0.068	1.049	0.082
House-holds	0.162	0.242	0.214	0.299	0.389	0.468	0.565	0.529	0.560	0.887	0.716	1.238

Table X.6: Inverse Matrix, 11-Sector Closed Model: Northern Region

	1	2	3	4	5	6	7	8	9	10	11	House-holds
1	1.008	0.009	0.012	0.083	0.012	0.025	0.015	0.021	0.014	0.022	0.019	0.029
2	0.117	1.159	0.081	0.304	0.073	0.125	0.102	0.122	0.097	0.138	0.125	0.203
3	0.003	0.004	1.017	0.015	0.056	0.013	0.007	0.011	0.007	0.008	0.011	0.010
4	0.117	0.129	0.164	1.184	0.162	0.346	0.216	0.294	0.200	0.314	0.265	0.411
5	0.026	0.036	0.071	0.041	1.038	0.039	0.048	0.047	0.078	0.058	0.094	0.070
6	0.029	0.030	0.038	0.032	0.057	1.030	0.046	0.125	0.058	0.125	0.061	0.051
7	0.133	0.162	0.187	0.183	0.150	0.276	1.273	0.262	0.248	0.258	0.278	0.376
8	0.055	0.079	0.092	0.112	0.109	0.121	0.124	1.112	0.098	0.132	0.116	0.174
9	0.038	0.059	0.072	0.079	0.075	0.103	0.182	0.117	1.161	0.154	0.144	0.220
10	0.002	0.004	0.004	0.005	0.005	0.007	0.008	0.008	0.008	1.010	0.010	0.017
11	0.025	0.036	0.035	0.047	0.048	0.063	0.075	0.074	0.072	0.098	1.090	0.151
House-holds	0.220	0.362	0.341	0.458	0.480	0.629	0.730	0.727	0.708	0.917	0.894	1.523

Table X.7: Inverse Matrix, 11-Sector Closed Model: Far North Region

	1	2	3	4	5	6	7	8	9	10	11	House-holds
1	1.010	0.009	0.011	0.088	0.012	0.023	0.015	0.018	0.015	0.026	0.020	0.030
2	0.135	1.172	0.080	0.437	0.080	0.142	0.108	0.122	0.105	0.177	0.143	0.222
3	0.001	0.001	1.019	0.004	0.001	0.012	0.001	0.002	0.001	0.003	0.002	0.002
4	0.129	0.123	0.145	1.166	0.154	0.308	0.197	0.236	0.190	0.337	0.263	0.398
5	0.018	0.022	0.039	0.025	1.024	0.017	0.023	0.021	0.051	0.036	0.061	0.023
6	0.024	0.023	0.019	0.024	0.051	1.017	0.031	0.071	0.050	0.136	0.045	0.027
7	0.094	0.103	0.174	0.109	0.074	0.167	1.163	0.143	0.139	0.142	0.147	0.163
8	0.037	0.051	0.068	0.075	0.068	0.071	0.069	1.060	0.051	0.073	0.058	0.077
9	0.018	0.025	0.062	0.040	0.034	0.048	0.108	0.055	1.088	0.092	0.073	0.099
10	0.001	0.001	0.001	0.001	0.001	0.002	0.002	0.002	0.002	1.003	0.003	0.004
11	0.012	0.014	0.018	0.021	0.022	0.028	0.035	0.033	0.033	0.061	1.042	0.068
House-holds	0.167	0.244	0.317	0.341	0.386	0.498	0.592	0.546	0.581	0.899	0.764	1.269

Table X.8: Inverse Matrix, 11-Sector Closed Model: North West Region

	1	2	3	4	5	6	7	8	9	10	11	Households
1	1.001	0.002	0.003	0.068	0.003	0.006	0.004	0.004	0.005	0.008	0.006	0.010
2	0.053	1.026	0.003	0.009	0.003	0.004	0.005	0.005	0.005	0.008	0.006	0.011
3	0.000	0.000	1.030	0.007	0.001	0.012	0.000	0.001	0.001	0.002	0.001	0.001
4	0.008	0.011	0.019	1.020	0.015	0.050	0.023	0.024	0.023	0.049	0.033	0.051
5	0.002	0.003	0.010	0.004	1.002	0.002	0.004	0.003	0.009	0.007	0.012	0.004
6	0.018	0.009	0.014	0.016	0.035	1.008	0.022	0.096	0.035	0.131	0.030	0.015
7	0.031	0.043	0.046	0.040	0.021	0.049	1.058	0.049	0.046	0.047	0.044	0.055
8	0.016	0.018	0.035	0.032	0.041	0.032	0.029	1.022	0.021	0.027	0.020	0.027
9	0.007	0.012	0.023	0.019	0.018	0.023	0.053	0.026	1.046	0.060	0.038	0.061
10	0.000	0.000	0.001	0.001	0.001	0.001	0.001	0.001	0.001	1.002	0.001	0.002
11	0.010	0.015	0.024	0.022	0.023	0.028	0.037	0.037	0.037	0.072	1.046	0.082
Households	0.116	0.206	0.316	0.294	0.307	0.373	0.474	0.454	0.491	0.797	0.604	1.120

Table X.9: Inverse Matrix, 11-Sector Closed Model: Central West Region

	1	2	3	4	5	6	7	8	9	10	11	Households
1	1.006	0.012	0.007	0.079	0.011	0.015	0.017	0.016	0.019	0.028	0.021	0.039
2	0.112	1.082	0.001	0.024	0.002	0.002	0.002	0.002	0.002	0.004	0.003	0.005
3	0.000	0.000	1.001	0.001	0.000	0.008	0.000	0.001	0.000	0.001	0.000	0.000
4	0.007	0.013	0.014	1.014	0.012	0.025	0.017	0.016	0.018	0.032	0.024	0.037
5	0.012	0.022	0.018	0.020	1.020	0.012	0.017	0.015	0.039	0.033	0.065	0.016
6	0.020	0.019	0.019	0.020	0.049	1.011	0.025	0.076	0.035	0.137	0.038	0.022
7	0.076	0.090	0.139	0.095	0.064	0.114	1.142	0.124	0.116	0.136	0.122	0.170
8	0.034	0.054	0.066	0.058	0.074	0.067	0.062	1.053	0.063	0.075	0.060	0.088
9	0.009	0.018	0.014	0.013	0.017	0.022	0.028	0.024	1.031	0.053	0.032	0.059
10	0.001	0.002	0.001	0.001	0.002	0.002	0.002	0.002	0.002	1.004	0.003	0.005
11	0.019	0.032	0.020	0.024	0.032	0.038	0.049	0.045	0.052	0.086	1.059	0.106
Households	0.186	0.362	0.215	0.263	0.350	0.427	0.518	0.487	0.583	0.864	0.654	1.202

Table X.10. Inverse Matrix, 11-Sector Closed Model: South West Region

	1	2	3	4	5	6	7	8	9	10	11	Households
1	1.012	0.016	0.014	0.311	0.019	0.033	0.027	0.026	0.028	0.045	0.034	0.058
2	0.139	1.124	0.066	0.139	0.037	0.049	0.053	0.055	0.056	0.087	0.067	0.119
3	0.000	0.001	1.024	0.002	0.009	0.013	0.001	0.002	0.001	0.002	0.002	0.001
4	0.031	0.039	0.035	1.083	0.043	0.089	0.060	0.059	0.061	0.104	0.078	0.128
5	0.009	0.014	0.030	0.015	1.019	0.010	0.013	0.011	0.028	0.022	0.042	0.015
6	0.022	0.022	0.029	0.028	0.067	1.015	0.029	0.089	0.039	0.140	0.041	0.027
7	0.085	0.093	0.106	0.117	0.069	0.133	1.149	0.133	0.126	0.137	0.129	0.166
8	0.038	0.056	0.065	0.092	0.074	0.075	0.071	1.058	0.065	0.083	0.067	0.101
9	0.015	0.022	0.022	0.027	0.027	0.035	0.067	0.039	1.059	0.084	0.051	0.087
10	0.001	0.001	0.001	0.001	0.001	0.002	0.002	0.002	0.002	1.003	0.002	0.004
11	0.017	0.022	0.017	0.027	0.028	0.034	0.044	0.040	0.045	0.073	1.052	0.092
Households	0.191	0.292	0.226	0.350	0.376	0.458	0.555	0.525	0.586	0.893	0.684	1.247

Table X.11: Inverse Matrix, 11-Sector Closed Model: Queensland

	1	2	3	4	5	6	7	8	9	10	11	House-holds
1	1.028	0.031	0.036	0.152	0.028	0.069	0.034	0.044	0.030	0.060	0.043	0.058
2	0.134	1.154	0.080	0.205	0.056	0.113	0.071	0.084	0.066	0.117	0.090	0.132
3	0.008	0.009	1.035	0.037	0.057	0.030	0.012	0.016	0.011	0.019	0.017	0.017
4	0.257	0.281	0.329	1.418	0.248	0.633	0.303	0.398	0.266	0.537	0.385	0.507
5	0.030	0.037	0.068	0.053	1.050	0.048	0.048	0.046	0.076	0.071	0.095	0.068
6	0.030	0.031	0.036	0.038	0.068	1.033	0.043	0.091	0.060	0.144	0.058	0.043
7	0.120	0.145	0.194	0.208	0.150	0.288	1.218	0.229	0.225	0.279	0.267	0.341
8	0.059	0.078	0.101	0.121	0.102	0.128	0.106	1.096	0.081	0.124	0.098	0.129
9	0.042	0.055	0.101	0.097	0.076	0.115	0.203	0.109	1.175	0.177	0.143	0.195
10	0.001	0.001	0.001	0.001	0.001	0.002	0.002	0.002	0.002	1.003	0.002	0.004
11	0.024	0.029	0.037	0.048	0.044	0.061	0.064	0.061	0.062	0.102	1.079	0.126
House-holds	0.242	0.337	0.412	0.548	0.503	0.708	0.717	0.690	0.699	1.062	0.904	1.478

APPENDIX XI: INVERSE MATRICES FOR THE NON-UNIFORM TABLES (OPEN MODEL)

Table XI.1: Inverse Matrix, 36-Sector Open Model: Moreton Region

	1	2A	2B	3A	3B	4A1	4A2	4A3	4A4	4A5	4B1	4B2	4B3	4B4	4C1	4C2	4D1
1	1.002	0.001	0.001	0.000	0.001	0.155	0.011	0.009	0.009	0.001	0.000	0.001	0.000	0.000	0.000	0.000	0.000
2A	0.033	1.029	0.002	0.000	0.000	0.042	0.123	0.038	0.188	0.035	0.001	0.002	0.001	0.000	0.000	0.000	0.001
2B	0.001	0.002	1.001	0.033	0.002	0.002	0.003	0.001	0.008	0.002	0.114	0.022	0.015	0.002	0.001	0.002	0.002
3A	0.002	0.002	0.002	1.004	0.004	0.004	0.003	0.002	0.003	0.003	0.004	0.003	0.008	0.002	0.003	0.004	0.031
3B	0.001	0.001	0.002	0.035	1.011	0.001	0.002	0.001	0.003	0.004	0.001	0.002	0.002	0.001	0.005	0.003	0.011
4A1	0.013	0.005	0.008	0.001	0.005	1.003	0.074	0.056	0.061	0.009	0.002	0.008	0.002	0.001	0.002	0.003	0.002
4A2	0.001	0.001	0.001	0.000	0.001	0.001	1.004	0.025	0.008	0.026	0.001	0.001	0.001	0.000	0.001	0.001	0.009
4A3	0.018	0.007	0.008	0.000	0.001	0.004	0.009	1.236	0.036	0.005	0.001	0.001	0.014	0.002	0.000	0.000	0.001
4A4	0.031	0.035	0.005	0.000	0.000	0.008	0.048	0.040	1.020	0.082	0.001	0.000	0.001	0.000	0.001	0.000	0.001
4A5	0.001	0.000	0.000	0.000	0.000	0.001	0.000	0.000	0.001	1.001	0.000	0.000	0.000	0.000	0.000	0.000	0.000
4B1	0.002	0.008	0.006	0.008	0.003	0.002	0.004	0.002	0.004	0.007	1.078	0.200	0.010	0.002	0.004	0.014	0.005
4B2	0.001	0.002	0.005	0.002	0.002	0.001	0.002	0.001	0.002	0.003	0.030	1.022	0.002	0.001	0.004	0.006	0.002
4B3	0.005	0.039	0.006	0.004	0.017	0.006	0.025	0.028	0.022	0.033	0.008	0.012	1.230	0.142	0.012	0.006	0.004
4B4	0.001	0.003	0.001	0.001	0.002	0.001	0.005	0.004	0.002	0.029	0.001	0.001	0.026	1.031	0.003	0.001	0.001
4C1	0.010	0.008	0.028	0.030	0.095	0.005	0.009	0.005	0.009	0.009	0.016	0.009	0.013	0.008	1.047	0.052	0.017
4C2	0.005	0.007	0.029	0.018	0.016	0.007	0.014	0.010	0.013	0.013	0.024	0.013	0.020	0.008	0.015	1.012	0.017
4D1	0.002	0.002	0.005	0.011	0.027	0.003	0.014	0.003	0.006	0.011	0.006	0.019	0.004	0.003	0.046	0.060	1.005

4D2	0.001	0.001	0.002	0.002	0.004	0.001	0.003	0.001	0.002	0.002	0.002	0.004	0.002	0.002	0.022	0.010	0.011
4D3	0.010	0.011	0.018	0.030	0.023	0.026	0.130	0.018	0.049	0.105	0.023	0.052	0.019	0.009	0.066	0.106	0.027
4E	0.004	0.004	0.003	0.035	0.041	0.005	0.019	0.004	0.008	0.055	0.008	0.017	0.005	0.003	0.009	0.009	0.026
4F1	0.075	0.073	0.089	0.023	0.074	0.022	0.031	0.024	0.032	0.027	0.053	0.036	0.040	0.019	0.028	0.037	0.035
4F2	0.001	0.003	0.006	0.001	0.002	0.001	0.011	0.002	0.003	0.003	0.005	0.020	0.004	0.001	0.002	0.003	0.003
4F3	0.000	0.000	0.001	0.000	0.001	0.000	0.000	0.000	0.001	0.000	0.000	0.002	0.003	0.000	0.001	0.001	0.001
4F4	0.003	0.004	0.020	0.005	0.039	0.004	0.023	0.014	0.017	0.014	0.007	0.023	0.010	0.008	0.016	0.025	0.004
4F5	0.000	0.000	0.002	0.000	0.001	0.000	0.001	0.001	0.001	0.001	0.001	0.001	0.003	0.002	0.001	0.001	0.001
5A1	0.014	0.018	0.011	0.061	0.025	0.013	0.022	0.022	0.017	0.025	0.039	0.021	0.029	0.016	0.023	0.023	0.048
5A2	0.000	0.000	0.000	0.001	0.001	0.000	0.001	0.005	0.001	0.001	0.001	0.001	0.001	0.001	0.003	0.002	0.003
5A3	0.006	0.007	0.001	0.003	0.006	0.002	0.003	0.002	0.003	0.007	0.002	0.001	0.003	0.001	0.001	0.001	0.002
6	0.022	0.022	0.013	0.030	0.021	0.014	0.031	0.021	0.025	0.032	0.036	0.022	0.033	0.019	0.015	0.014	0.018
7	0.065	0.070	0.123	0.067	0.152	0.063	0.106	0.112	0.088	0.127	0.063	0.085	0.071	0.135	0.093	0.082	0.053
8A1	0.035	0.049	0.037	0.058	0.075	0.066	0.110	0.085	0.094	0.085	0.081	0.068	0.053	0.033	0.059	0.048	0.128
8A2	0.000	0.000	0.000	0.000	0.001	0.000	0.000	0.000	0.000	0.000	0.000	0.000	0.000	0.000	0.000	0.000	0.000
9	0.012	0.015	0.021	0.023	0.120	0.017	0.037	0.036	0.029	0.039	0.068	0.052	0.037	0.052	0.043	0.030	0.022
10	0.000	0.000	0.000	0.000	0.000	0.000	0.000	0.000	0.000	0.000	0.000	0.000	0.000	0.000	0.000	0.000	0.000
11A	0.003	0.000	0.000	0.001	0.001	0.001	0.000	0.000	0.000	0.000	0.000	0.000	0.000	0.000	0.000	0.000	0.000
11B	0.000	0.000	0.000	0.000	0.001	0.000	0.000	0.000	0.000	0.000	0.000	0.000	0.000	0.000	0.000	0.000	0.000

Table XI.1 (continued)

	4D2	4D3	4E	4F1	4F2	4F3	4F4	4F5	5A1	5A2	5A3	6	7	8A1	8A2	9	10	11A	11B
1	0.000	0.000	0.000	0.003	0.009	0.002	0.015	0.001	0.000	0.000	0.000	0.000	0.000	0.000	0.000	0.000	0.000	0.001	0.000
2A	0.000	0.000	0.000	0.002	0.040	0.003	0.005	0.000	0.000	0.000	0.000	0.000	0.000	0.000	0.000	0.000	0.000	0.001	0.001
2B	0.001	0.001	0.002	0.002	0.001	0.002	0.003	0.001	0.002	0.003	0.001	0.006	0.001	0.003	0.001	0.000	0.001	0.001	0.000
3A	0.007	0.004	0.014	0.013	0.002	0.001	0.003	0.005	0.041	0.063	0.005	0.004	0.002	0.004	0.001	0.002	0.002	0.003	0.005
3B	0.151	0.004	0.055	0.005	0.001	0.001	0.002	0.009	0.002	0.003	0.003	0.015	0.001	0.002	0.001	0.001	0.002	0.001	0.001
4A1	0.002	0.001	0.002	0.019	0.023	0.010	0.096	0.005	0.000	0.001	0.001	0.002	0.002	0.002	0.001	0.000	0.002	0.009	0.001
4A2	0.000	0.001	0.001	0.008	0.000	0.000	0.002	0.001	0.000	0.000	0.000	0.001	0.000	0.001	0.000	0.000	0.000	0.003	0.000
4A3	0.001	0.000	0.001	0.007	0.001	0.000	0.002	0.001	0.000	0.000	0.000	0.000	0.000	0.001	0.000	0.000	0.000	0.001	0.000
4A4	0.000	0.000	0.000	0.003	0.002	0.000	0.001	0.000	0.000	0.000	0.000	0.000	0.000	0.000	0.000	0.000	0.000	0.000	0.001
4A5	0.000	0.000	0.000	0.001	0.000	0.000	0.000	0.000	0.000	0.000	0.000	0.000	0.000	0.000	0.000	0.000	0.000	0.000	0.009
4B1	0.003	0.004	0.004	0.004	0.002	0.002	0.007	0.005	0.002	0.003	0.007	0.049	0.003	0.007	0.001	0.002	0.008	0.003	0.001
4B2	0.001	0.002	0.002	0.003	0.001	0.001	0.003	0.003	0.001	0.002	0.005	0.030	0.004	0.003	0.001	0.001	0.011	0.005	0.001
4B3	0.007	0.006	0.026	0.029	0.016	0.022	0.015	0.026	0.001	0.003	0.003	0.008	0.019	0.012	0.004	0.002	0.009	0.005	0.007
4B4	0.001	0.002	0.002	0.012	0.005	0.002	0.004	0.002	0.000	0.001	0.000	0.001	0.002	0.001	0.001	0.000	0.035	0.012	0.001
4C1	0.024	0.018	0.020	0.021	0.005	0.004	0.010	0.014	0.005	0.019	0.013	0.052	0.007	0.010	0.064	0.004	0.029	0.007	0.023
4C2	0.014	0.011	0.022	0.030	0.009	0.006	0.010	0.009	0.031	0.014	0.006	0.011	0.007	0.078	0.005	0.003	0.035	0.003	0.004
4D1	0.014	0.091	0.021	0.013	0.002	0.002	0.006	0.014	0.003	0.004	0.007	0.021	0.002	0.007	0.006	0.001	0.007	0.002	0.002

4D2	1.001	0.016	0.002	0.008	0.002	0.001	0.003	0.017	0.001	0.001	0.002	0.006	0.001	0.002	0.002	0.000	0.002	0.001	0.001
4D3	0.018	1.050	0.022	0.067	0.010	0.010	0.040	0.048	0.008	0.022	0.057	0.107	0.008	0.020	0.031	0.006	0.035	0.013	0.011
4E	0.022	0.009	1.096	0.014	0.004	0.004	0.008	0.005	0.005	0.009	0.018	0.127	0.003	0.010	0.009	0.005	0.015	0.006	0.005
4F1	0.035	0.020	0.041	1.103	0.022	0.016	0.077	0.036	0.011	0.020	0.019	0.042	0.014	0.059	0.007	0.009	0.027	0.016	0.025
4F2	0.002	0.002	0.001	0.002	1.153	0.088	0.024	0.003	0.000	0.001	0.000	0.002	0.001	0.004	0.001	0.000	0.002	0.003	0.005
4F3	0.000	0.000	0.000	0.000	0.001	1.010	0.004	0.001	0.000	0.000	0.000	0.000	0.001	0.000	0.000	0.000	0.005	0.000	0.000
4F4	0.009	0.006	0.007	0.028	0.005	0.070	1.014	0.043	0.002	0.005	0.003	0.008	0.005	0.014	0.006	0.001	0.008	0.004	0.006
4F5	0.000	0.001	0.001	0.001	0.000	0.002	0.005	1.003	0.000	0.000	0.000	0.001	0.002	0.000	0.000	0.000	0.001	0.002	0.000
5A1	0.042	0.021	0.036	0.031	0.017	0.015	0.026	0.018	1.005	0.074	0.084	0.016	0.014	0.013	0.013	0.034	0.020	0.029	0.057
5A2	0.002	0.003	0.004	0.002	0.001	0.001	0.001	0.002	0.001	1.000	0.001	0.002	0.001	0.001	0.000	0.000	0.001	0.003	0.001
5A3	0.002	0.001	0.003	0.003	0.003	0.002	0.002	0.002	0.001	0.001	1.000	0.002	0.002	0.002	0.001	0.012	0.001	0.014	0.017
6	0.016	0.016	0.037	0.027	0.019	0.016	0.022	0.018	0.026	0.049	0.140	1.014	0.023	0.069	0.016	0.041	0.111	0.042	0.013
7	0.073	0.061	0.090	0.114	0.061	0.049	0.105	0.095	0.025	0.082	0.048	0.131	1.038	0.082	0.060	0.067	0.040	0.062	0.064
8A1	0.095	0.055	0.127	0.058	0.050	0.031	0.040	0.040	0.059	0.132	0.023	0.072	0.043	1.030	0.047	0.015	0.028	0.019	0.018
8A2	0.000	0.000	0.000	0.000	0.000	0.000	0.000	0.000	0.000	0.000	0.000	0.000	0.001	0.000	1.000	0.005	0.002	0.000	0.001
9	0.034	0.032	0.041	0.042	0.024	0.049	0.045	0.054	0.010	0.032	0.010	0.032	0.131	0.032	0.015	1.102	0.043	0.013	0.067
10	0.000	0.000	0.000	0.000	0.000	0.000	0.000	0.000	0.000	0.000	0.000	0.000	0.000	0.000	0.000	0.000	1.000	0.000	0.000
11A	0.000	0.000	0.000	0.000	0.000	0.000	0.000	0.000	0.000	0.000	0.000	0.000	0.000	0.002	0.000	0.001	0.010	1.000	0.000
11B	0.000	0.000	0.001	0.000	0.000	0.000	0.000	0.000	0.001	0.000	0.000	0.001	0.002	0.002	0.000	0.001	0.000	0.000	1.004

Table XI.2: Inverse Matrix, 19-Sector Open Model: Wide Bay—Burnett Region

	1	2A	2B	3A	3B	4A	4B	4C	4D	4E	4F	5	6	7	8	9	10	11A	11B
1	1.007	0.000	0.001	0.000	0.000	0.127	0.000	0.000	0.000	0.000	0.003	0.000	0.000	0.000	0.000	0.000	0.000	0.001	0.000
2A	0.097	1.125	0.002	0.000	0.000	0.413	0.000	0.000	0.000	0.000	0.009	0.000	0.000	0.000	0.000	0.000	0.000	0.003	0.001
2B	0.000	0.002	1.001	0.057	0.006	0.001	0.126	0.001	0.001	0.002	0.003	0.002	0.008	0.001	0.006	0.000	0.003	0.002	0.000
3A	0.000	0.000	0.000	1.001	0.000	0.001	0.000	0.000	0.005	0.005	0.001	0.016	0.001	0.001	0.001	0.000	0.000	0.001	0.002
3B	0.000	0.000	0.001	0.020	1.009	0.000	0.000	0.000	0.002	0.033	0.001	0.001	0.008	0.000	0.001	0.000	0.001	0.000	0.000
4A	0.055	0.003	0.004	0.000	0.000	1.034	0.001	0.000	0.000	0.000	0.023	0.000	0.000	0.001	0.000	0.000	0.001	0.008	0.000
4B	0.003	0.012	0.005	0.010	0.003	0.006	1.055	0.010	0.005	0.004	0.006	0.004	0.064	0.005	0.008	0.003	0.025	0.013	0.001
4C	0.009	0.008	0.030	0.014	0.044	0.005	0.015	1.018	0.010	0.016	0.004	0.022	0.013	0.002	0.006	0.002	0.015	0.002	0.003
4D	0.001	0.001	0.002	0.005	0.008	0.002	0.003	0.026	1.022	0.006	0.004	0.002	0.014	0.001	0.002	0.001	0.004	0.001	0.001
4E	0.001	0.001	0.001	0.014	0.004	0.001	0.002	0.002	0.006	1.007	0.001	0.003	0.056	0.001	0.006	0.002	0.007	0.002	0.001
4F	0.001	0.001	0.003	0.000	0.000	0.001	0.001	0.000	0.001	0.000	1.003	0.000	0.001	0.001	0.001	0.000	0.001	0.002	0.002
5	0.012	0.014	0.004	0.045	0.022	0.013	0.012	0.012	0.022	0.023	0.011	1.019	0.007	0.009	0.007	0.027	0.015	0.030	0.056
6	0.020	0.020	0.013	0.029	0.014	0.017	0.021	0.013	0.013	0.032	0.012	0.049	1.008	0.019	0.095	0.039	0.117	0.041	0.008
7	0.061	0.059	0.136	0.059	0.119	0.055	0.063	0.047	0.034	0.050	0.041	0.025	0.082	1.081	0.065	0.055	0.021	0.043	0.042
8	0.026	0.038	0.024	0.042	0.043	0.054	0.049	0.051	0.043	0.088	0.017	0.052	0.040	0.026	1.014	0.014	0.012	0.012	0.010
9	0.005	0.005	0.009	0.008	0.039	0.011	0.014	0.011	0.010	0.012	0.016	0.004	0.008	0.069	0.007	1.045	0.024	0.004	0.029
10	0.000	0.000	0.000	0.000	0.000	0.000	0.000	0.000	0.000	0.000	0.000	0.000	0.000	0.000	0.000	0.000	1.000	0.000	0.000
11A	0.002	0.000	0.000	0.001	0.000	0.001	0.000	0.000	0.000	0.000	0.000	0.000	0.000	0.000	0.000	0.001	0.009	1.000	0.000
11B	0.000	0.000	0.000	0.000	0.001	0.002	0.000	0.000	0.000	0.000	0.000	0.000	0.000	0.003	0.000	0.001	0.000	0.000	1.003

Table XI.3: Inverse Matrix, 19-Sector Open Model: Darling Downs Region

	1	2A	2B	3A	3B	4A	4B	4C	4D	4E	4F	5	6	7	8	9	10	11A	11B
1	1.018	0.004	0.001	0.000	0.000	0.460	0.000	0.000	0.000	0.001	0.029	0.000	0.000	0.001	0.000	0.000	0.001	0.004	0.003
2A	0.097	1.095	0.000	0.000	0.000	0.134	0.000	0.000	0.000	0.000	0.012	0.000	0.000	0.000	0.000	0.000	0.000	0.001	0.002
2B	0.000	0.001	1.000	0.057	0.000	0.001	0.099	0.001	0.001	0.001	0.001	0.001	0.007	0.001	0.005	0.000	0.002	0.001	0.000
3A	0.000	0.000	0.000	1.000	0.000	0.000	0.000	0.000	0.000	0.001	0.000	0.005	0.000	0.000	0.000	0.000	0.000	0.000	0.001
3B	0.000	0.000	0.001	0.025	1.001	0.000	0.000	0.000	0.000	0.030	0.000	0.000	0.006	0.000	0.001	0.000	0.001	0.000	0.000
4A	0.041	0.008	0.002	0.000	0.000	1.067	0.001	0.000	0.000	0.001	0.014	0.000	0.000	0.001	0.000	0.000	0.001	0.010	0.007
4B	0.002	0.009	0.002	0.010	0.002	0.004	1.052	0.004	0.005	0.004	0.003	0.004	0.072	0.005	0.007	0.003	0.023	0.013	0.001
4C	0.007	0.008	0.010	0.006	0.027	0.005	0.003	1.008	0.004	0.003	0.001	0.001	0.007	0.001	0.003	0.001	0.005	0.001	0.002
4D	0.001	0.001	0.001	0.005	0.004	0.002	0.003	0.013	1.014	0.003	0.002	0.003	0.020	0.001	0.002	0.001	0.005	0.002	0.001
4E	0.001	0.001	0.001	0.011	0.003	0.001	0.002	0.001	0.001	1.005	0.001	0.003	0.044	0.001	0.004	0.001	0.005	0.002	0.000
4F	0.000	0.001	0.001	0.000	0.000	0.000	0.001	0.000	0.002	0.008	1.066	0.000	0.001	0.001	0.001	0.000	0.003	0.002	0.003
5	0.009	0.009	0.003	0.030	0.005	0.011	0.007	0.007	0.009	0.012	0.008	1.012	0.004	0.006	0.004	0.020	0.008	0.021	0.039
6	0.020	0.020	0.014	0.029	0.011	0.023	0.020	0.016	0.011	0.029	0.013	0.056	1.007	0.019	0.080	0.033	0.108	0.042	0.007
7	0.071	0.070	0.153	0.069	0.171	0.092	0.084	0.053	0.041	0.062	0.037	0.024	0.099	1.086	0.080	0.061	0.025	0.051	0.049
8	0.028	0.035	0.027	0.046	0.044	0.080	0.051	0.073	0.028	0.108	0.019	0.044	0.044	0.028	1.012	0.015	0.015	0.013	0.011
9	0.005	0.005	0.010	0.008	0.052	0.009	0.014	0.009	0.009	0.011	0.014	0.003	0.009	0.067	0.006	1.046	0.025	0.004	0.023
10	0.000	0.000	0.000	0.000	0.000	0.000	0.000	0.000	0.000	0.000	0.000	0.000	0.000	0.000	0.000	0.000	1.000	0.000	0.000
11A	0.003	0.000	0.000	0.001	0.001	0.001	0.000	0.000	0.000	0.000	0.000	0.000	0.000	0.000	0.000	0.001	0.007	1.000	0.000
11B	0.000	0.000	0.000	0.000	0.000	0.000	0.000	0.000	0.000	0.000	0.000	0.000	0.000	0.002	0.000	0.000	0.000	0.000	1.003

Table XI.4: Inverse Matrix, 19-Sector Open Model: Fitzroy Region

	1	2A	2B	3A	3B	4A	4B	4C	4D	4E	4F	5	6	7	8	9	10	11A	11B
1	1.013	0.002	0.004	0.000	0.000	0.402	0.000	0.000	0.001	0.000	0.023	0.000	0.000	0.001	0.000	0.000	0.000	0.004	0.003
2A	0.091	1.111	0.001	0.000	0.000	0.097	0.000	0.000	0.000	0.000	0.021	0.000	0.000	0.000	0.000	0.000	0.000	0.001	0.002
2B	0.000	0.000	1.000	0.011	0.001	0.001	0.011	0.000	0.000	0.001	0.001	0.001	0.001	0.000	0.001	0.000	0.000	0.000	0.000
3A	0.001	0.002	0.001	1.005	0.004	0.004	0.002	0.006	0.036	0.029	0.010	0.093	0.005	0.003	0.006	0.003	0.002	0.004	0.008
3B	0.000	0.000	0.002	0.008	1.020	0.001	0.001	0.002	0.007	0.120	0.009	0.001	0.016	0.000	0.002	0.001	0.002	0.001	0.001
4A	0.035	0.005	0.011	0.000	0.001	1.059	0.001	0.001	0.003	0.001	0.036	0.000	0.001	0.001	0.000	0.000	0.001	0.009	0.009
4B	0.003	0.017	0.008	0.009	0.005	0.005	1.049	0.012	0.004	0.010	0.009	0.003	0.060	0.008	0.013	0.003	0.023	0.012	0.002
4C	0.005	0.005	0.014	0.013	0.026	0.006	0.005	1.022	0.007	0.015	0.007	0.009	0.012	0.003	0.083	0.002	0.009	0.002	0.003
4D	0.004	0.004	0.007	0.022	0.023	0.013	0.022	0.138	1.091	0.017	0.099	0.010	0.098	0.005	0.025	0.004	0.024	0.008	0.005
4E	0.001	0.001	0.000	0.012	0.017	0.001	0.001	0.001	0.001	1.060	0.001	0.002	0.032	0.001	0.004	0.001	0.004	0.001	0.000
4F	0.002	0.002	0.002	0.001	0.007	0.002	0.003	0.003	0.007	0.003	1.021	0.000	0.001	0.001	0.001	0.001	0.002	0.004	0.003
5	0.011	0.012	0.005	0.043	0.026	0.013	0.010	0.016	0.032	0.031	0.027	1.014	0.009	0.009	0.010	0.027	0.014	0.026	0.051
6	0.021	0.020	0.011	0.028	0.017	0.020	0.017	0.011	0.011	0.037	0.024	0.041	1.008	0.020	0.123	0.038	0.118	0.041	0.008
7	0.066	0.063	0.132	0.054	0.115	0.078	0.070	0.063	0.027	0.073	0.071	0.025	0.090	1.084	0.065	0.060	0.024	0.045	0.045
8	0.021	0.028	0.019	0.032	0.038	0.047	0.029	0.026	0.021	0.105	0.027	0.040	0.034	0.026	1.018	0.011	0.012	0.009	0.009
9	0.005	0.006	0.010	0.008	0.035	0.010	0.017	0.014	0.010	0.015	0.019	0.005	0.010	0.076	0.011	1.051	0.026	0.005	0.031
10	0.000	0.000	0.000	0.000	0.000	0.000	0.000	0.001	0.005	0.000	0.000	0.000	0.000	0.000	0.000	0.000	1.000	0.000	0.000
11A	0.002	0.000	0.000	0.001	0.000	0.001	0.000	0.000	0.004	0.000	0.000	0.000	0.000	0.000	0.001	0.001	0.013	1.000	0.000
11B	0.000	0.000	0.000	0.000	0.001	0.000	0.000	0.000	0.001	0.001	0.000	0.001	0.000	0.003	0.001	0.001	0.000	0.000	1.003

Table XI.5: Inverse Matrix, 19-Sector Open Model: Mackay Region

	1	2A	2B	3A	3B	4A	4B	4C	4D	4E	4F	5	6	7	8	9	10	11A	11B
1	1.002	0.000	0.001	0.000	0.000	0.061	0.000	0.000	0.000	0.000	0.001	0.000	0.000	0.000	0.000	0.000	0.000	0.000	0.000
2A	0.096	1.119	0.006	0.000	0.000	0.532	0.001	0.000	0.000	0.000	0.009	0.000	0.000	0.001	0.000	0.000	0.000	0.004	0.001
2B	0.000	0.000	1.000	0.021	0.000	0.000	0.028	0.000	0.000	0.001	0.000	0.001	0.001	0.000	0.002	0.000	0.001	0.000	0.000
3A	0.001	0.001	0.001	1.003	0.001	0.001	0.001	0.001	0.001	0.015	0.005	0.051	0.001	0.002	0.004	0.002	0.001	0.003	0.006
3B	0.000	0.000	0.001	0.015	1.000	0.000	0.000	0.000	0.000	0.023	0.002	0.001	0.006	0.000	0.001	0.000	0.001	0.000	0.000
4A	0.039	0.002	0.012	0.000	0.001	1.013	0.001	0.000	0.000	0.000	0.018	0.000	0.000	0.001	0.000	0.000	0.001	0.008	0.000
4B	0.002	0.011	0.010	0.009	0.002	0.006	1.044	0.007	0.003	0.004	0.003	0.003	0.053	0.004	0.007	0.002	0.020	0.014	0.001
4C	0.008	0.006	0.021	0.012	0.058	0.004	0.005	1.013	0.007	0.011	0.009	0.009	0.011	0.002	0.016	0.001	0.007	0.002	0.003
4D	0.000	0.000	0.000	0.001	0.000	0.000	0.000	0.002	1.002	0.000	0.001	0.001	0.005	0.003	0.001	0.000	0.001	0.000	0.000
4E	0.001	0.001	0.000	0.009	0.001	0.000	0.001	0.001	0.000	1.002	0.001	0.002	0.027	0.001	0.003	0.001	0.003	0.001	0.000
4F	0.046	0.040	0.011	0.001	0.026	0.022	0.003	0.004	0.004	0.007	1.056	0.000	0.001	0.001	0.001	0.000	0.001	0.004	0.002
5	0.013	0.016	0.006	0.045	0.010	0.014	0.010	0.012	0.012	0.024	0.041	1.021	0.006	0.009	0.008	0.034	0.015	0.030	0.060
6	0.021	0.018	0.009	0.027	0.012	0.014	0.016	0.009	0.010	0.031	0.027	0.048	1.005	0.018	0.077	0.032	0.120	0.042	0.007
7	0.070	0.065	0.133	0.059	0.166	0.056	0.074	0.052	0.043	0.066	0.060	0.029	0.093	1.084	0.072	0.067	0.024	0.048	0.042
8	0.019	0.026	0.017	0.029	0.037	0.036	0.028	0.027	0.021	0.069	0.020	0.036	0.029	0.022	1.016	0.010	0.011	0.009	0.008
9	0.004	0.004	0.007	0.006	0.043	0.011	0.010	0.009	0.007	0.010	0.008	0.003	0.007	0.050	0.007	1.035	0.021	0.003	0.019
10	0.000	0.000	0.000	0.000	0.000	0.000	0.000	0.000	0.000	0.000	0.000	0.000	0.000	0.000	0.000	0.000	1.000	0.000	0.000
11A	0.002	0.000	0.000	0.001	0.000	0.001	0.000	0.000	0.000	0.000	0.000	0.000	0.000	0.000	0.001	0.001	0.009	1.000	0.000
11B	0.000	0.000	0.000	0.000	0.001	0.002	0.000	0.000	0.000	0.000	0.000	0.000	0.000	0.003	0.002	0.001	0.000	0.000	1.002

Table XI.6: Inverse Matrix, 19-Sector Open Model: Northern Region

	1	2A	2B	3A	3B	4A	4B	4C	4D	4E	4F	5	6	7	8	9	10	11A	11B
1	1.004	0.001	0.002	0.000	0.000	0.103	0.000	0.000	0.000	0.000	0.002	0.000	0.000	0.000	0.000	0.000	0.000	0.001	0.000
2A	0.088	1.107	0.007	0.000	0.000	0.335	0.000	0.000	0.000	0.000	0.006	0.000	0.000	0.000	0.000	0.000	0.001	0.002	0.001
2B	0.000	0.001	1.000	0.025	0.002	0.001	0.026	0.000	0.000	0.001	0.001	0.002	0.001	0.000	0.002	0.000	0.000	0.000	0.000
3A	0.001	0.001	0.001	1.005	0.003	0.002	0.002	0.002	0.008	0.028	0.004	0.052	0.004	0.003	0.005	0.003	0.001	0.003	0.007
3B	0.000	0.000	0.001	0.016	1.007	0.000	0.001	0.004	0.044	0.049	0.004	0.002	0.012	0.000	0.002	0.001	0.002	0.001	0.001
4A	0.043	0.005	0.020	0.001	0.000	1.026	0.001	0.000	0.000	0.000	0.017	0.000	0.000	0.001	0.000	0.000	0.002	0.007	0.000
4B	0.002	0.015	0.006	0.004	0.006	0.006	1.040	0.005	0.002	0.011	0.009	0.002	0.026	0.008	0.007	0.001	0.007	0.006	0.002
4C	0.006	0.005	0.028	0.013	0.024	0.006	0.008	1.014	0.009	0.015	0.007	0.019	0.008	0.004	0.070	0.002	0.034	0.002	0.003
4D	0.003	0.003	0.006	0.018	0.022	0.004	0.016	0.083	1.065	0.018	0.053	0.008	0.074	0.003	0.014	0.003	0.017	0.006	0.004
4E	0.002	0.001	0.001	0.030	0.035	0.001	0.003	0.001	0.005	1.083	0.002	0.005	0.074	0.002	0.009	0.003	0.007	0.004	0.001
4F	0.003	0.002	0.005	0.001	0.008	0.001	0.004	0.001	0.006	0.002	1.015	0.000	0.001	0.001	0.002	0.000	0.002	0.006	0.004
5	0.016	0.020	0.010	0.069	0.030	0.016	0.021	0.017	0.032	0.047	0.030	1.017	0.012	0.015	0.014	0.046	0.016	0.038	0.075
6	0.022	0.018	0.009	0.031	0.019	0.016	0.021	0.009	0.014	0.037	0.020	0.041	1.010	0.021	0.100	0.035	0.094	0.046	0.009
7	0.079	0.071	0.149	0.073	0.165	0.070	0.089	0.067	0.053	0.080	0.077	0.030	0.121	1.093	0.083	0.073	0.031	0.057	0.057
8	0.030	0.038	0.027	0.050	0.060	0.058	0.044	0.032	0.061	0.118	0.031	0.053	0.052	0.040	1.027	0.017	0.027	0.014	0.014
9	0.007	0.007	0.011	0.010	0.048	0.012	0.021	0.011	0.010	0.016	0.019	0.005	0.013	0.077	0.012	1.059	0.022	0.006	0.028
10	0.000	0.000	0.000	0.000	0.000	0.000	0.000	0.000	0.000	0.000	0.000	0.000	0.000	0.000	0.000	0.000	1.000	0.000	0.000
11A	0.003	0.000	0.000	0.001	0.001	0.001	0.000	0.000	0.000	0.000	0.000	0.000	0.000	0.000	0.001	0.001	0.006	1.000	0.000
11B	0.000	0.000	0.000	0.000	0.001	0.002	0.000	0.000	0.000	0.001	0.000	0.001	0.000	0.002	0.001	0.001	0.000	0.000	1.003

Table XI.7: Inverse Matrix, 19-Sector Open Model: Far North Region

	1	2A	2B	3A	3B	4A	4B	4C	4D	4E	4F	5	6	7	8	9	10	11A	11B
1	1.004	0.001	0.001	0.000	0.000	0.101	0.000	0.000	0.000	0.000	0.004	0.000	0.000	0.000	0.000	0.000	0.000	0.001	0.001
2A	0.098	1.121	0.006	0.000	0.000	0.456	0.001	0.000	0.000	0.000	0.016	0.000	0.000	0.001	0.000	0.000	0.000	0.003	0.006
2B	0.001	0.002	1.002	0.000	0.008	0.002	0.149	0.004	0.001	0.002	0.001	0.001	0.011	0.001	0.004	0.001	0.003	0.002	0.000
3A	0.000	0.000	0.000	1.000	0.000	0.000	0.000	0.000	0.000	0.000	0.000	0.000	0.000	0.000	0.000	0.000	0.000	0.000	0.000
3B	0.001	0.001	0.001	0.000	1.019	0.001	0.001	0.002	0.036	0.080	0.008	0.001	0.015	0.000	0.001	0.001	0.002	0.001	0.000
4A	0.042	0.006	0.014	0.000	0.000	1.021	0.002	0.000	0.000	0.000	0.036	0.000	0.000	0.001	0.000	0.000	0.001	0.008	0.012
4B	0.003	0.012	0.014	0.000	0.003	0.007	1.111	0.025	0.006	0.005	0.006	0.004	0.080	0.005	0.009	0.003	0.025	0.011	0.001
4C	0.006	0.006	0.039	0.000	0.028	0.006	0.019	1.015	0.011	0.015	0.012	0.024	0.011	0.003	0.050	0.002	0.020	0.003	0.007
4D	0.001	0.001	0.004	0.000	0.010	0.001	0.005	0.044	1.033	0.011	0.014	0.004	0.021	0.001	0.004	0.001	0.007	0.002	0.002
4E	0.001	0.001	0.000	0.000	0.004	0.001	0.002	0.001	0.002	1.006	0.001	0.002	0.045	0.001	0.004	0.002	0.005	0.002	0.000
4F	0.023	0.020	0.005	0.000	0.000	0.010	0.001	0.000	0.000	0.000	1.001	0.000	0.000	0.000	0.000	0.000	0.000	0.000	0.001
5	0.016	0.019	0.009	0.000	0.033	0.017	0.028	0.016	0.032	0.023	0.022	1.017	0.010	0.013	0.011	0.041	0.020	0.035	0.074
6	0.020	0.018	0.008	0.000	0.012	0.015	0.026	0.009	0.013	0.026	0.018	0.042	1.007	0.019	0.059	0.037	0.117	0.038	0.008
7	0.072	0.069	0.137	0.000	0.134	0.064	0.076	0.073	0.049	0.079	0.055	0.025	0.105	1.087	0.074	0.065	0.027	0.050	0.048
8	0.026	0.036	0.024	0.000	0.048	0.054	0.051	0.032	0.059	0.112	0.031	0.044	0.043	0.033	1.026	0.016	0.018	0.012	0.012
9	0.005	0.006	0.009	0.000	0.038	0.012	0.022	0.012	0.012	0.016	0.011	0.004	0.010	0.062	0.012	1.043	0.022	0.005	0.029
10	0.000	0.000	0.000	0.000	0.000	0.000	0.000	0.000	0.000	0.000	0.000	0.000	0.000	0.000	0.000	0.000	1.000	0.000	0.000
11A	0.003	0.000	0.000	0.000	0.000	0.001	0.000	0.000	0.000	0.000	0.000	0.000	0.000	0.000	0.002	0.001	0.012	1.000	0.000
11B	0.000	0.000	0.000	0.000	0.001	0.002	0.000	0.000	0.000	0.001	0.000	0.001	0.000	0.003	0.002	0.001	0.000	0.000	1.003

Table XI.8: Inverse Matrix, 19-Sector Open Model: North West Region

	1	2A	2B	3A	3B	4A	4B	4C	4D	4E	4F	5	6	7	8	9	10	11A	11B
1	1.000	0.000	0.000	0.000	0.000	0.175	0.000	0.000	0.000	0.000	0.040	0.000	0.000	0.000	0.000	0.000	0.000	0.000	0.000
2A	0.054	1.062	0.000	0.000	0.000	0.015	0.000	0.000	0.000	0.000	0.002	0.000	0.000	0.000	0.000	0.000	0.000	0.000	0.001
2B	0.000	0.000	1.000	0.000	0.000	0.001	0.000	0.000	0.000	0.000	0.009	0.000	0.000	0.000	0.000	0.000	0.000	0.000	0.000
3A	0.000	0.000	0.000	1.000	0.000	0.000	0.000	0.000	0.000	0.000	0.000	0.000	0.000	0.000	0.000	0.000	0.000	0.000	0.000
3B	0.000	0.000	0.000	0.000	1.030	0.000	0.000	0.000	0.000	0.067	0.000	0.000	0.012	0.000	0.001	0.000	0.001	0.001	0.000
4A	0.001	0.000	0.002	0.000	0.000	1.005	0.000	0.000	0.000	0.000	0.045	0.000	0.000	0.000	0.000	0.000	0.000	0.001	0.000
4B	0.000	0.000	0.000	0.000	0.000	0.000	1.003	0.000	0.000	0.000	0.000	0.000	0.000	0.000	0.000	0.000	0.007	0.007	0.000
4C	0.001	0.000	0.000	0.000	0.003	0.000	0.001	1.002	0.001	0.000	0.001	0.000	0.003	0.000	0.001	0.000	0.001	0.000	0.001
4D	0.000	0.000	0.000	0.000	0.001	0.000	0.001	0.006	1.005	0.001	0.004	0.001	0.020	0.000	0.002	0.001	0.003	0.001	0.000
4E	0.000	0.000	0.000	0.000	0.001	0.000	0.000	0.000	0.000	1.001	0.000	0.000	0.010	0.000	0.001	0.000	0.001	0.000	0.000
4F	0.000	0.000	0.000	0.000	0.000	0.000	0.000	0.000	0.000	0.000	1.000	0.000	0.000	0.000	0.000	0.000	0.000	0.000	0.000
5	0.002	0.003	0.002	0.000	0.009	0.003	0.001	0.003	0.003	0.004	0.000	1.001	0.001	0.002	0.002	0.008	0.004	0.005	0.015
6	0.017	0.013	0.001	0.000	0.009	0.014	0.010	0.007	0.010	0.022	0.018	0.031	1.003	0.016	0.089	0.028	0.121	0.039	0.004
7	0.025	0.021	0.040	0.000	0.031	0.032	0.038	0.019	0.017	0.025	0.020	0.006	0.031	1.035	0.027	0.022	0.008	0.015	0.014
8	0.014	0.020	0.009	0.000	0.028	0.024	0.011	0.019	0.018	0.076	0.020	0.034	0.023	0.018	1.011	0.009	0.008	0.006	0.005
9	0.001	0.001	0.001	0.000	0.005	0.003	0.004	0.004	0.003	0.004	0.004	0.001	0.002	0.028	0.002	1.019	0.016	0.001	0.009
10	0.000	0.000	0.000	0.000	0.000	0.000	0.000	0.000	0.000	0.000	0.000	0.000	0.000	0.000	0.000	0.000	1.000	0.000	0.000
11A	0.001	0.000	0.000	0.000	0.000	0.000	0.000	0.000	0.000	0.000	0.000	0.000	0.000	0.000	0.002	0.001	0.014	1.000	0.000
11B	0.000	0.000	0.000	0.000	0.001	0.000	0.000	0.000	0.000	0.001	0.000	0.000	0.000	0.003	0.002	0.000	0.000	0.000	1.002

Table XI.9: Inverse Matrix, 36-Sector Open Model: Queensland

	1	2A	2B	3A	3B	4A1	4A2	4A3	4A4	4A5	4B1	4B2	4B3	4B4	4C1	4C2	4D1	4D2
1	1.007	0.001	0.004	0.000	0.002	0.604	0.043	0.033	0.001	0.003	0.001	0.004	0.001	0.001	0.001	0.001	0.001	0.001
2A	0.118	1.120	0.005	0.000	0.001	0.113	0.263	0.166	0.702	0.146	0.001	0.002	0.002	0.000	0.001	0.001	0.003	0.001
2B	0.001	0.002	1.001	0.041	0.006	0.003	0.003	0.001	0.002	0.002	0.154	0.036	0.016	0.001	0.002	0.003	0.004	0.003
3A	0.002	0.003	0.002	1.005	0.004	0.006	0.004	0.003	0.002	0.004	0.004	0.003	0.010	0.002	0.004	0.004	0.045	0.011
3B	0.003	0.003	0.005	0.038	1.026	0.003	0.005	0.002	0.002	0.006	0.004	0.010	0.005	0.003	0.037	0.018	0.034	0.347
4A1	0.011	0.002	0.006	0.001	0.002	1.007	0.071	0.054	0.002	0.004	0.002	0.005	0.002	0.001	0.001	0.002	0.001	0.001
4A2	0.001	0.001	0.001	0.000	0.000	0.001	1.004	0.025	0.001	0.029	0.001	0.000	0.001	0.000	0.001	0.001	0.009	0.000
4A3	0.015	0.003	0.006	0.000	0.001	0.010	0.008	1.234	0.002	0.002	0.001	0.001	0.012	0.001	0.000	0.000	0.001	0.001
4A4	0.035	0.015	0.005	0.000	0.000	0.024	0.063	0.054	1.012	0.124	0.001	0.001	0.001	0.000	0.001	0.000	0.001	0.000
4A5	0.001	0.000	0.000	0.000	0.000	0.001	0.000	0.000	0.000	1.001	0.000	0.000	0.000	0.000	0.000	0.000	0.000	0.000
4B1	0.003	0.011	0.006	0.010	0.003	0.003	0.005	0.004	0.007	0.009	1.071	0.238	0.011	0.002	0.005	0.017	0.006	0.004
4B2	0.001	0.002	0.004	0.002	0.001	0.002	0.002	0.001	0.001	0.003	0.031	1.021	0.002	0.001	0.004	0.007	0.002	0.001
4B3	0.006	0.031	0.003	0.002	0.010	0.007	0.022	0.025	0.020	0.026	0.004	0.009	1.130	0.077	0.008	0.004	0.003	0.006
4B4	0.001	0.002	0.001	0.000	0.001	0.001	0.003	0.002	0.001	0.013	0.000	0.001	0.016	1.022	0.002	0.000	0.000	0.001
4C1	0.012	0.010	0.022	0.020	0.052	0.009	0.008	0.005	0.007	0.006	0.013	0.007	0.009	0.005	1.032	0.043	0.014	0.024
4C2	0.005	0.007	0.024	0.016	0.013	0.010	0.014	0.010	0.007	0.011	0.024	0.013	0.017	0.007	0.015	1.010	0.017	0.015
4D1	0.001	0.002	0.003	0.007	0.014	0.002	0.007	0.002	0.001	0.005	0.004	0.011	0.002	0.001	0.034	0.040	1.003	0.011

4D2	0.005	0.005	0.006	0.006	0.016	0.005	0.011	0.003	0.003	0.008	0.007	0.024	0.008	0.007	0.102	0.047	0.061	0.090
4D3	0.006	0.007	0.010	0.022	0.012	0.019	0.083	0.011	0.005	0.068	0.017	0.032	0.012	0.006	0.045	0.073	0.020	1.036
4E	0.003	0.003	0.002	0.034	0.042	0.005	0.012	0.003	0.003	0.034	0.006	0.014	0.004	0.002	0.008	0.006	0.022	0.008
4F1	0.072	0.071	0.061	0.015	0.040	0.050	0.032	0.024	0.046	0.023	0.035	0.027	0.026	0.010	0.019	0.022	0.026	0.015
4F2	0.001	0.002	0.004	0.001	0.001	0.001	0.004	0.002	0.001	0.002	0.003	0.012	0.004	0.001	0.001	0.002	0.002	0.003
4F3	0.000	0.000	0.001	0.000	0.001	0.000	0.000	0.000	0.000	0.000	0.000	0.001	0.002	0.000	0.000	0.001	0.001	0.000
4F4	0.002	0.002	0.010	0.002	0.018	0.003	0.013	0.008	0.002	0.008	0.004	0.012	0.005	0.004	0.009	0.012	0.003	0.004
4F5	0.000	0.000	0.001	0.000	0.000	0.000	0.000	0.001	0.000	0.000	0.000	0.001	0.002	0.001	0.001	0.000	0.000	0.000
5A1	0.014	0.017	0.010	0.062	0.034	0.019	0.023	0.023	0.014	0.024	0.034	0.021	0.027	0.013	0.025	0.022	0.051	0.023
5A2	0.000	0.000	0.000	0.000	0.000	0.000	0.001	0.004	0.002	0.001	0.000	0.000	0.000	0.000	0.002	0.001	0.003	0.002
5A3	0.005	0.006	0.000	0.002	0.006	0.004	0.003	0.003	0.005	0.006	0.001	0.001	0.002	0.001	0.001	0.001	0.002	0.001
6	0.024	0.023	0.013	0.032	0.020	0.026	0.035	0.025	0.019	0.032	0.036	0.023	0.031	0.018	0.018	0.014	0.021	0.018
7	0.065	0.065	0.113	0.063	0.122	0.090	0.106	0.113	0.056	0.125	0.057	0.083	0.062	0.129	0.090	0.080	0.055	0.063
8A1	0.037	0.048	0.036	0.059	0.070	0.082	0.111	0.091	0.062	0.078	0.083	0.072	0.048	0.030	0.074	0.047	0.135	0.058
8A2	0.000	0.000	0.000	0.000	0.000	0.000	0.000	0.000	0.005	0.001	0.000	0.000	0.000	0.000	0.000	0.000	0.000	0.000
9	0.010	0.011	0.015	0.016	0.066	0.018	0.028	0.028	0.019	0.028	0.040	0.037	0.025	0.037	0.032	0.022	0.018	0.026
10	0.000	0.000	0.000	0.000	0.000	0.000	0.000	0.000	0.000	0.000	0.000	0.000	0.000	0.000	0.000	0.000	0.000	0.000
11A	0.003	0.000	0.000	0.001	0.001	0.002	0.000	0.000	0.001	0.000	0.000	0.000	0.000	0.000	0.000	0.000	0.000	0.000
11B	0.000	0.000	0.000	0.000	0.001	0.000	0.001	0.001	0.003	0.001	0.000	0.000	0.000	0.000	0.000	0.000	0.000	0.000

Table XI.9 (continued)

	4D3	4E	4F1	4F2	4F3	4F4	4F5	5A1	5A2	5A3	6	7	8A1	8A2	9	10	11A	11B
1	0.001	0.001	0.011	0.053	0.008	0.071	0.003	0.000	0.000	0.000	0.001	0.001	0.001	0.000	0.000	0.001	0.006	0.001
2A	0.000	0.000	0.007	0.018	0.002	0.013	0.003	0.000	0.000	0.000	0.001	0.000	0.001	0.000	0.000	0.001	0.002	0.002
2B	0.001	0.003	0.002	0.001	0.003	0.004	0.002	0.003	0.005	0.002	0.009	0.001	0.005	0.001	0.001	0.002	0.001	0.001
3A	0.005	0.020	0.017	0.004	0.002	0.004	0.007	0.058	0.090	0.007	0.004	0.003	0.006	0.001	0.002	0.002	0.003	0.007
3B	0.032	0.077	0.021	0.004	0.002	0.007	0.041	0.004	0.006	0.006	0.027	0.001	0.005	0.003	0.001	0.005	0.002	0.002
4A1	0.001	0.001	0.018	0.005	0.007	0.097	0.003	0.000	0.001	0.000	0.001	0.002	0.001	0.000	0.000	0.002	0.009	0.001
4A2	0.001	0.000	0.007	0.000	0.000	0.002	0.000	0.000	0.000	0.000	0.001	0.000	0.000	0.000	0.000	0.000	0.003	0.000
4A3	0.000	0.001	0.009	0.003	0.001	0.002	0.001	0.000	0.000	0.000	0.000	0.000	0.000	0.000	0.000	0.000	0.001	0.000
4A4	0.000	0.000	0.004	0.002	0.000	0.003	0.000	0.000	0.000	0.000	0.000	0.000	0.000	0.000	0.000	0.000	0.001	0.001
4A5	0.000	0.000	0.001	0.000	0.000	0.000	0.000	0.000	0.000	0.000	0.000	0.000	0.000	0.000	0.000	0.000	0.000	0.009
4B1	0.004	0.005	0.005	0.002	0.002	0.008	0.007	0.003	0.005	0.008	0.057	0.004	0.010	0.001	0.002	0.009	0.004	0.001
4B2	0.003	0.002	0.003	0.001	0.001	0.004	0.003	0.001	0.002	0.005	0.031	0.004	0.004	0.001	0.001	0.011	0.005	0.001
4B3	0.005	0.019	0.021	0.012	0.017	0.011	0.019	0.001	0.003	0.002	0.005	0.015	0.009	0.003	0.001	0.005	0.003	0.005
4B4	0.001	0.001	0.008	0.004	0.001	0.003	0.001	0.000	0.000	0.000	0.001	0.001	0.001	0.000	0.000	0.024	0.011	0.000
4C1	0.014	0.014	0.014	0.004	0.003	0.007	0.011	0.004	0.014	0.009	0.034	0.004	0.008	0.040	0.003	0.019	0.004	0.013
4C2	0.010	0.021	0.027	0.008	0.005	0.010	0.009	0.031	0.015	0.006	0.010	0.006	0.080	0.005	0.002	0.031	0.003	0.004
4D1	0.063	0.014	0.008	0.001	0.001	0.003	0.010	0.002	0.003	0.004	0.013	0.001	0.005	0.003	0.001	0.004	0.001	0.001

4D2	1.008	0.009	0.043	0.010	0.003	0.018	0.096	0.003	0.005	0.008	0.027	0.002	0.008	0.006	0.002	0.008	0.003	0.003
4D3	0.014	0.015	0.042	0.008	0.006	0.028	0.033	0.006	0.017	0.042	0.084	0.006	0.015	0.020	0.004	0.024	0.009	0.007
4E	0.026	1.095	0.011	0.004	0.003	0.006	0.006	0.005	0.008	0.016	0.105	0.003	0.010	0.008	0.004	0.012	0.005	0.003
4F1	0.030	0.025	1.083	0.023	0.011	0.069	0.030	0.007	0.012	0.012	0.027	0.008	0.033	0.004	0.005	0.017	0.011	0.015
4F2	0.001	0.003	0.001	1.108	0.078	0.014	0.007	0.000	0.001	0.000	0.001	0.001	0.003	0.000	0.000	0.002	0.003	0.005
4F3	0.000	0.000	0.000	0.001	1.006	0.002	0.000	0.000	0.000	0.000	0.000	0.000	0.000	0.000	0.000	0.004	0.000	0.000
4F4	0.007	0.004	0.017	0.004	0.057	1.008	0.026	0.001	0.003	0.001	0.004	0.003	0.007	0.003	0.000	0.004	0.002	0.003
4F5	0.000	0.000	0.001	0.000	0.001	0.003	1.002	0.000	0.000	0.000	0.000	0.001	0.000	0.000	0.000	0.000	0.001	0.000
5A1	0.050	0.037	0.034	0.024	0.014	0.027	0.021	1.006	0.077	0.086	0.015	0.014	0.012	0.012	0.034	0.020	0.029	0.060
5A2	0.001	0.003	0.002	0.001	0.000	0.001	0.002	0.001	1.000	0.000	0.001	0.001	0.001	0.000	0.000	0.001	0.002	0.001
5A3	0.002	0.003	0.003	0.003	0.001	0.002	0.001	0.000	0.001	1.000	0.002	0.001	0.001	0.001	0.010	0.001	0.012	0.014
6	0.021	0.039	0.028	0.021	0.016	0.023	0.020	0.028	0.053	0.144	1.015	0.023	0.090	0.016	0.040	0.113	0.043	0.012
7	0.089	0.085	0.108	0.041	0.043	0.104	0.099	0.025	0.081	0.047	0.124	1.053	0.075	0.056	0.064	0.035	0.059	0.058
8A1	0.107	0.130	0.058	0.035	0.028	0.041	0.047	0.062	0.137	0.023	0.070	0.042	1.029	0.045	0.014	0.027	0.018	0.017
8A2	0.000	0.000	0.000	0.000	0.000	0.000	0.000	0.000	0.000	0.000	0.000	0.001	0.000	1.000	0.005	0.002	0.000	0.001
9	0.034	0.029	0.031	0.021	0.035	0.034	0.042	0.008	0.024	0.008	0.024	0.109	0.022	0.010	1.083	0.037	0.010	0.050
10	0.000	0.000	0.000	0.000	0.000	0.000	0.000	0.000	0.000	0.000	0.000	0.000	0.000	0.000	0.000	1.000	0.000	0.000
11A	0.000	0.000	0.000	0.000	0.000	0.000	0.000	0.000	0.000	0.000	0.000	0.000	0.001	0.000	0.001	0.010	1.000	0.000
11B	0.001	0.001	0.000	0.000	0.000	0.000	0.000	0.001	0.000	0.000	0.001	0.002	0.002	0.000	0.001	0.000	0.000	1.003

APPENDIX XII: INVERSE MATRICES FOR THE NON-UNIFORM TABLES (CLOSED MODEL)

Table XII.1: Inverse Matrix, 36-Sector Closed Model: Moreton Region

	1	2A	2B	3A	3B	4A1	4A2	4A3	4A4	4A5	4B1	4B2	4B3	4B4	4C1	4C2	4D1	4D2	4D3
1	1.005	0.004	0.008	0.005	0.007	0.160	0.019	0.017	0.015	0.008	0.009	0.011	0.007	0.010	0.009	0.008	0.007	0.005	0.008
2A	0.037	1.035	0.013	0.008	0.011	0.049	0.135	0.052	0.197	0.047	0.014	0.017	0.012	0.017	0.014	0.013	0.012	0.009	0.013
2B	0.001	0.002	1.002	0.034	0.003	0.002	0.004	0,002	0.009	0.003	0.115	0.023	0.016	0.003	0.002	0.003	0.003	0.002	0.002
3A	0.002	0.003	0.003	1.005	0.005	0.005	0.005	0.004	0.004	0.005	0.006	0.005	0.010	0.004	0.005	0.006	0.033	0.009	0.006
3B	0.001	0.001	0.003	0.035	1.011	0.001	0.003	0.001	0.003	0.004	0.002	0.003	0.003	0.002	0.005	0.003	0.011	0.151	0.004
4A1	0.029	0.028	0.052	0.030	0.045	1.031	0.119	0.110	0.097	0.053	0.055	0.066	0.047	0.064	0.054	0.052	0.043	0.034	0.048
4A2	0.006	0.008	0.013	0.009	0.012	0.009	1.017	0.041	0.018	0.038	0.016	0.017	0.013	0.018	0.016	0.015	0.021	0.010	0.014
4A3	0.022	0.013	0.018	0.007	0.010	0.011	0.020	1.249	0.045	0.015	0.014	0.015	0.025	0.017	0.013	0.012	0.011	0.009	0.012
4A4	0.034	0.039	0.013	0.006	0.008	0.014	0.056	0.051	1.026	0.090	0.011	0.012	0.009	0.012	0.010	0.010	0.009	0.006	0.009
4A5	0.006	0.007	0.013	0.009	0.012	0.009	0.014	0.016	0.012	1.014	0.016	0.017	0.013	0.019	0.015	0.015	0.013	0.010	0.014
4B1	0.003	0.010	0.009	0.010	0.005	0.003	0.006	0.005	0.006	0.010	1.081	0.204	0.012	0.006	0.007	0.017	0.007	0.005	0.007
4B2	0.003	0.004	0.009	0.005	0.006	0.004	0.006	0.007	0.005	0.007	0.035	1.028	0.006	0.008	0.009	0.011	0.006	0.004	0.007
4B3	0.008	0.042	0.012	0.008	0.023	0.010	0.032	0.037	0.027	0.040	0.016	0.021	1.237	0.152	0.020	0.013	0.011	0.012	0.013
4B4	0.006	0.009	0.013	0.008	0.013	0.009	0.017	0.018	0.012	0.041	0.015	0.017	0.038	1.048	0.018	0.014	0.012	0.010	0.014
4C1	0.013	0.012	0.036	0.035	0.103	0.010	0.018	0.016	0.015	0.017	0.026	0.020	0.022	0.020	1.057	0.062	0.025	0.030	0.027
4C2	0.012	0.017	0.047	0.030	0.032	0.019	0.033	0.032	0.028	0.031	0.046	0.037	0.039	0.035	0.037	1.032	0.034	0.027	0.030
4D1	0.003	0.004	0.007	0.013	0.030	0.005	0.016	0.006	0.008	0.014	0.009	0.023	0.007	0.006	0.049	0.062	1.007	0.016	0.094
4D2	0.001	0.001	0.002	0.002	0.005	0.001	0.003	0.002	0.002	0.003	0.002	0.005	0.003	0.003	0.002	0.011	0.011	1.002	0.017

4D3	0.014	0.016	0.029	0.037	0.033	0.033	0.141	0.031	0.058	0.116	0.036	0.067	0.031	0.025	0.079	0.118	0.037	0.026	1.062
4E	0.005	0.006	0.007	0.037	0.045	0.007	0.022	0.008	0.010	0.059	0.012	0.021	0.009	0.008	0.013	0.013	0.029	0.024	0.013
4F1	0.081	0.081	0.104	0.034	0.088	0.032	0.047	0.043	0.044	0.043	0.071	0.056	0.056	0.041	0.046	0.054	0.050	0.047	0.037
4F2	0.002	0.004	0.009	0.002	0.004	0.002	0.013	0.005	0.005	0.005	0.008	0.024	0.006	0.005	0.005	0.006	0.006	0.004	0.005
4F3	0.002	0.003	0.006	0.004	0.006	0.004	0.006	0.007	0.005	0.006	0.007	0.009	0.008	0.008	0.007	0.007	0.006	0.004	0.006
4F4	0.006	0.007	0.027	0.009	0.044	0.008	0.029	0.022	0.022	0.020	0.014	0.032	0.016	0.017	0.023	0.031	0.010	0.013	0.012
4F5	0.001	0.001	0.003	0.001	0.002	0.001	0.002	0.003	0.002	0.002	0.003	0.003	0.004	0.004	0.003	0.002	0.002	0.001	0.002
5A1	0.021	0.028	0.031	0.074	0.044	0.026	0.043	0.046	0.033	0.045	0.062	0.047	0.049	0.044	0.047	0.045	0.066	0.057	0.043
5A2	0.001	0.001	0.002	0.001	0.002	0.001	0.002	0.007	0.002	0.002	0.002	0.002	0.002	0.002	0.004	0.003	0.004	0.003	0.004
5A3	0.008	0.010	0.006	0.007	0.011	0.006	0.009	0.009	0.008	0.013	0.009	0.009	0.008	0.009	0.008	0.007	0.008	0.006	0.008
6	0.027	0.030	0.028	0.040	0.035	0.024	0.047	0.041	0.038	0.047	0.055	0.042	0.049	0.042	0.034	0.031	0.032	0.028	0.033
7	0.116	0.143	0.258	0.158	0.278	0.151	0.248	0.281	0.200	0.265	0.229	0.268	0.210	0.333	0.256	0.235	0.183	0.176	0.209
8A1	0.049	0.069	0.075	0.084	0.111	0.091	0.150	0.133	0.125	0.124	0.128	0.119	0.092	0.088	0.105	0.091	0.164	0.124	0.097
8A2	0.003	0.005	0.009	0.006	0.009	0.006	0.009	0.011	0.007	0.009	0.011	0.012	0.009	0.013	0.011	0.010	0.008	0.007	0.010
9	0.048	0.065	0.114	0.086	0.207	0.078	0.135	0.153	0.105	0.134	0.182	0.177	0.133	0.188	0.156	0.136	0.111	0.105	0.134
10	0.001	0.001	0.002	0.001	0.001	0.001	0.002	0.002	0.001	0.002	0.002	0.002	0.002	0.002	0.002	0.002	0.001	0.001	0.002
11A	0.011	0.011	0.021	0.015	0.020	0.014	0.022	0.026	0.017	0.021	0.025	0.028	0.021	0.030	0.025	0.023	0.020	0.016	0.023
11B	0.012	0.017	0.031	0.021	0.029	0.020	0.033	0.039	0.026	0.032	0.038	0.042	0.032	0.046	0.038	0.035	0.030	0.024	0.034
Households	0.202	0.287	0.536	0.358	0.496	0.348	0.558	0.667	0.439	0.546	0.652	0.721	0.548	0.779	0.643	0.604	0.509	0.407	0.585

	4E	4F1	4F2	4F3	4F4	4F5	5A1	5A2	5A3	6	7	8A1	8A2	9	10	11A	11B	House-holds
1	0.008	0.009	0.016	0.011	0.023	0.009	0.006	0.009	0.008	0.010	0.010	0.009	0.009	0.009	0.015	0.015	0.009	0.019
2A	0.014	0.012	0.052	0.018	0.018	0.014	0.010	0.015	0.013	0.017	0.016	0.015	0.015	0.015	0.024	0.023	0.016	0.032
2B	0.003	0.002	0.002	0.004	0.005	0.002	0.003	0.004	0.002	0.007	0.002	0.004	0.002	0.002	0.003	0.003	0.002	0.003
3A	0.016	0.015	0.004	0.003	0.005	0.007	0.042	0.066	0.007	0.006	0.004	0.006	0.003	0.004	0.005	0.006	01007	0.005
3B	0.055	0.006	0.001	0.001	0.002	0.009	0.002	0.004	0.003	0.016	0.001	0.003	0.002	0.001	0.003	0.002	0.002	0.002
4A1	0.052	0.056	0.068	0.066	0.144	0.058	0.038	0.059	0.049	0.063	0.063	0.059	0.056	0.059	0.093	0.095	0.058	0.122
4A2	0.015	0.018	0.013	0.016	0.016	0.016	0.011	0.017	0.014	0.018	0.018	0.017	0.016	0.017	0.026	0.027	0.017	0.035
4A3	0.013	0.016	0.012	0.014	0.013	0.013	0.009	0.014	0.012	0.015	0.015	0.014	0.014	0.014	0.022	0.021	0.014	0.029
4A4	0.010	0.010	0.010	0.011	0.010	0.010	0.007	0.011	0.009	0.012	0.012	0.011	0.011	0.011	0.018	0.017	0.012	0.023
4A5	0.015	0.012	0.013	0.017	0.014	0.016	0.011	0.017	0.014	0.018	0.018	0.017	0.017	0.017	0.027	0.025	0.026	0.036
4B1	0.007	0.007	0.005	0.005	0.010	0.009	0.004	0.007	0.010	0.053	0.007	0.011	0.005	0.006	0.013	0.008	0.005	0.008
4B2	0.007	0.007	0.006	0.007	0.008	0.008	0.005	0.008	0.009	0.036	0.010	0.009	0.007	0.007	0.020	0.013	0.007	0.012
4B3	0.034	0.035	0.023	0.031	0.023	0.034	0.007	0.013	0.010	0.018	0.028	0.021	0.013	0.011	0.024	0.018	0.016	0.019
4B4	0.015	0.022	0.017	0.018	0.017	0.016	0.011	0.016	0.014	0.018	0.019	0.017	0.016	0.016	0.059	0.035	0.016	0.033
4C1	0.030	0.028	0.013	0.015	0.019	0.024	0.012	0.030	0.022	0.064	0.018	0.021	0.074	0.015	0.046	0.023	0.034	0.023
4C2	0.043	0.045	0.028	0.029	0.030	0.030	0.047	0.038	0.026	0.037	0.032	0.102	0.028	0.027	0.073	0.039	0.028	0.050
4D1	0.024	0.015	0.004	0.005	0.008	0.017	0.005	0.007	0.010	0.024	0.005	0.010	0.009	0.005	0.012	0.007	0.006	0.007
4D2	0.003	0.009	0.002	0.002	0.004	0.018	0.001	0.002	0.002	0.007	0.001	0.002	0.003	0.001	0.003	0.002	0.002	0.002

4D3	0.035	0.077	0.021	0.024	0.052	0.061	0.017	0.036	0.069	0.123	0.024	0.035	0.045	0.021	0.057	0.034	0.026	0.031
4E	1.100	0.017	0.007	0.009	0.012	0.009	0.008	0.013	0.022	0.132	0.008	0.015	0.013	0.010	0.022	0.013	0.009	0.010
4F1	0.058	1.116	0.038	0.035	0.094	0.054	0.025	0.040	0.036	0.064	0.035	0.079	0.027	0.029	0.059	0.045	0.045	0.042
4F2	0.004	0.005	1.155	0.091	0.026	0.007	0.003	0.004	0.003	0.005	0.005	0.007	0.004	0.004	0.007	0.008	0.008	0.007
4F3	0.007	0.005	0.006	1.017	0.009	0.007	0.005	0.007	0.006	0.008	0.008	0.007	0.007	0.007	0.016	0.011	0.007	0.015
4F4	0.014	0.033	0.011	0.078	1.021	0.050	0.007	0.013	0.010	0.017	0.014	0.022	0.014	0.009	0.021	0.016	0.014	0.017
4F5	0.002	0.002	0.002	0.004	0.007	1.005	0.001	0.002	0.002	0.003	0.004	0.002	0.002	0.002	0.004	0.005	0.002	0.004
5A1	0.059	0.048	0.037	0.041	0.048	0.042	1.022	0.100	0.106	0.043	0.042	0.038	0.038	0.061	0.061	0.068	0.083	0.055
5A2	0.006	0.003	0.002	0.002	0.002	0.004	0.002	1.002	0.002	0.003	0.003	0.003	0.002	0.002	0.004	0.005	0.003	0.003
5A3	0.010	0.008	0.009	0.009	0.008	0.008	0.006	0.009	1.007	0.010	0.010	0.009	0.008	0.020	0.013	0.025	0.025	0.016
6	0.055	0.040	0.035	0.036	0.039	0.037	0.039	0.069	0.158	1.036	0.044	0.090	0.035	0.062	0.143	0.072	0.033	0.043
7	0.249	0.229	0.203	0.228	0.255	0.261	0.144	0.265	0.200	0.324	1.249	0.262	0.235	0.250	0.324	0.329	0.242	0.382
8A1	0.172	0.090	0.090	0.081	0.082	0.086	0.093	0.183	0.066	0.126	0.097	1.081	0.096	0.066	0.108	0.094	0.068	0.107
8A2	0.010	0.007	0.009	0.012	0.010	0.011	0.008	0.012	0.010	0.012	0.013	0.011	1.011	0.017	0.020	0.017	0.012	0.024
9	0.150	0.121	0.121	0.172	0.149	0.167	0.092	0.157	0.115	0.165	0.262	0.155	0.135	1.228	0.238	0.196	0.190	0.262
10	0.002	0.001	0.002	0.002	0.002	0.002	0.001	0.002	0.002	0.002	0.002	0.002	0.002	0.002	1.003	0.003	0.002	0.004
11A	0.024	0.018	0.022	0.027	0.023	0.025	0.018	0.028	0.023	0.029	0.029	0.029	0.026	0.029	0.053	1.041	0.027	0.058
11B	0.037	0.027	0.033	0.041	0.035	0.038	0.028	0.042	0.035	0.045	0.046	0.043	0.040	0.042	0.065	0.061	1.044	0.087
House-holds	0.627	0.454	0.559	0.703	0.593	0.653	0.469	0.719	0.599	0.762	0.751	0.705	0.689	0.720	1.117	1.051	0.702	1.504

Table XII.2: Inverse Matrix, 19-Sector Closed Model: Wide Bay—Burnett Region

	1	2A	2B	3A	3B	4A	4B	4C	4D	4E	4F	5	6	7	8	9	10	11A	11B	House-holds
1	1.010	0.005	0.011	0.006	0.007	0.134	0.013	0.013	0.009	0.011	0.014	0.009	0.012	0.013	0.013	0.013	0.020	0.020	0.012	0.028
2A	0.117	1.154	0.064	0.035	0.043	0.456	0.077	0.077	0.058	0.067	0.075	0.056	0.071	0.081	0.077	0.079	0.124	0.119	0.076	0.173
2B	0.002	0.004	1.006	0.060	0.010	0.005	0.132	0.008	0.006	0.007	0.008	0.007	0.014	0.007	0.012	0.007	0.013	0.011	0.006	0.014
3A	0.000	0.000	0.000	1.001	0.001	0.001	0.001	0.001	0.005	0.005	0.001	0.016	0.001	0.001	0.001	0.001	0.001	0.001	0.002	0.001
3B	0.000	0.000	0.001	0.020	1.009	0.001	0.001	0.001	0.003	0.033	0.001	0.001	0.008	0.000	0.001	0.001	0.001	0.001	0.000	0.000
4A	0.079	0.038	0.079	0.042	0.051	1.086	0.093	0.093	0.069	0.081	0.101	0.067	0.085	0.098	0.093	0.095	0.149	0.147	0.090	0.207
4B	0.007	0.018	0.018	0.017	0.012	0.015	1.071	0.027	0.017	0.018	0.020	0.016	0.080	0.022	0.025	0.020	0.051	0.037	0.017	0.037
4C	0.015	0.016	0.047	0.024	0.056	0.017	0.036	1.040	0.026	0.035	0.022	0.037	0.033	0.025	0.028	0.024	0.050	0.035	0.024	0.049
4D	0.001	0.001	0.003	0.006	0.009	0.003	0.005	0.027	1.023	0.007	0.005	0.004	0.016	0.002	0.004	0.002	0.007	0.004	0.002	0.004
4E	0.002	0.002	0.002	0.015	0.005	0.002	0.004	0.003	0.007	1.008	0.002	0.004	0.058	0.003	0.008	0.004	0.010	0.005	0.003	0.004
4F	0.001	0.001	0.003	0.001	0.001	0.001	0.002	0.001	0.002	0.001	1.003	0.001	0.001	0.002	0.002	0.001	0.002	0.003	0.003	0.002
5	0.016	0.019	0.015	0.051	0.029	0.021	0.025	0.025	0.032	0.034	0.022	1.029	0.020	0.023	0.021	0.041	0.036	0.050	0.069	0.030
6	0.024	0.024	0.023	0.035	0.021	0.024	0.034	0.026	0.022	0.043	0.023	0.058	1.019	0.032	0.107	0.052	0.138	0.060	0.020	0.028
7	0.080	0.087	0.196	0.093	0.160	0.097	0.137	0.122	0.089	0.115	0.104	0.079	0.150	1.159	0.139	0.132	0.141	0.155	0.114	0.167
8	0.035	0.051	0.053	0.059	0.063	0.074	0.085	0.087	0.070	0.120	0.047	0.078	0.073	0.064	1.050	0.051	0.070	0.066	0.045	0.081
9	0.016	0.022	0.045	0.028	0.063	0.036	0.058	0.056	0.043	0.050	0.054	0.036	0.049	0.116	0.051	1.090	0.095	0.071	0.072	0.099
10	0.000	0.001	0.001	0.001	0.001	0.001	0.002	0.002	0.001	0.001	0.001	0.001	0.001	0.002	0.002	0.002	1.003	0.002	0.002	0.004
11A	0.004	0.002	0.005	0.003	0.004	0.004	0.006	0.006	0.004	0.005	0.005	0.004	0.006	0.006	0.006	0.007	0.019	1.009	0.006	0.013
11B	0.005	0.006	0.014	0.008	0.010	0.011	0.017	0.017	0.013	0.015	0.014	0.012	0.016	0.020	0.017	0.018	0.027	0.025	1.019	0.037
House-holds	0.144	0.213	0.455	0.254	0.309	0.316	0.556	0.562	0.419	0.488	0.473	0.407	0.517	0.588	0.562	0.575	0.900	0.842	0.544	1.259

Table XII.3: Inverse Matrix, 19-Sector Closed Model: Darling Downs Region

	1	2A	2B	3A	3B	4A	4B	4C	4D	4E	4F	5	6	7	8	9	10	11A	11B	House-holds
1	1.026	0.013	0.027	0.014	0.013	0.479	0.028	0.028	0.023	0.027	0.052	0.021	0.028	0.033	0.030	0.032	0.046	0.050	0.032	0.069
2A	0.134	1.138	0.115	0.060	0.059	0.220	0.126	0.126	0.104	0.116	0.118	0.093	0.125	0.143	0.132	0.141	0.204	0.206	0.131	0.306
2B	0.001	0.001	1.002	0.058	0.001	0.002	0.100	0.002	0.002	0.003	0.002	0.003	0.008	0.002	0.006	0.002	0.005	0.004	0.002	0.004
3A	0.000	0.000	0.000	1.000	0.000	0.000	0.000	0.000	0.001	0.001	0.000	0.005	0.000	0.000	0.000	0.000	0.000	0.000	0.001	0.000
3B	0.000	0.000	0.001	0.025	1.001	0.000	0.000	0.000	0.000	0.030	0.000	0.001	0.006	0.000	0.001	0.000	0.001	0.001	0.000	0.000
4A	0.059	0.029	0.057	0.029	0.028	1.109	0.061	0.061	0.050	0.057	0.065	0.045	0.060	0.070	0.064	0.068	0.099	0.109	0.069	0.147
4B	0.006	0.013	0.012	0.015	0.007	0.011	1.063	0.014	0.013	0.013	0.012	0.012	0.082	0.017	0.018	0.014	0.040	0.030	0.012	0.026
4C	0.011	0.012	0.021	0.012	0.032	0.013	0.015	1.020	0.014	0.014	0.011	0.010	0.019	0.015	0.016	0.014	0.025	0.021	0.014	0.030
4D	0.002	0.003	0.007	0.008	0.007	0.006	0.009	0.019	1.019	0.009	0.007	0.008	0.026	0.008	0.008	0.008	0.015	0.011	0.007	0.015
4E	0.001	0.001	0.002	0.012	0.004	0.002	0.003	0.003	0.003	1.007	0.002	0.004	0.045	0.003	0.006	0.003	0.007	0.005	0.002	0.004
4F	0.004	0.005	0.014	0.007	0.007	0.010	0.014	0.014	0.014	0.020	1.078	0.010	0.014	0.016	0.015	0.015	0.025	0.024	0.017	0.033
5	0.010	0.011	0.007	0.032	0.007	0.014	0.012	0.012	0.013	0.016	0.012	1.015	0.009	0.011	0.009	0.025	0.016	0.029	0.043	0.012
6	0.024	0.025	0.026	0.035	0.018	0.033	0.033	0.029	0.022	0.042	0.025	0.066	1.021	0.034	0.094	0.048	0.130	0.064	0.021	0.033
7	0.103	0.108	0.254	0.121	0.222	0.167	0.194	0.164	0.132	0.163	0.130	0.105	0.208	1.211	0.196	0.184	0.204	0.230	0.162	0.267
8	0.040	0.049	0.064	0.065	0.063	0.108	0.092	0.114	0.062	0.146	0.054	0.074	0.085	0.074	1.055	0.061	0.081	0.080	0.053	0.100
9	0.020	0.022	0.055	0.032	0.075	0.043	0.064	0.059	0.050	0.056	0.056	0.040	0.058	0.124	0.058	1.102	0.105	0.085	0.074	0.121
10	0.000	0.001	0.002	0.001	0.001	0.001	0.002	0.002	0.001	0.002	0.001	0.001	0.002	0.002	0.002	0.002	1.003	0.003	0.002	0.004
11A	0.005	0.002	0.007	0.004	0.004	0.006	0.007	0.007	0.006	0.007	0.006	0.005	0.007	0.008	0.008	0.009	0.019	1.012	0.007	0.017
11B	0.006	0.007	0.018	0.010	0.010	0.014	0.020	0.020	0.016	0.018	0.017	0.015	0.020	0.024	0.021	0.022	0.032	0.032	1.023	0.048
House-holds	0.160	0.185	0.495	0.259	0.251	0.369	0.540	0.541	0.447	0.496	0.456	0.400	0.536	0.612	0.566	0.606	0.877	0.878	0.555	1.314

Table XII.4: Inverse Matrix, 19-Sector Closed Model: Fitzroy Region

	1	2A	2B	3A	3B	4A	4B	4C	4D	4E	4F	5	6	7	8	9	10	11A	11B	House-holds
1	1.020	0.011	0.023	0.011	0.016	0.418	0.023	0.022	0.021	0.018	0.040	0.018	0.025	0.028	0.030	0.027	0.042	0.043	0.029	0.059
2A	0.100	1.122	0.025	0.013	0.020	0.117	0.029	0.027	0.025	0.022	0.042	0.023	0.031	0.035	0.037	0.034	0.053	0.051	0.033	0.074
2B	0.000	0.000	1.000	0.011	0.002	0.001	0.011	0.000	0.001	0.001	0.001	0.001	0.001	0.000	0.002	0.000	0.001	0.001	0.000	0.000
3A	0.003	0.003	0.004	1.007	0.007	0.007	0.006	0.010	0.039	0.032	0.013	0.096	0.009	0.007	0.011	0.007	0.009	0.010	0.012	0.009
3B	0.001	0.001	0.003	0.009	1.021	0.001	0.002	0.003	0.008	0.121	0.010	0.002	0.017	0.002	0.004	0.002	0.004	0.003	0.002	0.003
4A	0.053	0.029	0.058	0.027	0.039	1.099	0.058	0.055	0.053	0.044	0.078	0.046	0.062	0.071	0.074	0.067	0.107	0.109	0.073	0.147
4B	0.004	0.019	0.011	0.011	0.007	0.008	1.052	0.015	0.007	0.013	0.012	0.007	0.064	0.013	0.018	0.007	0.030	0.018	0.006	0.010
4C	0.013	0.016	0.034	0.025	0.042	0.023	0.029	1.045	0.028	0.034	0.025	0.029	0.038	0.033	0.114	0.030	0.054	0.044	0.030	0.063
4D	0.025	0.032	0.063	0.054	0.069	0.060	0.090	0.202	1.149	0.069	0.149	0.065	0.170	0.087	0.112	0.083	0.148	0.126	0.080	0.174
4E	0.002	0.003	0.004	0.014	0.021	0.004	0.005	0.005	0.005	1.063	0.005	0.006	0.037	0.006	0.010	0.007	0.012	0.009	0.006	0.012
4F	0.003	0.003	0.005	0.002	0.010	0.004	0.006	0.006	0.010	0.006	1.023	0.003	0.005	0.005	0.006	0.005	0.008	0.010	0.007	0.009
5	0.015	0.017	0.016	0.049	0.034	0.022	0.022	0.028	0.043	0.041	0.036	1.024	0.022	0.025	0.026	0.042	0.038	0.048	0.065	0.033
6	0.024	0.024	0.019	0.033	0.024	0.027	0.027	0.021	0.019	0.045	0.031	0.049	1.019	0.032	0.135	0.049	0.136	0.059	0.019	0.026
7	0.088	0.093	0.191	0.088	0.163	0.128	0.141	0.131	0.088	0.128	0.123	0.083	0.167	1.170	0.157	0.143	0.155	0.169	0.124	0.183
8	0.026	0.034	0.032	0.040	0.049	0.058	0.045	0.041	0.034	0.117	0.038	0.053	0.050	0.044	1.037	0.029	0.040	0.036	0.026	0.039
9	0.016	0.019	0.037	0.024	0.057	0.033	0.050	0.045	0.039	0.041	0.043	0.031	0.046	0.116	0.054	1.090	0.087	0.063	0.068	0.086
10	0.001	0.001	0.001	0.001	0.001	0.001	0.002	0.002	0.006	0.001	0.002	0.001	0.002	0.002	0.002	0.002	1.003	0.003	0.002	0.004
11A	0.005	0.003	0.007	0.005	0.006	0.007	0.008	0.008	0.011	0.006	0.006	0.007	0.009	0.010	0.011	0.010	0.027	1.014	0.009	0.021
11B	0.007	0.009	0.017	0.010	0.015	0.015	0.021	0.020	0.019	0.016	0.016	0.017	0.023	0.028	0.027	0.025	0.038	0.036	1.026	0.053
House-holds	0.154	0.205	0.407	0.232	0.337	0.351	0.496	0.470	0.427	0.379	0.367	0.400	0.532	0.601	0.638	0.579	0.916	0.864	0.551	1.275

Table XII.5: Inverse Matrix, 19-Sector Closed Model: Mackay Region

	1	2A	2B	3A	3B	4A	4B	4C	4D	4E	4F	5	6	7	8	9	10	11A	11B	House-holds
1	1.006	0.005	0.008	0.004	0.005	0.066	0.010	0.010	0.008	0.007	0.007	0.008	0.009	0.011	0.010	0.011	0.018	0.017	0.011	0.024
2A	0.126	1.165	0.075	0.042	0.049	0.584	0.095	0.098	0.076	0.069	0.066	0.074	0.091	0.107	0.101	0.106	0.169	0.162	0.103	0.233
2B	0.000	0.000	1.000	0.021	0.000	0.000	0.028	0.001	0.000	0.001	0.001	0.002	0.002	0.000	0.002	0.000	0.001	0.001	0.000	0.001
3A	0.001	0.002	0.001	1.003	0.001	0.002	0.002	0.002	0.002	0.016	0.006	0.052	0.002	0.003	0.005	0.003	0.003	0.004	0.007	0.002
3B	0.000	0.000	0.001	0.015	1.000	0.000	0.000	0.000	0.000	0.024	0.002	0.001	0.006	0.000	0.001	0.000	0.001	0.001	0.000	0.000
4A	0.088	0.075	0.121	0.066	0.077	1.096	0.150	0.155	0.120	0.108	0.108	0.117	0.144	0.170	0.159	0.167	0.267	0.257	0.161	0.369
4B	0.003	0.012	0.012	0.010	0.003	0.008	1.048	0.010	1.006	0.007	0.005	0.006	0.056	0.008	0.011	0.006	0.026	0.019	0.004	0.008
4C	0.009	0.008	0.023	0.013	0.060	0.006	0.008	1.016	0.009	0.013	0.011	0.011	0.013	0.005	0.018	0.004	0.012	0.006	0.005	0.006
4D	0.000	0.000	0.000	0.001	0.000	0.000	0.001	0.002	1.002	0.001	0.001	0.001	0.006	0.001	0.001	0.001	0.002	0.001	0.001	0.001
4E	0.001	0.002	0.002	0.011	0.002	0.002	0.004	0.004	0.003	1.004	0.002	0.004	0.030	0.004	0.006	0.004	0.008	0.006	0.003	0.007
4F	0.048	0.043	0.015	0.004	0.029	0.026	0.009	0.011	0.009	0.011	1.060	0.005	0.007	0.008	0.007	0.007	0.012	0.015	0.009	0.016
5	0.018	0.022	0.015	0.050	0.016	0.021	0.022	0.025	0.022	0.033	0.048	1.031	0.018	0.024	0.021	0.048	0.038	0.051	0.073	0.031
6	0.024	0.022	0.015	0.031	0.017	0.019	0.024	0.018	0.017	0.037	0.032	0.055	1.014	0.028	0.086	0.042	0.135	0.057	0.017	0.022
7	0.088	0.093	0.174	0.085	0.196	0.088	0.131	0.111	0.089	0.108	0.094	0.074	0.148	1.149	0.133	0.131	0.126	0.144	0.104	0.141
8	0.023	0.032	0.026	0.035	0.043	0.043	0.040	0.040	0.031	0.078	0.027	0.046	0.041	0.036	1.029	0.024	0.033	0.030	0.021	0.031
9	0.015	0.020	0.030	0.019	0.059	0.029	0.041	0.042	0.032	0.033	0.027	0.028	0.037	0.086	0.041	1.070	0.077	0.056	0.053	0.078
10	0.000	0.001	0.001	0.001	0.001	0.001	0.001	0.001	0.001	0.001	0.001	0.001	0.001	0.001	0.001	0.001	1.002	0.002	0.001	0.003
11A	0.004	0.003	0.005	0.003	0.004	0.004	0.006	0.006	0.005	0.005	0.004	0.005	0.006	0.007	0.007	0.008	0.020	1.011	0.007	0.015
11B	0.009	0.013	0.020	0.012	0.014	0.017	0.027	0.028	0.022	0.020	0.016	0.021	0.026	0.033	0.030	0.031	0.048	0.045	1.031	0.066
House-holds	0.161	0.240	0.362	0.218	0.255	0.274	0.494	0.514	0.399	0.359	0.298	0.388	0.477	0.559	0.528	0.554	0.883	0.828	0.534	1.224

Table XII.6: Inverse Matrix, 19-Sector Closed Model: Northern Region

	1	2A	2B	3A	3B	4A	4B	4C	4D	4E	4F	5	6	7	8	9	10	11A	11B	House-holds
1	1.009	0.008	0.012	0.007	0.009	0.112	0.013	0.018	0.014	0.013	0.013	0.011	0.014	0.016	0.016	0.015	0.020	0.024	0.014	0.033
2A	0.118	1.157	0.069	0.044	0.058	0.388	0.080	0.111	0.085	0.079	0.079	0.067	0.090	0.101	0.104	0.097	0.129	0.148	0.092	0.209
2B	0.001	0.001	1.001	0.026	0.003	0.002	0.028	0.002	0.002	0.003	0.003	0.003	0.002	0.002	0.004	0.002	0.002	0.003	0.002	0.004
3A	0.002	0.003	0.003	1.006	0.005	0.004	0.004	0.005	0.010	0.030	0.006	0.054	0.006	0.005	0.008	0.005	0.005	0.007	0.009	0.006
3B	0.001	0.001	0.002	0.017	1.007	0.001	0.002	0.005	0.045	0.050	0.005	0.002	0.013	0.001	0.003	0.001	0.003	0.002	0.001	0.002
4A	0.089	0.082	0.116	0.069	0.089	1.108	0.123	0.171	0.132	0.122	0.130	0.103	0.138	0.156	0.160	0.150	0.199	0.231	0.141	0.322
4B	0.005	0.020	0.011	0.008	0.011	0.011	1.047	0.015	0.010	0.018	0.015	0.007	0.033	0.017	0.016	0.010	0.018	0.018	0.010	0.018
4C	0.008	0.010	0.034	0.017	0.029	0.011	0.016	1.024	0.017	0.023	0.014	0.026	0.017	0.013	0.080	0.011	0.046	0.016	0.012	0.020
4D	0.005	0.006	0.011	0.021	0.026	0.008	0.022	0.091	1.072	0.024	0.059	0.013	0.081	0.011	0.022	0.010	0.026	0.017	0.010	0.015
4E	0.003	0.004	0.005	0.033	0.038	0.005	0.007	0.008	0.010	1.087	0.006	0.009	0.080	0.008	0.015	0.008	0.015	0.012	0.006	0.012
4F	0.004	0.004	0.007	0.003	0.011	0.004	0.008	0.006	0.010	0.006	1.018	0.003	0.005	0.066	0.007	0.005	0.008	0.013	0.008	0.010
5	0.026	0.036	0.031	0.084	0.049	0.034	0.047	0.054	0.060	0.074	0.054	1.040	0.042	0.048	0.048	0.078	0.059	0.086	0.106	0.070
6	0.029	0.029	0.023	0.041	0.032	0.028	0.039	0.034	0.033	0.054	0.036	0.056	1.030	0.044	0.123	0.057	0.123	0.079	0.030	0.047
7	0.132	0.159	0.259	0.151	0.266	0.164	0.228	0.261	0.203	0.218	0.206	0.147	0.278	1.270	0.265	0.244	0.256	0.312	0.217	0.367
8	0.054	0.078	0.077	0.086	0.107	0.101	0.108	0.121	0.130	0.182	0.091	0.107	0.125	0.121	1.111	0.096	0.131	0.132	0.087	0.169
9	0.038	0.058	0.075	0.055	0.107	0.067	0.103	0.125	0.098	0.097	0.095	0.074	0.105	0.180	0.119	1.159	0.154	0.156	0.122	0.216
10	0.002	0.004	0.005	0.004	0.005	0.004	0.006	0.009	0.007	0.006	0.006	0.005	0.007	0.008	0.008	0.008	1.010	0.012	0.007	0.017
11A	0.006	0.005	0.006	0.005	0.006	0.006	0.008	0.011	0.009	0.008	0.007	0.007	0.009	0.010	0.011	0.011	0.019	1.015	0.009	0.021
11B	0.019	0.030	0.038	0.027	0.035	0.034	0.048	0.067	0.052	0.048	0.045	0.041	0.055	0.063	0.064	0.059	0.078	0.088	1.058	0.126
House-holds	0.215	0.355	0.444	0.314	0.409	0.378	0.564	0.786	0.605	0.561	0.524	0.475	0.637	0.715	0.736	0.693	0.911	1.033	0.647	1.487

Table XII.7: Inverse Matrix, 19-Sector Closed Model: Far North Region

	1	2A	2B	3A	3B	4A	4B	4C	4D	4E	4F	5	6	7	8	9	10	11A	11B	House-holds
1	1.008	0.006	0.011	0.002	0.008	0.108	0.014	0.013	0.010	0.011	0.012	0.010	0.013	0.014	0.014	0.014	0.022	0.022	0.015	0.031
2A	0.126	1.162	0.071	0.016	0.055	0.505	0.098	0.092	0.068	0.073	0.078	0.067	0.089	0.101	0.095	0.099	0.155	0.151	0.102	0.216
2B	0.002	0.003	1.004	0.001	0.010	0.003	0.153	0.007	0.004	0.005	0.004	0.004	0.014	0.004	0.007	0.004	0.009	0.007	0.003	0.007
3A	0.000	0.000	0.000	1.000	0.000	0.000	0.000	0.000	0.000	0.000	0.000	0.000	0.000	0.000	0.000	0.000	0.000	0.000	0.000	0.000
3B	0.001	0.001	0.002	0.000	1.019	0.001	0.001	0.003	0.036	0.080	0.008	0.001	0.016	0.001	0.002	0.001	0.003	0.002	0.001	0.001
4A	0.082	0.064	0.105	0.023	0.078	1.092	0.139	0.130	0.097	0.103	0.122	0.094	0.125	0.143	0.134	0.140	0.219	0.216	0.147	0.304
4B	0.010	0.022	0.029	0.004	0.016	0.018	1.133	0.047	0.022	0.022	0.020	0.019	0.100	0.028	0.031	0.026	0.060	0.044	0.023	0.050
4C	0.008	0.009	0.044	0.001	0.033	0.010	0.027	1.023	0.017	0.021	0.017	0.030	0.018	0.011	0.057	0.010	0.032	0.015	0.014	0.017
4D	0.002	0.003	0.006	0.001	0.012	0.003	0.008	0.047	1.035	0.014	0.016	0.006	0.024	0.005	0.007	0.004	0.012	0.007	0.005	0.007
4E	0.002	0.002	0.003	0.001	0.006	0.003	0.005	0.004	0.005	1.009	0.003	0.004	0.048	0.005	0.007	0.005	0.011	0.007	0.004	0.008
4F	0.024	0.022	0.007	0.001	0.003	0.012	0.005	0.004	0.003	0.003	1.004	0.003	0.004	0.004	0.004	0.004	0.006	0.006	0.005	0.008
5	0.019	0.023	0.016	0.002	0.039	0.022	0.038	0.026	0.039	0.031	0.029	1.025	0.019	0.024	0.022	0.052	0.037	0.051	0.085	0.024
6	0.024	0.023	0.016	0.002	0.019	0.021	0.037	0.020	0.021	0.035	0.025	0.050	1.013	0.031	0.070	0.049	0.135	0.056	0.020	0.026
7	0.093	0.099	0.186	0.012	0.176	0.102	0.148	0.142	0.100	0.133	0.101	0.075	0.171	1.162	0.145	0.139	0.143	0.160	0.119	0.161
8	0.037	0.050	0.047	0.006	0.068	0.071	0.085	0.065	0.084	0.138	0.053	0.067	0.074	0.069	1.059	0.051	0.073	0.064	0.045	0.076
9	0.018	0.024	0.038	0.007	0.063	0.035	0.066	0.054	0.043	0.050	0.039	0.034	0.051	0.108	0.056	1.088	0.093	0.073	0.073	0.099
10	0.001	0.001	0.001	0.000	0.001	0.001	0.002	0.002	0.001	0.001	0.001	0.001	0.002	0.002	0.002	0.002	1.003	0.003	0.002	0.004
11A	0.005	0.003	0.005	0.001	0.005	0.005	0.007	0.007	0.005	0.006	0.005	0.005	0.007	0.008	0.009	0.008	0.024	1.011	0.007	0.016
11B	0.007	0.010	0.016	0.004	0.015	0.014	0.023	0.022	0.017	0.018	0.015	0.016	0.022	0 027	0.025	0.024	0.037	0.035	1.025	0.051
House-holds	1.166	0.240	0.377	0.094	0.323	0.291	0.564	0.538	0.399	0.426	0.359	0.389	0.517	0.588	0.553	0.578	0.902	0.861	0.557	1.260

Table XII.8: Inverse Matrix, 19-Sector Closed Model: North West Region

	1	2A	2B	3A	3B	4A	4B	4C	4D	4E	4F	5	6	7	8	9	10	11A	11B	House-holds
1	1.001	0.002	0.002	0.000	0.003	0.177	0.005	0.004	0.002	0.003	0.043	0.003	0.004	0.005	0.004	0.005	0.008	0.007	0.004	0.011
2A	0.055	1.064	0.001	0.000	0.002	0.017	0.003	0.003	0.001	0.002	0.004	0.002	0.002	0.003	0.003	0.003	0.005	0.005	0.004	0.007
2B	0.000	0.001	1.001	0.000	0.001	0.002	0.002	0.001	0.001	0.001	0.010	0.001	0.001	0.002	0.002	0.002	0.003	0.003	0.002	0.004
3A	0.000	0.000	0.000	1.000	0.000	0.000	0.000	0.000	0.000	0.000	0.000	0.000	0.000	0.000	0.000	0.000	0.000	0.000	0.000	0.000
3B	0.000	0.000	0.000	0.000	1.030	0.000	0.000	0.000	0.000	0.067	0.000	0.000	0.012	0.000	0.001	0.001	0.002	0.001	0.000	0.000
4A	0.003	0.005	0.005	0.000	0.006	1.010	0.009	0.007	0.004	0.006	0.050	0.006	0.007	0.009	0.009	0.009	0.015	0.015	0.008	0.021
4B	0.001	0.001	0.001	0.000	0.001	0.001	1.005	0.002	0.001	0.001	0.001	0.001	0.002	0.002	0.002	0.002	0.011	0.010	0.002	0.005
4C	0.001	0.001	0.001	0.000	0.005	0.001	0.002	1.003	0.002	0.001	0.002	0.001	0.004	0.002	0.002	0.002	0.004	0.003	0.002	0.004
4D	0.002	0.004	0.003	0.000	0.005	0.004	0.007	0.012	1.008	0.006	0.009	0.005	0.026	0.007	0.009	0.008	0.015	0.012	0.007	0.016
4E	0.000	0.001	0.000	0.000	0.002	0.001	0.001	0.001	0.001	1.002	0.001	0.001	0.011	0.001	0.002	0.002	0.003	0.002	0.001	0.003
4F	0.000	0.000	0.000	0.000	0.000	0.000	0.000	0.000	0.000	0.000	1.000	0.000	0.000	0.000	0.000	0.000	0.000	0.000	0.000	0.000
5	0.002	0.004	0.002	0.000	0.010	0.004	0.003	0.004	0.003	0.005	0.001	1.002	0.002	0.004	0.003	0.009	0.007	0.008	0.016	0.004
6	0.019	0.016	0.004	0.000	0.013	0.017	0.016	0.012	0.012	0.026	0.021	0.035	1.008	0.022	0.095	0.034	0.131	0.049	0.010	0.014
7	0.031	0.033	0.049	0.000	0.046	0.045	0.060	0.038	0.028	0.040	0.034	0.021	0.049	1.058	0.049	0.046	0.047	0.051	0.036	0.054
8	0.017	0.026	0.014	0.000	0.035	0.031	0.022	0.028	0.023	0.083	0.027	0.041	0.032	0.029	1.022	0.021	0.027	0.024	0.016	0.026
9	0.007	0.015	0.011	0.000	0.023	0.017	0.030	0.026	0.015	0.020	0.020	0.018	0.022	0.053	0.026	1.046	0.060	0.042	0.034	0.061
10	0.000	0.001	0.000	0.000	0.001	0.001	0.001	0.001	0.000	0.001	0.001	0.001	0.001	0.001	0.001	0.001	1.002	0.002	0.001	0.002
11A	0.003	0.003	0.002	0.000	0.003	0.003	0.005	0.004	0.002	0.003	0.003	0.003	0.004	0.005	0.006	0.005	0.022	1.008	0.004	0.011
11B	0.008	0.016	0.011	0.000	0.020	0.017	0.030	0.025	0.014	0.019	0.018	0.020	0.024	0.033	0.031	0.031	0.051	0.048	1.031	0.071
House-holds	0.117	0.251	0.175	0.000	0.314	0.269	0.470	0.395	0.219	0.296	0.283	0.304	0.369	0.469	0.450	0.487	0.794	0.749	0.447	1.110

Table XII.9: Inverse Matrix, 36-Sector Closed Model: Queensland

	1	2A	2B	3A	3B	4A1	4A2	4A3	4A4	4A5	4B1	4B2	4B3	4B4	4C1	4C2	4D1	4D2
1	1.019	0.018	0.032	0.019	0.026	0.628	0.073	0.069	0.024	0.031	0.036	0.042	0.027	0.039	0.037	0.034	0.029	0.027
2A	0.142	1.153	0.059	0.036	0.049	0.159	0.321	0.237	0.747	0.202	0.069	0.076	0.052	0.076	0.070	0.065	0.056	0.052
2B	0.001	0.003	1.003	0.042	0.007	0.004	0.005	0.003	0.003	0.004	0.156	0.038	0.018	0.004	0.004	0.005	0.005	0.005
3A	0.003	0.004	0.004	1.006	0.006	0.007	0.006	0.006	0.004	0.006	0.007	0.006	0.012	0.005	0.007	0.007	0.047	0.013
3B	0.003	0.003	0.006	0.039	1.027	0.004	0.007	0.004	0.004	0.007	0.005	0.012	0.006	0.005	0.038	0.019	0.036	0.349
4A1	0.030	0.028	0.049	0.030	0.041	1.044	0.118	0.111	0.038	0.049	0.056	0.065	0.041	0.062	0.057	0.053	0.045	0.043
4A2	0.004	0.005	0.008	0.005	0.007	0.007	1.011	0.034	0.006	0.036	0.009	0.010	0.007	0.010	0.010	0.009	0.016	0.007
4A3	0.020	0.009	0.017	0.008	0.010	0.019	0.019	1.248	0.011	0.013	0.015	0.016	0.022	0.016	0.014	0.013	0.011	0.011
4A4	0.051	0.036	0.040	0.024	0.032	0.055	0.101	0.101	1.041	0.160	0.045	0.049	0.033	0.049	0.046	0.042	0.036	0.034
4A5	0.003	0.003	0.005	0.003	0.004	0.005	0.006	0.007	0.004	1.006	0.006	0.007	0.005	0.007	0.006	0.006	0.005	0.005
4B1	0.005	0.013	0.011	0.013	0.007	0.007	0.010	0.009	0.011	0.013	1.076	0.244	0.014	0.008	0.010	0.022	0.010	0.008
4B2	0.003	0.004	0.007	0.004	0.004	0.004	0.005	0.005	0.004	0.006	0.035	1.026	0.005	0.005	0.007	0.010	0.005	0.004
4B3	0.009	0.034	0.009	0.006	0.014	0.012	0.027	0.032	0.025	0.031	0.011	0.016	1.134	0.084	0.014	0.010	0.008	0.011
4B4	0.006	0.008	0.011	0.007	0.010	0.010	0.015	0.016	0.010	0.024	0.014	0.015	0.026	1.036	0.015	0.013	0.011	0.011
4C1	0.015	0.014	0.030	0.025	0.059	0.016	0.016	0.015	0.013	0.014	0.023	0.017	0.016	0.015	1.042	0.052	0.021	0.031
4C2	0.010	0.014	0.035	0.023	0.023	0.019	0.026	0.025	0.016	0.023	0.038	0.028	0.027	0.022	0.029	1.024	0.029	0.026
4D1	0.002	0.002	0.004	0.008	0.015	0.003	0.008	0.003	0.002	0.007	0.005	0.013	0.003	0.003	0.036	C.041	1.005	0.012

4D2	0.006	0.006	0.009	0.008	0.018	0.007	0.013	0.007	0.006	0.011	0.010	0.027	0.011	0.011	0.105	0.050	0.063	1.011
4D3	0.009	0.010	0.016	0.025	0.017	0.024	0.089	0.019	0.010	0.074	0.024	0.040	0.018	0.014	0.052	0.080	0.026	0.020
4E	0.004	0.004	0.005	0.035	0.044	0.007	0.015	0.006	0.005	0.036	0.008	0.017	0.006	0.005	0.011	0.008	0.024	0.028
4F1	0.077	0.078	0.072	0.022	0.050	0.060	0.044	0.039	0.055	0.035	0.049	0.042	0.037	0.026	0.034	0.035	0.037	0.041
4F2	0.002	0.003	0.006	0.002	0.003	0.003	0.006	0.004	0.003	0.004	0.005	0.015	0.005	0.003	0.004	0.004	0.004	0.003
4F3	0.001	0.001	0.002	0.001	0.002	0.002	0.002	0.003	0.002	0.002	0.003	0.004	0.003	0.003	0.003	0.003	0.003	0.002
4F4	0.003	0.004	0.014	0.005	0.021	0.006	0.017	0.012	0.005	0.011	0.008	0.017	0.008	0.009	0.013	0.016	0.006	0.011
4F5	0.001	0.001	0.002	0.001	0.001	0.001	0.001	0.002	0.001	0.001	0.001	0.002	0.002	0.002	0.002	0.001	0.001	0.001
5A1	0.022	0.028	0.028	0.074	0.050	0.035	0.042	0.047	0.029	0.042	0.056	0.046	0.043	0.039	0.048	0.043	0.069	0.067
5A2	0.001	0.001	0.001	0.001	0.001	0.001	0.002	0.006	0.002	0.002	0.002	0.002	0.001	0.002	0.003	0.003	0.004	0.002
5A3	0.007	0.008	0.005	0.005	0.010	0.008	0.008	0.008	0.009	0.011	0.007	0.007	0.006	0.007	0.007	0.006	0.006	0.007
6	0.030	0.032	0.028	0.041	0.033	0.038	0.051	0.045	0.031	0.048	0.054	0.044	0.045	0.038	0.037	0.031	0.036	0.035
7	0.118	0.138	0.232	0.142	0.228	0.192	0.234	0.269	0.155	0.247	0.206	0.246	0.170	0.295	0.242	0.221	0.173	0.201
8A1	0.053	0.070	0.073	0.083	0.103	0.114	0.151	0.140	0.093	0.117	0.130	0.122	0.082	0.082	0.121	0.091	0.172	0.142
8A2	0.004	0.005	0.008	0.005	0.007	0.007	0.009	0.010	0.012	0.009	0.010	0.010	0.007	0.011	0.010	0.009	0.008	0.007
9	0.040	0.053	0.083	0.061	0.126	0.076	0.101	0.117	0.076	0.099	0.125	0.130	0.087	0.132	0.120	0.103	0.085	0.098
10	0.001	0.001	0.001	0.001	0.001	0.001	0.001	0.002	0.001	0.001	0.002	0.002	0.001	0.002	0.002	0.002	0.001	0.001
11A	0.011	0.011	0.018	0.013	0.017	0.017	0.020	0.024	0.016	0.019	0.023	0.025	0.017	0.025	0.023	0.022	0.018	0.017
11B	0.012	0.016	0.026	0.017	0.024	0.023	0.029	0.035	0.025	0.028	0.033	0.036	0.024	0.037	0.034	0.031	0.026	0.025
House-holds	0.230	0.314	0.514	0.340	0.458	0.440	0.556	0.674	0.430	0.531	0.645	0.704	0.469	0.720	0.660	0.610	0.509	0.488

Table XII.9 (continued)

	4D3	4E	4F1	4F2	4F3	4F4	4F5	5A1	5A2	5A3	6	7	8A1	8A2	9	10	11A	11B	House-holds
1	0.031	0.034	0.034	0.080	0.044	0.101	0.036	0.025	0.038	0.031	0.040	0.039	0.039	0.035	0.037	0.058	0.060	0.037	0.079
2A	0.061	0.066	0.052	0.070	0.072	0.073	0.069	0.049	0.074	0.061	0.076	0.075	0.074	0.068	0.073	0.112	0.109	0.073	0.154
2B	0.003	0.005	0.003	0.002	0.005	0.006	0.004	0.005	0.007	0.003	0.011	0.003	0.007	0.003	0.003	0.005	0.004	0.003	0.004
3A	0.007	0.022	0.019	0.005	0.004	0.006	0.010	0.060	0.092	0.010	0.007	0.006	0.008	0.004	0.005	0.006	0.007	0.009	0.006
3B	0.034	0.078	0.023	0.005	0.003	0.009	0.043	0.005	0.008	0.007	0.029	0.003	0.007	0.005	0.003	0.008	0.005	0.004	0.004
4A1	0.049	0.053	0.054	0.047	0.063	0.145	0.056	0.039	0.060	0.049	0.062	0.062	0.061	0.055	0.059	0.091	0.095	0.057	0.124
4A2	0.009	0.009	0.013	0.007	0.009	0.010	0.009	0.006	0.010	0.008	0.010	0.010	0.010	0.009	0.010	0.015	0.017	0.010	0.020
4A3	0.012	0.014	0.018	0 014	0.015	0.014	0.014	0.010	0.015	0.012	0.016	0.015	0.015	0.014	0.015	0.023	0.022	0.014	0.031
4A4	0.039	0.043	0.034	0.036	0.045	0.042	0.043	0.032	0.048	0.040	0.050	0.049	0.048	0.044	0.047	0.073	0.070	0.047	0.100
4A5	0.006	0.006	0.005	0.005	0.006	0.006	0.006	0.004	0.007	0.006	0.007	0.007	0.007	0.006	0.007	0.010	0.010	0.016	0.014
4B1	0.009	0.010	0.008	0.006	0.007	0.013	0.012	0.006	0.010	0.013	0.063	0.009	0.015	0.007	0.008	0.017	0.012	0.007	0.012
4B2	0.006	0.006	0.006	0.004	0.005	0.007	0.007	0.004	0.006	0.008	0.035	0.009	0.008	0.005	0.006	0.017	0.011	0.005	0.009
4B3	0.010	0.025	0.025	0.017	0.024	0.017	0.026	0.006	0.010	0.008	0.012	0.022	0.016	0.010	0.008	0.016	0.013	0.012	0.015
4B4	0.013	0.013	0.016	0.014	0.015	0.014	0.014	0.010	0.015	0.012	0.015	0.016	0.015	0.014	0.014	0.046	0.032	0.014	0.030
4C1	0.023	0.023	0.021	0.012	0.013	0.016	0.021	0.011	0.025	0.017	0.044	0.015	0.019	0.049	0.013	0.035	0.020	0.023	0.022
4C2	0.023	0.035	0.036	0.019	0.020	0.022	0.022	0.041	0.030	0.018	0.026	0.0[illegible]1	0.096	0.019	0.018	0.054	0.025	0.018	0.032
4D1	0.064	0.015	0.009	0.002	0.003	0.005	0.012	0.003	0.004	0.005	0.014	0.003	0.006	0.004	0.002	0.007	0.003	0.003	0.003

4D2	0.092	0.012	0.045	0.012	0.007	0.020	0.099	0.005	0.008	0.011	0.030	0.005	0.011	0.009	0.005	0.013	0.008	0.006	0.007
4D3	1.042	0.022	0.047	0.013	0.014	0.034	0.040	0.011	0.025	0.048	0.092	0.014	0.023	0.027	0.012	0.036	0.021	0.014	0.017
4E	0.010	1.098	0.013	0.006	0.006	0.008	0.008	0.007	0.011	0.018	0.108	0.006	0.013	0.011	0.007	0.017	0.010	0.006	0.006
4F1	0.027	0.039	1.093	0.033	0.025	0.081	0.044	0.017	0.027	0.024	0.043	0.023	0.048	0.018	0.020	0.040	0.033	0.030	0.032
4F2	0.005	0.005	0.003	1.109	0.080	0.016	0.010	0.002	0.003	0.003	0.004	0.004	0.005	0.003	0.003	0.006	0.007	0.008	0.005
4F3	0.002	0.003	0.002	0.003	1.009	0.005	0.003	0.002	0.003	0.002	0.003	0.003	0.003	0.003	0.003	0.008	0.004	0.003	0.006
4F4	0.008	0.008	0.020	0.007	0.062	1.012	0.031	0.004	0.007	0.005	0.009	0.007	0.012	0.008	0.005	0.012	0.009	0.008	0.010
4F5	0.001	0.001	0.001	0.001	0.002	0.004	1.003	0.001	0.001	0.001	0.002	0.002	0.001	0.001	0.001	0.002	0.003	0.001	0.002
5A1	0.044	0.058	0.049	0.041	0.038	0.047	0.043	1.022	0.101	0.106	0.040	0.039	0.037	0.035	0.059	0.057	0.064	0.084	0.051
5A2	0.003	0.004	0.002	0.002	0.002	0.002	0.003	0.002	1.002	0.002	0.002	0.002	0.002	0.002	0.002	0.003	0.004	0.002	0.003
5A3	0.006	0.008	0.006	0.007	0.007	0.007	0.007	0.004	0.007	1.005	0.008	0.007	0.007	0.006	0.016	0.010	0.021	0.020	0.013
6	0.035	0.057	0.041	0.036	0.035	0.039	0.038	0.041	0.073	0.161	1.035	0.043	0.110	0.035	0.060	0.143	0.073	0.031	0.042
7	0.195	0.228	0.207	0.155	0.195	0.235	0.244	0.131	0.243	0.179	0.290	1.216	0.237	0.206	0.224	0.281	0.294	0.213	0.337
8A1	0.100	0.175	0.089	0.071	0.076	0.082	0.092	0.095	0.188	0.065	0.122	0.093	1.080	0.091	0.064	0.103	0.092	0.065	0.105
8A2	0.008	0.009	0.006	0.007	0.010	0.008	0.009	0.007	0.010	0.008	0.011	0.011	0.010	1.010	0.015	0.017	0.015	0.010	0.021
9	0.101	0.111	0.088	0.086	0.122	0.108	0.125	0.069	0.117	0.083	0.119	0.202	0.114	0.096	1.174	0.177	0.144	0.138	0.193
10	0.001	0.002	0.001	0.001	0.002	0.001	0.002	0.001	0.002	0.001	0.002	0.002	0.002	0.002	0.002	1.003	0.003	0.002	0.004
11A	0.020	0.022	0.015	0.018	0.023	0.020	0.022	0.016	0.025	0.020	0.025	0.025	0.026	0.023	0.025	0.048	1.036	0.024	0.051
11B	0.029	0.032	0.022	0.025	0.033	0.029	0.032	0.024	0.036	0.029	0.037	0.038	0.037	0.033	0.035	0.054	0.052	1.037	0.074
Households	0.571	0.618	0.429	0.493	0.657	0.565	0.624	0.460	0.702	0.573	0.719	0.708	0.699	0.648	0.689	1.059	1.016	0.668	1.458

BIBLIOGRAPHY

Australian Bureau of Statistics. *Australian National Accounts – Input–Output Tables 1968–69 (Preliminary)*. Canberra, 1976

Australian Bureau of Statistics. *Australian National Accounts, 1975–76*. Canberra, 1976

Bacharach, M. *Biproportional Matrices and Input–Output Change*. Cambridge University Press, 1970

Barker, T. S. 'An Analysis of the Updated 1963 Input–Output Transactions Tables' in R. I. G. Allen and W. F. Gossling (eds.), *Estimating and Projecting Input–Output Coefficients*. Input–Output Publishing Company, 1975

Blin, J. and Cohen, C. 'Technological Similarity and Aggregation in Input–Output Systems: A Cluster-Analytic Approach'. Discussion Paper No. 163, Graduate School of Management, Northwestern University, Evanston, Illinois, 1976

Boster, R. S. and Martin, W. E. 'The Value of Primary versus Secondary Data in Interindustry Analysis: A Study in the Economics of the Economic Models', *Annals of Regional Science*, 6, 2 (1972), 35–43

Bourque, P. J. *et al*. *The Washington Economy: An Input–Output Study*. University of Washington, 1967

Brownrigg, M. 'The Regional Income Multiplier: An Attempt to Complete the Model', *Scottish Journal of Political Economy*, XVIII, 3 (1971), 281–97

Brownrigg, M. *A Study of Economic Impact: The University of Stirling*. Scottish Academic Press, 1974

Cambridge Department of Applied Economics. *Input–Output Relationships 1954–66*. Chapman and Hall, London, 1963

Central Statistical Office (UK). *Provisional Input–Output Tables for 1968*. 1971

Commonwealth Bureau of Census and Statistics. *Australian National Accounts – Input–Output Tables 1962–63*. Canberra, 1973

Consad Research Corp. *Research Federal Procurement Study*. Office of Economic Regional, US Department of Commerce, Wash., DC, 1967

Cutbush, G. C. 'Input–Output Analysis and Regional Economic Planning'. M.Ec. dissertation, University of New England, Armidale, 1973

Czamanski, S., and Malizia, E. 'Applicability and Limitations in the Use of National Input–Output Tables for Regional Studies', *Papers and Proceedings of the Regional Science Association*, 23 (1969), 65–77

Department of Economic Affairs (UK). 'Use of an Input–Output Model in the Preparation of the British National Plan' in Economic Commission for Europe, *Macroeconomic Models for Planning and Policy Making*. UN, Geneva, 1967

Dickinson, J. 'An Interindustry Model of the Northern Region of Queensland', paper presented to the Input–Output Workshop of the Second Meeting of the Australian and New Zealand Section of the Regional Science Association, Sydney, 1977

Edwards, G. C. 'An Input–Output Model of the Tasmanian Economy', paper presented to the Input–Output Workshop of the Second Meeting of the Australian and New Zealand Section of the Regional Science Association, Sydney, 1977

Evans, W. D., and Hoffenberg, M. 'The Interindustry Relations Study for 1947', *Review of Economics and Statistics*, XXXIV, 2 (1952), 97–142

Friedlander, D. 'A Technique for Estimating a Contingency Table Given the Marginal Totals and Some Supplementary Data', *Journal of the Royal Statistical Society*, Series A (1961), 412–20

Goldman, M. R. Comment on Czamanski and Malizia (1969), *Papers and Proceedings of the Regional Science Association*, 23 (1969), 79–80

Government Gas Engineer and Chief Gas Examiner. *Annual Report*. Brisbane, 1975

Greig, M. A. 'The Regional Income and Employment Effects of a Pulp and Paper Mill', *Scottish Journal of Political Economy* (1971)

Hansen, W. L. and Tiebout, C. M. 'An Intersectoral Flows Analysis of the California Economy', *Review of Economics and Statistics*, 45, 4 (1963), 409–18

Harvey, M. E. *The Impact of the Wool Crisis on the Bourke Economy Between 1968/69 and 1970/71: A Regional Input–Output Study*. Department of Agricultural Economics and Business Management, Miscellaneous Publication No. 2, University of New England, Armidale, 1976

Hewings, G. J. D. 'Regional Input–Output Models Using National Data: The Structure of the West Midlands Economy', *Annals of Regional Science*, 3 (1969), 179–91

Hewings, G. J. D. 'Regional Input–Output Models in the UK: Some Problems and Prospects for the Use of Nonsurvey Techniques', *Regional Studies*, 5 (1971a), 11–22

Hewings, G. J. D. 'Nonsurvey Input–Output Tables for S.E. Kent Using 1963 and 1968 UK Input–Output Data'. Discussion Paper 5, S.E. Kent Regional Input–Output Study, Centre for Research in the Social Sciences, University of Kent at Canterbury, 1971b

Hirsch, W. Z. 'Interindustry Relations of a Metropolitan Area', *Review of Economics and Statistics*, 41, 3 (1959), 360–9

Huxley, S. J. *Interregional Trade Flows in Queensland 1970–71*, Vols. I and II, Co-ordinator General's Department, Brisbane, 1973

Isard, W. 'Regional Commodity Balances and Interregional Commodity Flows', *American Economic Review*, XLIII (1953), 167–80

Isard, W., and Keunne, R. 'The Impact of Steel upon the Greater New York–Philadelphia Industrial Region', *Review of Economics and Statistics*, 34 (1953), 289–301

Isard, W., and Langford, T. W. *Regional Input–Output Study. Recollections, Reflections and Diverse Notes on the Philadelphia Experience*. MIT Press, Cambridge, Mass., 1971

Jensen, R. C. 'An Interindustry Study of the Central Queensland Economy', *Economic Record*, 52, 30 (1976), 315–38

Jensen, R. C. 'Some Accounting Procedures and their Effects on Input–Output Multipliers', *Annals of Regional Science*, forthcoming

Jensen, R. C., and McGaurr, D. 'Reconciliation of Purchases and Sales Estimates in an Input–Output Table', *Urban Studies*, 13 (1976), 59–65

Jensen, R. C., and McGaurr, D. 'Reconciliation Techniques in Input–Output Analysis: Some Comparisons and Implications', *Urban Studies*, 14 (1977), 327–37

Jones, L. L., Sporleder, T. L., and Mustafa, G. 'A Source of Bias in Regional Input–Output Models Estimates from National Coefficients', *Annals of Regional Science*, 7, 1 (1973), 67–74

Kokat, R. *The Economic Component of a Regional Socioeconomic Model*. IBM Technical Report, 17–210, 1966

Lecomber, R. 'A Critique of Methods of Adjusting, Updating and Projecting Matrices, Together with Some New Proposals'. Discussion Paper in Economics No. 40, Conference on Input–Output and Throughput, Norwich, 1971

Malizia, E. E., and Bond, D. L. 'Empirical Tests of the RAS Method of Interindustry Coefficient Adjustment', *Journal of Regional Science*, 14 (1974)

Mandeville, T. D. *Linking APMAA to Representative Regional Input–Output Models*. Aggregative Programming Model for Australian Agriculture Research Report No. 8. Department of Agricultural

Economics, University of New England, Armidale, 1975

Mandeville, T. D., Jensen, R. C., and Karunaratne, N. D. *An Inter-industry Input–Output System for the Regions of Queensland, Studies 2 and 3: Application of the Methodology to the Bowen Basin Area of Queensland*. Report to the Queensland Co-ordinator General's Department, 1977

Mandeville, T. D., and Powell, R. A. *Structural Interrelationships in a NSW Wheat–Sheep Region*, Department of Agricultural Economics and Business Management. Bulletin 22, University of New England, Armidale, 1976

Matuszewski, T. I., Pitts, P. R., and Sawyer, J. A. 'Linear Programming Estimates of Changes in Input Coefficients', *The Canadian Journal of Economics and Political Science*, 30 (1964), 203–10

McGaurr, D. 'Measuring a City's Dependence on Its Region: An Input–Output Study of the City of Toowoomba', paper presented to the First Meeting of the Australian and New Zealand Section of the Regional Science Association, Brisbane, 1976

McGaurr, D. 'An Interindustry Study of the Economy of Toowoomba', unpublished M.Econ. thesis, University of Queensland, 1977

McMenamin, D. G., and Haring, J. E. 'An Appraisal of Non survey Techniques for Estimating Regional Input–Output Models', *Journal of Regional Science*, 14, 2 (1974), 191–205

Miernyk, W. H. 'Comments on Czamanski and Malizia', *Papers and Proceedings of the Regional Science Association*, 23 (1969), 81–2

Miernyk, W. H. *The Projection of Technical Coefficients for Medium Term Forecasting*. MR-20, Regional Research Institute, West Virginia University, 1975

Miernyk, W. H. 'Comment on Recent Developments in Regional Input–Output Analysis', *International Regional Science Review*, 1, 2 (1976), 47–55

Miernyk, W. H. *et al. Simulating Regional Economic Development: An Interindustry Analysis of the West Virginia Economy*. Heath Lexington, 1970

Miller, R. 'The Impact of the Aluminum Industry on the Pacific Northwest: A Regional Input–Output Analysis', *Review of Economics and Statistics*, 34 (1957), 200–9

Moore, F. T., and Petersen, J. 'Regional Analysis: An Interindustry Model of Utah', *Review of Economics and Statistics*, 37 (1955), 368–83

Morrison, W. I., and Smith, P. 'Nonsurvey Input–Output Techniques at the Small Area Level: An Evaluation', *Journal of Regional Science*, 14, 1 (1974) 1–14

Mules, T. J. *Interindustry Analysis and the South Australian Wool Industry*. M.Ec. thesis, University of Adelaide, 1967

O'Connor, R., and Henry, E. W. *Input–Output Analysis and Its Applications*. Charles Griffin, 1975

Parker, M. L. *An Interindustry Study of the Western Australian Economy*. Agricultural Economic Research Report No. 6, University of Western Australia Press, 1967

Richardson, H. *Input–Output and Regional Economics*. Weidenfeld and Nicolson, London, 1972

Schaffer, W. 'Estimating Regional Input–Output Coefficients'. Georgia Institute of Technology, Discussion Paper 16, 1970

Schaffer, W. A. (ed.). *On the Use of Input–Output Models for Regional Planning*. Studies in Applied Regional Science, Vol. 1, Martinus Nijhoff, Leiden, 1976

Schaffer, W., and Chu, K. 'Non-Survey Techniques for Constructing Regional Interindustry Models', *Papers and Proceedings of the Regional Science Association*, 23 (1969a), 83–101

Schaffer, W. A., and Chu, K. 'Simulating Regional Interindustry Models for Western States', A Program on Regional Industrial Development. Discussion Paper 14, Georgia Institute of Technology, Georgia, 1969b

Shen, T. Y. 'An Input–Output Table with Regional Weights', *Papers and Proceedings of the Regional Science Association*, 6 (1960), 113–19

Smith, P. S., and Morrison, W. I. *Simulating the Urban Economy*. Pion, London, 1974

State Electricity Commission of Queensland. *Annual Report*, Brisbane, 1975

Stone, R., and Leicester, C. S. 'An Exercise in Projecting Industrial Needs for Labour'. Cambridge, 1966

Su, T. T. 'A Note on Regional Input–Output Models', *Southern Economic Journal*, 36 (1970), 325–7

Tiebout, C. M. 'An Empirical Regional Input–Output Projection Model', *Review of Economics and Statistics*, 51 (1969), 334–40

Theil, H. *Economics and Information Theory*. North Holland Publishing Co., Amsterdam, 1967

United Nations. *A System of National Accounts*. Studies in Methods, Series F, No. 2, Rev. 3, New York, 1968

Walderhaug, A. 'State Input–Output Tables Derived from National

Data', *1971 Proceedings of the Business and Economic Statistics Section of the American Statistical Association*, Washington, 77–86, 1972

West, G., and Jensen, R. C. 'Some Effects of Errors in Coefficients on Input–Output Multipliers', paper presented to the Input–Output Workshop of the Second Meeting of the Australian and New Zealand Section of the Regional Science Association, Sydney, 1977

INDEX